SCHOOLWISE

SCHOOLWISE

A Parent's Guide to Getting the Best Education for Your Child

Martha C. Brown

JEREMY P. TARCHER, INC.
Los Angeles
Distributed by St. Martin's Press
New York

Chapter 3, "Make That Talk with the Teacher Count," is adapted
from an article by Martha Brown for *Working Mother* magazine,
September 1982 issue. Copyright © 1982 by McCall Publishing
Company. Reprinted with permission.

Library of Congress Cataloging in Publication Data

Brown, Martha Cluverius.
   A parent's guide to getting the best education for your child.

   Bibliography: p. 233
   Includes index.
      1. Home and school—United States.   I. Title.
LC225.3.B76   1985   370.19'3   85–17195
ISBN 0-87477-364-4

Jeremy P. Tarcher, Inc.
9110 Sunset Blvd.
Los Angeles, CA 90069

Design by Cynthia Eyring

Manufactured in the United States of America
10 9 8 7 6 5 4 3 2 1

First Edition

*To Jim, Annette, Dee, and Amanda, who
were patient and helpful beyond measure.*

ACKNOWLEDGMENTS

This book could not have been written without the help of the dozens of students, teachers, parents, and others concerned with education who have spoken freely about their experiences working in and dealing with public schools in many types of communities. Though I can't thank them individually, they know of my appreciation.

I also wish to thank those who answered numerous technical questions, sent material that greatly helped with my research, or offered valuable advice for parents and enthusiastic support during the months of work on this book: Michael Brunner, research associate, National Institute of Education (NIE); Nancy Berla and the staff of the National Committee for Citizens in Education (NCCE), Columbia, Maryland; Samuel L. Blumenfeld, Boston; Charles M. Richardson, director, Learning Foundations, Dix Hills, New York; Dennis Gray, deputy director, the Council for Basic Education (CBE), Washington, D.C.; Leslie Kaplan-Hodes, special education teacher, Chicago; Dr. S. Jay Samuels, Center for Research in Human Learning, University of Minnesota, Minneapolis; Bettina Rubicam, president, Reading Reform Foundation (RRF), Scottsdale, Arizona; Dr. Vance Grant, National Center for Educational Statistics (NCES); Charlotte Lockhart, Illinois chairman, RRF; Erica G. Kenney, legislative assistant to Senator Edward Zorinsky (Nebraska); M. Blouke Carus, president, Open Court Publishing Co., LaSalle, Illinois; Ross Zerchykov, vice president, Institute for Responsive Education (IRE), Boston; Joseph M. James, Jr., principal, Thornton Township High School, Harvey, Illinois; Daniel Safran, Institute for the Study of Parent Involvement, Oakland, California; Charlotte Scott, parent and teacher, Flossmoor, Illinois; Jerry L. Lambert of Stinespring, Lambert, Schroeder & Associates, Chicago; Barbara Cueter, National Forum for Educational Awareness, Birmingham, Michigan; Dr. Robert T. McGee, superintendent, Denton (Texas) Independent School District; Chip Shields, college/career counselor, Homewood-Flossmoor High School, Flossmoor, Illinois; Mary C. Jackson, director, School Advisory Council Assistance Project, University of South Carolina, Columbia, South Carolina; Larry Gelfius and Ardeth Livingstone, Homewood (Illinois) Public Library; Lou Kerr, reference librarian, Governors State University, University Park, Illinois; Robert Abbott, supervisor of special education, Waukegan, Illinois.

CONTENTS

CONTENTS

INTRODUCTION

Today millions of American parents are concerned as never before about their children's schooling. Thanks to the nationwide reports on our educational problems, parents are less likely to believe educators who say, "*Our* schools are just fine. The *real* problems are in the next district [or in the next state—or in the inner city]."

As a former public school teacher and as a parent, I have listened to scores of concerned parents voice their frustrations in dealing with the schools. They hesitate to speak up for fear school people will treat their child unfavorably. They can't get straight (or even intelligible) answers to questions about their child's progress or school programs. When they do speak up about classroom chaos or low academic standards, administrators too often ignore them.

But I have also talked with other parents who seem to have a knack for getting the best that school has to offer for their children. You will meet them in this book: parents who, when the principal refused to act, devised a simple scheme to get an impossible teacher out of their children's class; parents who insisted on having one school in their district devoted to teaching reading, writing, and math by methods known to be most effective in helping children learn; parents who have learned how to get their questions answered and how to see that their child gets the program, or the teacher, or the special help he needs.

In my talks with parents in all parts of the country, many of them from small towns and suburbs, I have not noted the "parent apathy" educators so often complain about. I did not find apathy, either, in big-city parent advocate groups that were struggling to get good reading instruction and competent principals in their schools. All too often the same school people who complain loudly of parent apathy one week refuse to answer interested parents' questions or to consider their suggestions the next week.

How can parents—both as individuals and in organized groups—gain more of a say in their children's schools? Two principal answers came from my talks with parents and with leaders of school improvement groups around the country. First, parents must

1

be persistent in asking questions—about discipline, or curriculum, or any area where changes seem needed in their schools. Second, parents must not take educators too seriously when they say that the ways of learning are too complex for ordinary parents and citizens to understand.

I heard the current version of this argument from a professor of education who holds an influential post in a major university. He told me the public is making a big mistake in "supposing that education depends on a foundation of simplified skills." "You mean reading, writing, and math?" I asked. "Yes," he replied. "We have to concentrate on teaching the higher skills, like critical thinking."

If they truly want to help students learn to think critically, it is difficult to understand why so many educators deliberately downgrade fundamental skills. Children who are not taught to read and write fluently and to deal accurately with numbers are being denied the tools of independent, critical thought. They can only accept *uncritically* the ideas of others. They grow into adults who accept opinion as fact and propaganda as truth.

Today millions of students leave school barely able to read, write, and do simple math after ten or twelve years in the classroom. Colleges find it necessary to run courses to help their students understand textbooks and write simple English.

Parents (and everyone else concerned about education) must be highly skeptical when educators deny the need to concentrate on teaching reading, writing, and math—especially when test scores and other evidence show plainly that schools in all types of communities have done an inadequate job of teaching children these fundamental skills.

We've heard a good deal recently about the work of education commissions and committees and about state laws passed to upgrade schools. Necessary and helpful as these efforts are, you cannot assume they will guarantee improvements in your child's classroom.

Only people who support local schools and whose children attend them have a real stake in working for meaningful changes and in monitoring the job their school is doing. The aim of this book is to give you the information you need to do both—in addition to the parent-tested strategies which can help you to be an effective advocate for your child in school situations you may have to deal with today, tomorrow, or next month.

1

A Close Look
at Learning

1

FACING PROBLEMS IN THE PARENT-SCHOOL CONNECTION

No child in today's schools can afford to be without the support of informed parents. Yet millions of concerned parents hesitate to ask the questions or to insist on getting the answers they need to understand how well their children are learning.

When parents fail to speak up, children often lose out—even in good schools. A second-grader's reading problems go unsolved. A high school student signs up for the wrong courses, limiting college and career choices. A sixth-grader who has trouble with math gets easier work instead of real help.

Why do so many caring, intelligent parents lack the confidence they need to be good advocates for their children? A major reason for parent uneasiness is the conviction—earnestly promoted by educators—that since school people are trained and licensed education experts, parents have no need, and no right, to ask questions. When parents do ask about a child's progress or behavior, some school people evade the issue, saying, in effect, "Trust us." Parents may be told, "Don't worry about the math, as long as she's happy in school." Or "It's normal for kids to act that way these days."

Parents also remain silent for fear that the school will retaliate against their child. While this can happen, there is often less danger than parents imagine. In my talks with parents over the past fifteen years, I have heard only one or two say they regretted speaking up at school. A far larger number regretted not asking questions when they suspected a problem or not insisting on action by school people when a child needed help. As J. Cy Rowell, an associate professor at Texas Christian University and an educator concerned about parents' rights, says, "Act humble and apologetic, and you'll be treated accordingly." So will your child.

Finally, many parents eager to be good advocates for their children lack confidence because they don't know their rights in dealing with the schools. They are not aware, for example, that they have a legal right to see their child's scores on standardized tests and to have these scores explained in plain English. Millions of parents don't know they can visit their child's class any time during the day, provided they first notify the principal. (Parents in twenty-one states and the District of Columbia have this right; in other states individual districts regulate parents' visits to school. See chapter 10 for more information on parents' rights.) Frequently school people fail to inform parents of their rights. Parents must inform themselves.

HOW CAN PARENTS LEARN TO SPEAK UP?

Parents who are effective in dealing with the school trust their own common-sense judgments about their children, rather than automatically deferring to the "experts." Instead of keeping quiet for fear school people will treat their child unfairly, they take sensible precautions to minimize this danger. Finally, they learn their rights and the facts about how schools operate before an emergency—failing grades, fear of having a child mislabeled in "special ed," an incompetent teacher—arises.

Among the dozens of parents I talked to in the course of researching this book were many from all parts of the United States who had become successful advocates for their children and who believed other parents could do the same. Often they spoke with a sense of urgency about the need to communicate with the school and offer children active support even when things are going well. Nan, a New Jersey mother of five, says: "My own education was a disaster, partly because my mother didn't believe a parent should ever question the teacher or anyone else at school. As a result, I had some miserable experiences. Much as I wanted to help my own children when they started school, I wasn't too sure how to go about it, but I was determined to keep an eye on things. I found out that I could learn a lot in a short time just by visiting classes and talking to other parents. Now I don't hesitate to go to bat for my children—and I often succeed in getting school people to see things my way."

For some parents, the decision to "keep an eye on things" arose from serious doubts about what was going on at school. A midwestern parent, Pat, describes how she gained unsettling "inside" information firsthand. "In the late '70s our district had loads of money, and it was spend, spend, spend. They did all kinds of crazy things, including 'open' classrooms with as many as 200 kids, divided into 'pods.' One day I went in as a substitute teacher. They gave me a chalkboard on wheels and sent me into this big open space to teach a group of about twenty-five third-graders. When the first bell rang, the lights went out and everyone hit the floor. I hit the floor, too, scared to death. I thought we were having a raid or a disaster drill. It turned out they had trained the kids to do that every day because it was the only way they could get 200 of them sitting on the floor in one room to quiet down all at once. When it was time to teach math on my rolling chalkboard, I had to stop constantly to remind children they couldn't go scooting around the floor on their bottoms while we were having a lesson."

This experience convinced Pat she would have to watch carefully to make sure her own two children were not short-changed on learning, given the chaos in the classroom. She paid special attention to their progress and kept in close touch with their teachers. As a result of her success in communicating with school people and looking after the interests of her children, she became the neighborhood school "expert." She reports that she still gets requests for advice about school problems, though her own children are well beyond elementary school. Pat believes all children, regardless of the school situation, would be better off with more active support from parents. "From kindergarten on, right through high school, let the teacher know who you are. Let the counselor know who you are. Only a very few kids can do well on their own. The majority of those who get ahead in school are the ones whose parents make themselves known. Assuming they're pleasant and tactful, the parents who make the most noise are the ones whose children get the best attention. It pays to remember these [school] people are public servants."

Among the parents I talked to are several who are or have been teachers, administrators, or counselors. As a group the parent-educators were often more persistent in trying to get their children's school problems solved, yet they met with the same obstacles that other parents have to deal with. Often parent-educators were the most emphatic about the need for all parents to keep a watchful eye on what happens at school. Arlene, a former school guidance director and the mother of four children, says, "I *always* make it a point to visit classes. I figure that if my child is going to spend all that time with the person who is his teacher, I want to see for myself how the teacher does things, what the atmosphere of that class is. Parents have to realize that even though they won't always be able to get school problems solved, it is very important for them to *go through the process* of speaking up with suggestions, or complaining, or doing whatever it takes to make things better at school. Parents *must* let school people know they are determined enough to go through the process."

MIXED MESSAGES

A second problem in the parent-school connection is the continuing disagreement between educators on one side and parents on the other about what type of education our schools should provide.

Consider for a moment what you mean when you say you want your child to get an education in school. If by "education" you mean primarily learning to read, write, and do math, plus learning about science, geography, history, and government, your views probably match those of the majority of parents. A Gallup poll in 1979 reported good teaching, high standards, teaching of the basics, high scholarship, and homework ranked at the top of parents' school preferences—ahead of special programs, class size, and the physical condition of school buildings.

Educators, though, do not always rank scholarship as high as parents do. A study in the late '70s showed that at all levels of schooling—elementary, junior high, and high school—parents rated the intellectual goals of schooling as more important and the personal and social-development goals as less important than did school people. This survey took place before the full extent of the decline in public school academic achievement was widely known.

To understand how school people think, you need a brief look at the ideas they are exposed to during their college training. They are taught that the school should concern itself with the "whole child" and his social development—a philosophy dating back to the early 1900s and the founding of "progressive" education. Prospective teachers are often told by professors of education that teaching a child to read and write, helping him to develop intellectually, is no more important than teaching him physical education or how to be a useful member of a group. A textbook used in college courses for prospective teachers states: "Instead of requiring written reports, invite students to sign up for 10-minute blocks of time on designated days to give you an oral report. This will not only save the student the trouble of writing or typing a report and you [the teacher] the trouble of reading a report; it will also give you the opportunity to interact with each of your students on a person-to-person basis and to probe more deeply into interpretations."

Are prospective teachers being taught to consider the real needs of children? Which will benefit them more, learning to "interact" with the teacher or learning to think and write precisely? A recent in-service training course for teachers in one district in a western state is called "How to Take the Boredom Out of Math." When educators themselves speak of math as boring and of writing as being too much trouble, the decline in school achievement is not surprising. We rank first among developed nations on "measures of resource and resource allocation" for education. Yet in reading and other measures of achievement, we are twelfth, just above India. One third of U.S. adults are totally or functionally illiterate—unable to use a phone book or read a label on a medicine bottle.

Our brief look at the ideas school people are exposed to during their college training will help you to understand why they often send you and other parents mixed messages about taking an interest in your schools. All educators want citizens and parents to be interested enough to vote more tax money for schools and to send their children to school ready to behave and to learn whatever is being taught. Many educators, though, especially those who believe strongly in the theories we have been discussing, do *not* want parents to be too interested in *what* is being taught. These educators fear—rightly—that concerned parents will not approve of such classroom activities as "interacting" with the teacher at the expense of learning reading, writing, and math.

Many parents suspect—rightly—that children can't learn much

merely by being in the same room with the teacher, or by talking endlessly in group "discussions" with other equally uninstructed children, or by engaging in such random, "hands-on" activities as collecting "some things that interest you" at recess and pasting them on a tag board (as a popular guide for science teachers suggests). Unfortunately, most parents lack the information they need to question these teaching practices.

Yet the evidence is there: studies which show that this type of teaching does not help children to learn writing, or science, or anything else. You will read about it later in this book, along with other information which will help you decide whether your child is getting the education he needs—and what to do if he isn't. For example, in chapter 6 you will find simple tests to check your child's reading skills—regardless of his age—and suggestions for getting help if he needs it. In the final chapter you will learn strategies for working with other parents and citizens to bring about needed changes in your child's school.

Fortunately, there are in our schools a number of teachers who are working hard to teach children fundamental skills. Those capable teachers do not waste class time teaching by osmosis—turning children loose to interact with learning materials or with other children in class bull sessions. These teachers give children the structure and direction they must have in order to learn. They can make school better for your child and others. Often, though, they get little appreciation from those inside the school. In some cases, they may be under pressure to relax standards and deemphasize academic learning. Your child needs good teachers, and good teachers badly need your support.

Frank Armbruster, director of interdisciplinary studies at the Hudson Institute, refers to these hard workers in our schools as "common-sense" teachers. They are as eager as common-sense parents to have children learn basic skills and to have school people held accountable.

Grace Vaughan, an outstanding Texas teacher, says: "If a teacher isn't doing the job, I think the principal should tell him or her face-to-face to show improvement, and the principal should offer help. Then if there's no improvement, that teacher has to go. A superintendent should oust a principal whose school is below standard. We have to weed out bad teachers and principals. Then the rest of us could do the job."

MORE SAY, MORE SUCCESS

Traditionally, the views of educators have prevailed over the views of parents and taxpayers when it comes to deciding how schools will be run and what children will learn. My own experience as a teacher, as a parent, and as a listener (to parents, teachers, administrators, and professors of education) has convinced me that if parents had had more say in our schools, the current decline in academic achievement would not be so severe.

Among the brightest spots on the educational horizon is the generally superior track record of parents in predicting what will work and what won't work in helping children learn. Almost from the beginnings of the "new math" craze in the '60s, parents recognized it as an ineffective way of teaching the subject to children. Among parents who told me they thought it was a bad idea were many who had had no college training and many others who had advanced degrees in such subjects as engineering and physics. Yet educators continued to defend new math, to write new math textbooks, and to see that it was taught in the classroom for well over a decade. This despite widespread protests from parents and criticism from such prominent mathematicians as Dr. Morris Kline, a professor at New York University, formerly of the Institute for Advanced Study at Princeton. Many teachers also objected to the new math, but not strenuously enough. Often they had little choice, as they were given textbooks and curriculum plans based on it.

Parents also know successful school programs when they see them. In an Arizona school district parents waged a successful campaign to have one school devoted to strong emphasis on the basics, including the use of intensive phonics, the reading method research has proven superior in helping children learn. (See chapter 6.) Enrollment in this school was to be on a first-come basis. More than a dozen parents camped out for three nights to assure themselves a place in line to register their children. When registration was over, there was a long waiting list.

Test scores proved that the parents' enthusiasm was justified. Though their average score on a group intelligence test was no higher than the district average, second-graders in the basics school outscored second-graders in all of the district's thirty-one other schools in reading, math, and grammar on a standardized achievement test.

Other promising signs are the volunteer and nonprofit organizations which can give parents information on needed improvements in school curricula and on how to gain more of a say in local schools. You'll hear more about these organizations in later chapters.

A growing number of parents insist on having a greater say in their schools. Thanks to the support of legislators and some educators, who are finally convinced that parents who pay for and care about education can no longer be shut out, parents in some districts do have a real say in their children's schooling. For example, in Salt Lake City many parents have a permanent place on councils that run each neighborhood school. In other states, laws require that schools set up parent advisory groups. Parents in a number of cities, including Philadelphia, Milwaukee, and Houston, can choose what type of school to send their children to. Among the choices are "open" unstructured schools, "fundamental" schools, which stress discipline and teaching of basic skills, and creative-arts elementary schools.

HOW THIS BOOK CAN HELP

By giving you the facts and the strategies you need to deal confidently with school people, this book can help you become the strong advocate your child needs today. You will learn how other parents have solved the same types of school problems you might face this week or next month. To make this book work for you, the chapters have been organized into three parts: Part 1, A Close Look at Learning, deals with at-home learning and those important talks with the teacher. Part 2, You, Your Child, and School, will help you to solve specific problems your child may have in school. In Part 3, Parents' Rights and Parent Action, you'll learn what your rights are and how you can influence what goes on at school.

The premise of this book is that your common sense, your own years in school, and your experience as your child's first teacher, along with what you'll find in this book, will better enable you to deal confidently with your child's school years.

The following preview highlights some of the key questions answered in each chapter.

Chapter 2
Set the Stage for Learning

How can I encourage my child's language learning and at-home learning in general? How can I help my child evaluate information? What can I do about too much TV viewing?

Chapter 3
Make That Talk with the Teacher Count

How can I find out where my child really stands in reading and math? What if the teacher uses education terms I don't understand? How can I talk to school experts without feeling intimidated?

Chapter 4
Take the Mystery out of Test Scores

Can those standardized tests really show how smart my child is? What questions should I ask about her test scores? How do her scores on these tests affect the way she's taught in school?

Chapter 5
Learn the Basics of Helping with Homework

How can I get my child to do her homework without a nightly battle? How much should I help her? What can I do if my child doesn't understand her math homework and I don't either?

Chapter 6
Check Your Child's Progress

How should I discuss a report card with my child? How can I find out if he has learned how to read as well as he should? What can I do if the teacher promises help and doesn't give it?

Chapter 7
Recognizing Your Child's People Problems

What should I do to build my child's self-confidence? How can I help her to deal with a teacher she just plain doesn't like? How can I tell if my child is using drugs? How can I help my child adjust to a new school?

Chapter 8
Help Your Child Make the Most of High School

How can I make sure my child gets the right advice about choosing courses? How important are extracurricular activities? How can I find out about financial aid for college?

Chapter 9
Between Parent and Teacher

What does my child's teacher expect of him—and of me? How can I keep my child from losing out in reading or math if he's stuck with a bad teacher? Is there any way to get a bad teacher out of our school?

Chapter 10
Learn Your Rights *Before* Anything Goes Wrong

What part of my child's school record can I see? Can I complain about a bad school situation without risking possible retaliation by school people? Can I protest if the teacher asks my child to talk about private family matters in class?

Chapter 11
Learn the School Setup

What's the difference between the school board and the school administration? Who decides what my child will be taught in class? How do teachers' unions affect my child's education?

Chapter 12
How to Use Parent Power to Improve Your Schools

Will I really help my child by joining the parents' group? How can I compliment a really great teacher? What do school volunteers do?

Chapter 13
Make Your Vote Count for Better Education

How can I—and other parents—convince the school board that our schools should set higher standards? How can we elect a more responsive school board? How can I gain more of a say in laws affecting my children's school?

In the next chapter we'll discuss another important ingredient in the parent-school connection: home learning. You'll find suggestions to help you make informal teaching at home pay off for your child whether he's in second grade or high school.

2

SET THE STAGE FOR LEARNING

I started school late because I'd been ill,
so I was six or more when I went. The first day
I was there, the teacher wrote the word *see* on
the board and explained how to sound out the
letters and make the word.

She gave us pencil and paper to write it
out. I remember it was a short yellow pencil
with a chewed end.

And a great light came over me. It was the
first time I had really realized that this was a
code, and you could break it.

So I came tearing home, and my parents
had given me a copy of *Raggedy Man* [by
James Whitcomb Riley], and I sat there with it,
and they explained to me what the codes for
the other letters were, and within a couple of
weeks I could read it aloud with some fluency,
and this struck me as the greatest miracle that
ever happened in the world.

—DAN LACY,
senior vice president, McGraw-Hill

How can you set the stage so your child will become an eager
learner? Over the years, advice for parents on how to improve children's learning has ranged from the farfetched to the counterpro-

ductive. In the early 1900s, private "fresh air" schools were popular on the east coast, all the way up into chilly New England. Parents who could afford it were advised to bundle up their children and send them to classes conducted outside year-round. The brisk air was expected to produce rosy cheeks, good health, and alert minds.

Two or three decades later, parents got stern warnings not to help with school work—especially with reading—for fear of "confusing" children and upsetting what the school was trying to do. Some parents wisely ignored the warnings. In this chapter you'll find out how you can make a positive difference in your child's attitude and how you can boost his learning and set the stage for school success with casual, informal teaching at home.

Consider which of these two reactions to a youngster's bid for attention is more likely to help him become an eager learner:

Toddler: (After watching his mother vacuum for what he considers too long, he flips the switch and the vacuum stops. Grinning, he blurts out one of his very first sentences.) All through now?

First Mother: (Startled, too rushed to notice the sentence, pushes him aside.) Not now, dear. I'm busy!

Second Mother: (Startled, then laughing as she picks him up.) That's a good question! . . . But I guess the answer is no. We'll have to turn it on again. (She lets him flip the switch to "on" before directing his attention back to a box of toys.)

ACTIVE LISTENING
Children who have learned to talk continue to be very much influenced by their parents' "listening style." In studies at the University of Leeds (England), Dr. Joan Tough found that children accustomed to being listened to attentively were almost three times more likely to talk about facts and ideas not related to their immediate surroundings than were children not favored with good listening. The "unfavored" children were much more likely to limit their talk to calling attention to themselves and their needs. Dr. Tough also found that children favored with good listening used language imaginatively from three to five times as often as the "unfavored" children.

The message is clear: if you want your child to use language to "reach out" and learn, be a good listener. This is sometimes easier said than done, as any parent of a "chatterbox" knows, but it's worth the effort.

Being a good listener may mean more than simply being attentive. Ask questions along the way. For example, asking "What happened first?" or "And then what happened?" will help a younger child understand that every communication, even a brief story about the class trip to the zoo, has a beginning, a middle, and an end. Encouraging your child to think in this beginning-middle-end pattern will help him in writing, when he must learn to put ideas down in proper order, according to recent studies at Northwestern University.

You can also show your child that you're an interested listener and help him to expand his vocabulary by occasionally paraphrasing what he says. If he says, "Dan went on a plane," you can reply, "Dan took a limousine to the airport. He's flying to California to visit his aunt." But remember, a little questioning or paraphrasing goes a long way. Don't overdo it.

We've all seen the bumper sticker reading "Have you hugged your child today?" Perhaps we're just as much in need of one that asks "Have you talked to your child today?" One teacher told me about a study which showed that on the average parents spend less than an hour a week really talking to their children. "Talking" was defined as real conversation between parent and child, excluding routine talk about family schedules or the giving of directions.

Keep in mind that active listening on your part can help to sharpen the thinking of older children and teenagers. Several years ago, W. P. Cushman, the head of the English department at Baylor, a private school in Chattanooga, Tennessee, wrote a letter to parents about children's language learning at home. He suggested that parents make a deliberate effort to ask children questions requiring more than "yes" or "no" answers. In discussing a movie, book, party, or television show with your child, try to get beyond "short answer" conversation by asking why he enjoyed it (or didn't). Was it exciting? Funny? Dull?

Don't be discouraged if you still get a monosyllabic answer. Your questions may spur your child to give more thought to the next movie he sees or the next book he reads. And don't overlook the possibilities of that always-flattering question, "What do you think?," in stimulating your child to put his opinions and ideas into words. Cushman also urges parents to listen patiently to a child speak "about anything that interests *him*—even maddeningly detailed replays of games or retelling of stories."

READ TO YOUR CHILD

One thoughtful elementary school teacher gives his class a special test at the beginning of each school year. He reads aloud short passages from children's books and then asks students to describe in their own words the object, person, or scene described in the reading. Few children can do this readily. The teacher believes that television is to blame, since it supplies the picture, making it unnecessary for children to use their imaginations to "translate" words into pictures. To give them practice in visualizing what they read, he reads aloud often, calling on them afterwards to describe what they heard in their own words, an activity they come to enjoy. He reports that their ability to visualize does improve with practice and hopes this will make their own reading more vivid.

Children love being invited to share a book with Mother or Dad. Tailor the entertainment to your child by choosing books that match his age and interests. Even in a busy day, try to find time for half a chapter. Listening to you read aloud will lengthen your child's attention span, which is especially important in helping younger children adjust to school.

A child who reads well on his own still benefits from being read to. (Parents who read aloud to younger children report that older ones often listen in.) You may choose a more advanced book to read aloud to your child; hearing longer and more complex material than he can read on his own will enrich the language learning of any child and encourage him to try more challenging books. Don't make this the sole purpose of your reading, though, as pushing a child to read difficult books can take the fun out of reading for him.

Being read to will also give your child a feel for the language patterns he must use in writing. Hearing even the best speech from parents, teachers, and playmates will not help children learn these patterns, since spoken language differs in important ways from written language. Even the most correct conversation contains unfinished sentences and often has a loosely organized, off-the-cuff quality—which is all right for speech but not suitable for writing. Reading—or hearing—the structure and rhythm of book language will help your child to become a better writer.

ENCOURAGE YOUR CHILD
TO THINK INDEPENDENTLY

At times creating a good learning environment for your child may involve questioning what goes on at school. My eldest daughter once came home upset by a lesson on the population problem. It seemed that the teacher had talked at length about overcrowding and starvation, concluding with the view that the human race was headed for inevitable disaster because of overpopulation.

We discussed this at dinner, noting that there are a number of views on the subject. We explained to her that in fact today starvation is not always caused by overpopulation, since modern agriculture makes it possible to raise food efficiently. In some countries, though, a poor distribution system keeps people from getting enough food.

Later that evening my daughter told me, "Tomorrow I'm going to try to make Mary Jane feel better. There are eight kids in her family, and she felt so bad she couldn't keep from crying after class today."

At times, teachers may propagandize students rather than teaching them. Instead of teaching fundamental knowledge about a subject such as science or history, they may present controversial or "relevant" topics at great length. Sometimes teachers fail to present more than one side of controversial issues, and sometimes they don't get the facts straight before presenting them to students.

Textbooks, too, can contribute to children's getting distorted information. They sometimes contain slanted or inaccurate material. This is particularly true of social studies books. Teachers should know their subjects well enough to question the textbook and make needed adjustments in their teaching. Often, they do not.

A recent survey of seventy social studies textbooks by Jane Newitt of the Hudson Institute shows that they frequently present gloomy and misleading or inaccurate information about such issues as overpopulation, pollution, and dwindling resources. In *Why Are They Lying to Our Children?*, Dr. Herbert I. London points out that these claims often run counter to the facts. Dr. London offers parents the following guidelines to help children see the importance of finding out the truth, rather than blindly trusting what appears in print.

1. Examine textbooks not to censor but to raise questions that could serve as the basis of class discussion.

2. Give your child the information he needs to challenge inaccurate information and to have confidence in doing so.

3. Encourage questions and independent research: "How do you know that is true?"

You have a stake in seeing that your child is not given a one-sided or factually misleading view of the world. Try to avoid giving your child the impression that you're downgrading the teacher. Most important, you want your child to learn that knowing when to ask questions and how to evaluate information is a vital part of being educated. Seeing you take this approach will encourage him to do the same.

TRICKS OF THE TRADE TO PROMOTE LEARNING

As you're probably aware, your child is more likely to spend time reading if you do. In a detailed survey of the reading habits of more than 100 elementary school children, researchers found that almost all those who were avid readers had parents who were also avid readers.

Taking advantage of your child's tendency to imitate—not only your reading habits but your general approach to learning—is one of the most effective tricks of the parenting "trade." For example, when your child asks a question you can't answer and you respond with "let's look it up," he learns much more than how to use a reference book. Seeing you searching for an answer shows him that not knowing is nothing to be ashamed of and that learning isn't confined to school.

Actions speak louder than words, too, when it comes to encouraging your child to put his thoughts on paper. Seeing you write a letter or a report shows him the need for writing isn't limited to the classroom. In fact, you can give your child an important writing lesson simply by letting him see you crumple up the first copy of a letter or a report that didn't turn out right. Children often fail to realize that revision is a normal part of writing for everyone, grownups included.

Keep in mind that your child will imitate negative attitudes toward learning as well as positive ones. For example, if you dislike math, try not to pass this feeling on to your child. Hearing you say, "I never was any good at math," can make him feel that it's no use trying to learn. Instead, motivate your child by showing him the connection between school work and what happens later in life. Tell him about teachers or courses you remember as being especially valuable in preparing for a career or becoming interested in a hobby.

If you've seen the movie *Cheaper by the Dozen,* you'll recall the not-so-subtle devices Mr. Gilbreth used to make sure his children didn't waste a moment when they could be learning. Meals were occasions for lectures and quizzes, lists of formulas or French verbs to be memorized were posted on mirrors and closet doors, and the house was filled with all kinds of educational projects. This scheme worked pretty well for the Gilbreth children, probably because their mother and father—both industrial engineers—participated wholeheartedly in most of the projects.

In *Teach Your Own,* John Holt describes an awkward family dinner at which every word the parents spoke was obviously intended to teach something to the children. The awkwardness, I suspect, meant that the parents themselves weren't genuinely interested in what they were talking about. Putting on a front for children seldom works. Enthusiasm is the key ingredient in teaching anyone anything, and children sense when it's missing.

Whether these more obvious tricks of the trade to promote learning succeed depends on the individual parents and children. Regardless of what parents plan, though, much of the learning that takes place at home is apt to be as impromptu, incongruous, and exciting as children themselves. One muggy summer afternoon when she was eight, my daughter rushed into the house carrying a battered, dusty violin case.

"Julie's dad cleaned out their attic, and look what he found!" She opened the case and took out a small violin, cradling it on her shoulder. "They're selling it. Isn't it beautiful? I want it. It's a half-size. Buy it for me. Please!"

"But you don't buy a violin unless you're going to play it. They're not just to look at," I told her.

"Then I'll take lessons." Without a glance at the surprised expression on my face, she was out the door, racing back to Julie's with the good news.

I wasn't sure what to do next. No one in our family had had any musical training and I had no idea how to find a teacher, let alone recognize a good one. Thanks to luck and the man in the music store who put the instrument in playing condition, we found a wonderful violin teacher. Ten years, two violins, one piano, and many lessons and school concerts later, I admit that parental planning had nothing to do with any of this.

But planning—often it's more like scheming—does have a part in encouraging children to make the most of what's available at home:

Be sure there's plenty of reading material scattered around—books, newspapers, magazines, pamphlets, anything that offers fiction, poetry, or just plain interesting (to your child) information in printed form. Forget about neatness. Don't "hide" reading materials by stacking magazines on the coffee table or putting books away on the shelf with only the spines showing. If a magazine "just happens" to be open to a particularly intriguing article or story, your child may be too busy reading to guess what you've been up to.

You can't force a child to spend his spare time reading, but you can make reading more attractive by getting your child together with books and eliminating other distractions. At our house, we set up a "quiet time," making sure children were in their bedrooms for an hour or so before bedtime. Because there were books (but no television), in most cases reading was inevitable. You may want to begin "quiet time" by reading aloud.

A mother who travels on business told me she tapes bedtime stories for her daughter to play when she's away. Not as cozy as the traditional "read aloud," perhaps, but her daughter enjoys the novelty of hearing her mother on tape.

Encourage your child to write (perhaps during "quiet time") by giving him a notebook or diary in which to record events of the day, thoughts, jokes, poems—whatever strikes his fancy. Resist the temptation to peek and do *not* make critical comments about writing or spelling if your child invites you to read what he has written. As soon as your child learns to print in school, he can keep a simple diary, though you may have to search for widelined notebooks, or put one together yourself. The educator Bronson Alcott, father of Louisa May Alcott, started journals for each of his daughters when they were infants. The girls continued them when they learned to write.

Fostering your child's writing skills at home is particularly important, since schools do a very poor job of teaching composition. (See chapter 6.) In school most students are "over-workbooked" and underchallenged when it comes to real writing.

Be alert for meaningful opportunities for your child to write. Urge relatives to write to him, and urge your child to write letters instead of picking up the telephone. Check at school to find out whether your child could have a pen pal. Suggest that he write away for vacation folders and free samples. *All About Letters,* a U.S. Postal Service brochure, offers many suggestions on where and how to write. (Send $1.50 to the National Council of Teachers of English, 1111 Kenyon Rd., Urbana, IL 61801.) Older children can make written plans for family projects or vacations. They can also write captions for photograph albums or compose a running commentary on places visited during the trip.

Give books as gifts for birthdays and other occasions. This tells your child that you value books, and he is likely to follow your example.

Give your child a subscription to one of the children's magazines, preferably one that prints letters to the editor. Some children enjoy reading what other children write as much as they enjoy the articles or stories. Your child may write a letter or two himself for the thrill of seeing his words in print.

Teachers often say that children of all ages need to learn to follow directions more carefully. Such family activities as cooking from recipes and playing board games may help to boost your child's skill in following directions.

YOU CAN FIGHT TV—AND WIN!

A parent of five children ranging from junior high to college age says: "I've always censored what the children watch on television. If they ask me why I don't let them watch this show or that one, I tell them it's not something I want in the house because I find it offensive. I know they probably watch when I'm not home, but they've seen less of the really awful stuff than if I didn't censor, and they know what my standards are. I think that's important."

Nearly all parents I talked with shared this view, though few actively censored programs. However, not everyone agrees that television is all bad. "TV is good for children up to about grade 4. After that, the situation is reversed," according to Dr. Robert L. Thorndike of Teachers College, Columbia University. Dr. Thorndike expressed this view to explain in part why an observed increase in children's general intelligence made it necessary to adjust the average score upward on a widely used intelligence test (Stanford-Binet) in 1972. A possible explanation is that younger children are learning to read. Many ads on TV and some children's programs help them to learn the sounds which letters stand for—which is essential in learning to read. Consider, for example, ads for Ban deodorant. When the letters are flashed on the screen, while an announcer says "Ban," children learn the sight-sound relationship for two consonants, "b" and "n," plus the "short 'a' " vowel sound.

After age 9, though, TV is a time-waster that keeps children from developing reading and thinking skills. Many critics believe that the biggest problem with TV is not sex or violence, but its tendency to encourage passivity. Children must interact with a book to get the meaning. Television lays it all out, complete with pictures, so little thinking is required. In fact, a visual medium like television cannot show children that people *do* think. In books children can read and reflect on what characters are thinking.

If the verbal abilities of adults are affected by heavy viewing, as studies have shown, we can probably assume that the effect on children will be far greater. Some authorities believe that lack of adequate language skills can lead to emotional problems. What could be more frustrating than not being able to think things through or not being able to communicate well with fellow human beings?

It seems that if you want to help children avoid the worst effects of TV, avoiding objectionable programs is going only halfway. You have to reduce viewing time, too. These approaches have worked reasonably well in our home and in others:

Ban television viewing (or cut it down to a half hour) if there's school the next day. Limit viewing on weekends, vacations, and holidays to an hour or two. Children get choosy about what they watch if time is limited, but you can still censor if necessary.

Keep television out of children's bedrooms, where you can't control it.

Keep television out of eating areas, and refuse to schedule meals or other family activities around television programs.

Always have the television turned off unless someone makes a deliberate decision to watch a program. Don't keep a set running "for company" in an empty house.

Don't rush to have a broken television repaired. Cutting down the number of sets usually results in less viewing. When buying a new set, avoid the big-screen models.

Spend the money you saved when you bought a cheaper TV on books or on tapes of old-time radio shows. When children listen to "The Green Hornet"—or any other radio adventure show—they have to use their imagination to visualize what's happening. Radio does not encourage passivity in the way television does.

Consider not having a television in your home.

If heavy television viewing has become a habit in your family, you'll probably miss it when you cut down. Have good books, a new hobby, and games on hand to get everyone over the rough spots.

DON'T EXPECT A CARBON COPY

"You look for something of yourself in your child, and you often find it," says a father of three, but he adds, "The big shocker is that in other ways, a child who seems on surface much like you can be totally different."

Recognizing this is one thing. Guiding a child as she develops her own way of thinking and doing things can be far more difficult, particularly when you try to help her with planning for education and a career. How much real help can you give when you know nothing about what your child is interested in? I recall feeling helpless as we shopped for a violin or a piano for my daughter, uncertain what to look for, unable to accept the clerk's invitation to

"Go ahead and play something. See how it sounds to you." When a music teacher describes strong or weak points in a child's playing, I listen intently, hoping enthusiasm will make up for lack of real understanding.

An English professor speaks of advising his son on college plans. "He's starting a course that would lead to automotive engineering, and now he's had an offer of a job rebuilding engines and he wants to quit school. It's a really good job, and he's very good at what he does. He spent years out in the garage under the hood, and I didn't know what an expert he was becoming. I can't say I feel qualified in giving advice, but it seems the best thing would be to finish college. Right now, though, he's leaning toward the job. I know people in engineering, and he's had a chance to talk with them. But I know the decision has to be his."

A high school counselor says, "A good many parents are sympathetic to their children's interests. Other parents may be just as well meaning but they urge their children into fields which really interest *them*. Once in a while I get a call from parents who want my help in undercutting a child's plans because they don't approve. They say, 'He just can't want to major in English [or biology, or art, or whatever]. There's no future in it. Please talk him out of it. We want him to go into dentistry [or some other field].' "

We've all seen unhappy people who chose a college or a career they didn't like because a parent "expected" them to. As parents it's hard to realize that all the teaching and helping and guiding at home is ideally a no-strings-attached proposition, with children finally set free to follow their own interests—not ours.

The counselor continues, "Sometimes parents who really want to protect their children make them miserable. I know one very bright boy from a rather poor home who's making ambitious career plans. He has what it takes to carry them through—except that he gets negative messages from home. His mother keeps telling him he's 'only dreaming,' that 'life is all against you from the start.' I'm sure she's trying to save her son from disappointment, but instead she's discouraging him."

Two mistakes to avoid in dealing with your child and his interests, whether he's six or sixteen:

Don't label your child as stupid, or lazy, or as a quitter, or with any other undesirable trait. Your goal may be to help him to change, but the message can backfire. For example, you may tell your child he's being lazy in order to get him to do more. But to him it could seem as if you're making a final judgment that he is lazy and won't change. A counselor tells this true story. "Lois was extremely talented artistically, and she was also a pretty good student. She used to tell me, though, that her mother got upset with her at home for being so 'lazy' all the time. Of course no one here at school ever saw her as being lazy. She was very active, an all-round good kid. When Lois went off to college, everyone here had high hopes for her. She quit before the end of freshman year, though. I've always wondered whether all the talk about her being lazy had anything to do with it."

Don't predict the future with such remarks as "You don't have what it takes to be a dancer [baseball player, surgeon, or whatever]." Messages like this can be misinterpreted by a child, who may hear only "You don't have what it takes." If he hears this often enough, he'll believe it. Believing will make it so. On the other hand, belief in positive messages, plus determination, can overcome "impossible" obstacles. In the 1880s a young German girl auditioned as a singer. "My dear young lady, I advise you to go home and buy yourself a sewing machine. You have no future in music," she was told by a professor of voice. The girl did not buy a sewing machine. Instead she studied and practiced. Her career as an opera and concert singer brought her world recognition as the contralto Madame Ernestine Schumann-Heink. While not everyone either wants something so much, or has such faith in his own ability, no one can accomplish much of anything if he is discouraged from the start.

Says Illinois teacher Carolyn Hillebrand, noted for her skill and enthusiasm in working with young children: "Parents should always be aware of the need to nurture a child's self-image. Children need *honest* compliments, though. They can tell the difference."

In the next chapter, we'll discuss why good communication between you and the teacher can be important in laying a good foundation for your child's formal learning in school.

3

MAKE THAT TALK WITH THE TEACHER COUNT

School District 81 will hold parent conferences next week on Wednesday afternoon. You are scheduled to meet with your child's teacher at 3:45.

If you react to an announcement like this with a twinge of uneasiness, or even downright anxiety, you have lots of company. "Many parents are afraid they'll say something that might have an unfavorable effect on the way the teacher treats their child. Or they worry that the teacher will judge them as parents," says Sadie Hofstein, director of the Nassau County (New York) Mental Health Association and a specialist in parent education.

There is no sure cure for the anxiety most parents, even those who are teachers themselves, feel about discussing a child's progress—or possible lack of it—with the teacher. You're less likely to feel uneasy about a conference if you take definite steps to prepare for it, and if you learn how to overcome some of the barriers to good communication between parents and teachers.

WHY YOU SHOULD TALK WITH THE TEACHER

What if your school doesn't invite parents to meet individually with the teacher? Call for an appointment, even if your child is doing well. Parents can always ask for a conference with a child's teacher or counselor, even at the junior high and high school level. Especially in the first four or five grades, a written report really can't take the place of a face-to-face talk with the teacher to check on your child's progress—and to find out how good a job the school is doing. It's important, too, to establish a relationship with the teacher before you have to deal with possible problems. Some parents fear they'll be considered a nuisance or too pushy if they take the initiative in approaching the school. Most teachers don't see it that way. As a teacher, I was always pleased when parents of my junior high students wanted to meet with me. Kindergarten teacher Charlotte Scott agrees: "I find that the better I get to know parents, the more interested I am in working with their children."

Remember, a talk *with* the teacher is not the same as a talk *by* the teacher. Be ready to contribute more than a polite smile and a nod if you want to make sure your meeting with the teacher accomplishes all it should for your child. Keep in mind that your approach will help to set the tone of the conference. An air of self-assurance on your part will encourage the teacher to speak freely, to respect your opinions, and to respond positively to your requests for information. Act as if you consider yourself a partner in your child's education, and you're more likely to be treated that way.

But don't come on too strong and give the impression you're there to quiz the teacher. She may be uneasy about conferences, too, particularly if she's naturally shy or new to teaching. Says a teacher with twenty-five years' experience, "I know many teachers who feel that talking with parents is among the most difficult things they do."

PREPARE FOR A TALK WITH THE TEACHER

Before you talk with the teacher, talk with your child, who is an important authority on how he's doing in school. Look at his work for clues. Find out what he likes most and least, what he has problems with. Jot down notes and questions during the semester before the conference. One mother found that even when her children weren't eager to talk to her about school, she could learn a lot by listening to what they said to one another and to their friends.

When my own children were in elementary school, I always asked before going to a conference whether there was anything they wanted me to tell the teacher. Even when their messages weren't fit to deliver ("Tell him I wish he'd quit reading that dumb book to us every day!") they often gave me a child's-eye view of life in the classroom. Once my daughter said, "Ask him why he practically never calls on me to put math problems on the board anymore." When I brought this up (tactfully, of course) at the conference, the teacher smiled knowingly. "For the first few weeks of school your daughter and a few others volunteered so eagerly for board work that I'm afraid I called on them too often. Now I'm trying to make sure everyone gets an equal chance." My daughter was glad to hear the change didn't mean the teacher thought any less of her or her math.

Talking to your child before you see the teacher will make him less anxious about the conference. Children often worry about those mysterious meetings between parent and teacher. Reassure your child by giving him at least a partial recap of what the teacher said during your talk, though of course you may feel it's best to keep some of the discussion confidential.

Before your talk with the teacher, you'll also find it helpful to look over these questions suggested by the National Committee for Citizens in Education (NCCE), a nonprofit organization dedicated to strengthening parent-citizen involvement in the public schools. If the teacher doesn't answer these questions during your talk, you may want to bring them up yourself.

1. If your school issues a handbook, look it over before your talk with the teacher. It may suggest questions you'll want to ask or save conference time by answering some of your other questions.

2. Is your child working at grade level in reading and math, or is he performing above or below? (In an average fifth-grade classroom, for example, reading levels can range from the third to eighth grade.)

3. Ask to go over samples of your child's work with the teacher.

4. What tests has he been given, and what do the scores mean? Don't hesitate to ask for an explanation of testing terms such as "norm" and "percentile." Once you understand your child's score,

ask how it compares with that of other children in the same grade in your school. (See chapter 4 for more help in understanding tests.)

5. Does your child do his homework and class work regularly? Is it consistent with his test grades?

6. Does your child get along well with classmates in class and on the playground?

7. Has the teacher noticed any marked decline or improvement in his learning, or any changes in behavior, like squinting or fatigue, that could signal a medical problem? In discussing an older child, you may want to ask about symptoms suggestive of drug use.

8. Does your child need special help in any academic area?

9. Does the teacher advise any special program or placement?

THE CONFERENCE

A sincere compliment is a good conference opener. Are you pleased that the teacher stresses spelling or makes memorizing multiplication tables seem like a game? Tell her so. This will show that you really are interested in what goes on in the classroom. But avoid being overly chatty, since this wastes conference time.

Parents often feel that teachers are too hesitant about delivering bad news. One parent says, "I think teachers sometimes spend too much time accentuating the positive when they talk to parents about their children. Of course it's nice to hear the good things. But since time is limited, I want to find out right away if the teacher thinks my child is inattentive or needs extra help in a subject. I always try to let her know that she can speak frankly."

I once heard a kindergarten teacher in a phone conference with a parent. "I'm really not enjoying David in class right now. He's not cooperative when the children work at their tables and he doesn't quiet down when we have rest period."

She hung up the phone and turned to me: "He's frantic! He tears around the room whenever he feels like it. Nothing I do seems to work with him." I recall thinking that if David were my child, I would certainly want to know how bad the problem really was so I could help him. The kindergarten teacher's understatement to David's mother was a disservice to all concerned, most of all to him.

With the best of intentions, teachers often do sugarcoat bad news. For example: "He doesn't work independently" can mean a child cheats. "She's outspoken" can mean she's disrespectful. "He doesn't settle down to work" can mean he's disruptive. How can you make sure the teacher levels with you? Simply be direct—"Are we talking about cheating?" Your child won't get help unless someone names the problem. Says parent education expert Sadie Hofstein: "Teachers and parents both fear they'll be blamed for any problems a child has in school. It would be better if they were willing to trust one another and concentrate on doing what's best for the child."

If you're especially concerned about some aspect of your child's work or behavior, you may want to take the lead in discussing it. One mother explains how this approach worked for her: "In the first few weeks of fourth grade, my son had to stay after school several times for disturbing the class. I talked to him about it and I worried a lot. At the fall conference, I brought up his behavior right away. I could see that the teacher was relieved I hadn't waited for her to mention it. That talk helped me to develop a very good working relationship with her."

It's a rare parent, though, who gets every conference off to a good start and finds smooth sailing from there on. No amount of poise will keep you from being upset if the teacher says your child acts up or fails to do his work.

A magazine editor and former teacher recalls her reaction to bad news: "When the teacher told me about the problem my son was having in class, I was shocked to find myself feeling angry at *her*. I managed to hide my feelings, but I was drained when that conference was over."

A mother whose husband serves on the local school board had a similar experience: "I resented hearing that my daughter acted immature, always running to the teacher for help instead of trying to work things out for herself. I was tempted to tell the teacher he was mistaken. Later I was glad I hadn't. Taking a new look at the way my daughter behaved at home, I decided the teacher might be right."

Because the teacher has been trained to let parents vent their anger by talking it out, she will probably stay calm if your temper gets out of control. Stop talking as soon as you're aware of what's happening. Apologize; explain that you're overtired or terribly worried about whatever provoked the outburst. Nearly everyone responds to a sincere apology. Before you leave, try to calm yourself enough to say something like this: "I really am sorry, and I'd be grateful if we could get together again when I've had a chance to think things through."

How can you keep from being thrown off balance when the teacher brings up a problem? First, avoid acting guilty or apologetic. Saying "I knew I should have . . ." or "I knew I shouldn't have . . ." won't improve the situation or put you on an equal footing with the teacher in working to solve the problem. The teacher who brings up a difficulty your child is having in school is not being critical of you as a parent; she's asking for your help, even if she doesn't say so directly. Second, avoid jumping to conclusions. Suppose the teacher says, "Julie is too easily distracted." Calmly ask the teacher for an example of whatever behavior seems to be causing the problem. Then try to get answers to these questions: How does the behavior compare with what is normal for her age? How does the problem affect her school work? What does the teacher think should be done about the problem? What can you do to help? If you have a suggestion about handling the problem in class, don't hesitate to offer it tactfully.

If conference time runs out—or if you're too stunned to think about the problem clearly—arrange another meeting before you leave. Keep in mind that if after getting all the facts you have doubts about the way the teacher suggests handling the problem, you can ask for another opinion.

COMMUNICATIONS PROBLEMS
BETWEEN PARENT AND TEACHER

Though no two conferences are alike, several communications problems crop up frequently in talks between parents and teachers. Should you be pleased or worried if the teacher says your son works poorly in an "unstructured classroom situation"? Ask, and you'll learn that "unstructured" means children are expected to work at their own pace with varying degrees of guidance. If you don't ask for a translation when the teacher uses education terms you don't understand, you're liable to miss out on important information about your child. (See Glossary for an explanation of these terms.)

In this scene, the stage is set for another serious problem:

Mother: "How is Cheri doing in reading?"
Teacher: "She's doing well. She works well in class and her comprehension is good. Her grade-equivalent on the last test was 3.7."

Cheri is just beginning third grade, so the 3.7 sounds like cause for rejoicing. In Cheri's school district, though, most third-graders scored above 4.5 on that national test. When the teacher says Cheri is "doing well," she means that Cheri works hard in the lowest reading group in her class. But Cheri's mother leaves thinking her daughter is a very good reader.

Misunderstandings like this can occur all too easily. Like many teachers, Cheri's believes that where a child stands in relation to his classmates isn't important—as long as he works well at his own level. This view may make sense when it comes to creating a good climate for learning in the classroom, but a teacher who fails to make clear to parents exactly how a child's progress or ability compares with that of other children in the class is guilty of a serious deception. Echoing many complaints I've heard from other parents, one mother told me, "It wasn't until the next year [fourth grade] that I found out my son was well behind most of the class, and I decided he should have extra help in reading. I wish I had insisted on finding out sooner."

"I don't hesitate to say to parents, 'Yes, he did get a check for "satisfactory" in reading, but he is in the slow group,'" says an outstanding primary teacher of many years' experience. "Parents have a right to know and should know what level the group is. If parents aren't told, they should always ask the teacher. But they should *not* talk to their child about which group she's in."

How can you be sure you're getting the whole story? First, ask what the average score on that standardized test was for students in your child's grade *in your school or school district.* Next, find out what reading group your child is in. (See chapter 6 for what to do if your child needs extra help.)

Unfortunately, some teachers and other school people discourage parents from asking questions by implying they don't need the information or wouldn't understand it. If you find yourself in this frustrating situation during a talk with the teacher, remember that it's your legal right to have *all* of your child's test scores explained fully, so you can insist on it.

Usually you can persuade the teacher to give you the information you need simply by convincing her that you understand her point of view. Teachers say they avoid discussing how children are grouped because they're afraid parents will ask to have a child moved up, even if he isn't ready, or will nag a child who doesn't score high. First, let the teacher know that you understand children learn at different rates and that you won't raise the roof if your child isn't put in the advanced math group. Then explain that you do need to know where your child stands now, because it will help you in planning for him.

Deciding What to Tell the Teacher

You can concentrate so hard on getting information from the teacher that you forget she needs your input, too. "If little Dan is lively and talkative outside school, but timid and shy in kindergarten class, I would want to find out why. I like to compare notes with parents to make sure neither of us misses a clue," says a kindergarten teacher. What you tell the teacher about your child may help her to work better with him in class. Let her know about his hobbies, vacations, special interests.

You'll probably want to tell the teacher about a death or illness in the family or any other emergency which might disrupt your child's work or behavior at school. But some parents and some experts, including the late Dr. Haim Ginott, advise against letting the school know about chronic problems—such as an alcoholic parent—or an unusual family situation—like adoption. Teachers are not trained counselors, and the school could "label" a child and blame any difficulties he has at school on the situation at home.

Betty Felton, field staff director for United Parents Associations, Inc. of New York City, disagrees: "A parent who doesn't tell the school about a problem at home can miss out on valuable help. In New York City, for example, some schools will help a single parent find a teenaged 'homework helper' for younger children." In the late '70s a number of schools on the east coast and in the middle west started group counseling sessions for children of divorced parents.

TIME AND SCHEDULING PROBLEMS

Admittedly, all of this is a lot to cover in a brief talk. Many teachers, particularly in the early grades, say that the ten minutes or so usually set aside for reporting conferences is seldom enough. Try these tips for making every minute count:

Ask for an appointment early in the conference schedule, before the teacher feels "talked out."

If you come with questions, let the teacher know at the beginning of your talk, so they won't get lost in the shuffle. List them in order of importance beforehand.

Encourage the teacher to speak about problems early in your talk. Otherwise, she may leave bad news until last.

If time is up before you can ask about something you feel is especially important, plan for another talk: "I know other people are waiting to see you now, but I'd like to talk more about this. May I call for another appointment?"

If you can't keep an appointment because of your commuting schedule, a deadline at work, or a business trip, let the teacher know right away so you can set up another meeting, perhaps before or after school hours. Or a phone conference might be more convenient for you both. Ask the teacher to mail you copies of your child's papers and tests before the conference call. Although more than 17 million working mothers in this country have school children under thirteen years of age, half of the school districts that hold regular parent conferences do so during normal working hours, according to a 1980 survey by Phyllis L. Clay of the NCCE. A suburban elementary district schedules two of its yearly parent conferences during the day and the other two in the evening for the convenience of working parents. "When you already know the teacher and your child is doing well, cancelling the conference altogether may be all right," says one experienced elementary teacher. "The teacher is probably a working parent, too, and will understand."

"PROBLEM" CONFERENCES

So far we've been talking about routine conferences to discuss a child's school work. But much of what we've said also applies to school conferences requested by you or by the school to deal with a specific problem. Be sure to let the teacher know why you want to see her. "Parents sometimes ask for a meeting and then expect the teacher to figure out what it's all about without being told," says Carole Murray, a second-grade teacher whose experience spans twenty-five years in Chicago-area schools. "Whoever suggests the conference should carry the ball."

If the teacher, principal, or counselor calls to suggest a special conference, they should tell you the reason for the meeting right away. Whatever the difficulty, you'll deal with it better if you know well before the meeting what to expect. If you were too stunned to ask questions at first, call to find out. These suggestions can help you prepare for the meeting:

Unless there's a good reason for not doing so, talk the matter over with your child. If his behavior is involved, support him while you try to find out what it's all about.

Sometimes teachers and counselors like to include the child in a conference. If you want to suggest this, ask whether the teacher thinks it's a good idea in this case. If the teacher suggests a three-way conference and you're not sure you like the idea, ask what she hopes to accomplish by including your child. You may change your mind. Perhaps you can compromise by meeting alone with the teacher before or after the three-way talk.

If you feel you need moral support or advice during *any* conference at school, you can bring along a spouse, a friend, a legal advisor, or any other person you choose.

Find out beforehand which members of the school staff will attend the conference. A conference to discuss a special problem or plan a specialized program for your child can include several people, some of whom may be strangers to you, in addition to the teacher and the counselor or principal. *Do not* go alone to such a meeting. You will almost certainly be at a psychological disadvantage facing so many experts—a far from ideal situation if you must make a decision that may profoundly affect your child's education.

Schools may sometimes use such meetings not only to inform parents, but also to intimidate them. In *Parent Prerogatives,* guidance counselors Richard L. and Lynn Goetsch Weinberg suggest taking a tape recorder to any school meeting where you expect to be given important information by several people. Then you can replay the conference at your leisure and make whatever decision is necessary in a more relaxed frame of mind at home.

If school people object to your recorder, explain it's the only way you can be sure you have an accurate record of all the information you'll be given. An alternative is to hire a stenographer to make a verbatim record of the meeting for you.

Whether your talk with the teacher is a routine reporting conference or a special meeting, it may require some followup. If you and the teacher make plans to give your child special help in school or at home, set a date for plans to be carried out. After you've worked with your child at home for a week or two, you might call the teacher or send a note asking if your efforts are paying off for your child in class. If the teacher says she'll give you further information about anything you discussed, ask when you can expect to hear from her.

Taking the trouble to follow up after a conference lets the teacher know you're willing to work with her and want to keep the lines of communication open.

2

You,
Your Child,
and
School

4

TAKE THE MYSTERY OUT OF TEST SCORES

> From early childhood through entry into
> professional jobs, standardized tests make sig-
> nificant judgments about our children. Yet no
> portion of the public school system is less un-
> derstood than are the facts about standardized
> tests, their assets and their limitations . . . The
> present degree of the art of assessment is far
> less precise than we have been led to believe.
>
> —VIRGINIA SPARLING, testi-
> mony on behalf of National
> PTA before a House of Rep-
> resentatives hearing on truth
> in testing

"The number in the upper left corner of your printout is your
child's IQ score," the high school counselor told the 200 parents
who had come to pick up packets of tests and other materials for
their incoming freshmen children. The counselor went on to give
the "normal" range for IQ scores as anywhere from around 90 to
110. Actually, though, the numbers she pointed out were not IQ
scores at all. Since few parents in that group held printouts with
numbers above 60 or 70, most of those present would have had to
conclude that their children had subnormal intelligence.

When several parents talked with the counselor about the "IQ
scores," she insisted what she had said was correct. Finally, after

parents pointed out that the numbers looked strange indeed, she admitted that there "must have been some mistake." Those numbers in the upper left corner of the printouts were *percentile rankings* of IQ scores, not the scores themselves. However, no effort was made to inform the nearly 200 parents who did not hear her belated explanation.

You can learn two important lessons about tests from this scene with the counselor. The first is that most school people are not test experts. They do know more about standardized tests (the type we will discuss in this chapter) than most parents. Only school psychologists might be said to have expert knowledge about testing. Yet all school people—including kindergarten teachers, principals, junior high teachers, curriculum planners, and high school counselors—make extensive use, and sometimes misuse, of tests to decide your child's educational future. For example, IQ tests and achievement tests are used to group children at all levels of schooling—sometimes without your being aware of it. In high school these tests are often used to "track" students and to advise them on which courses to take (economics *or* a watered-down economics course called consumer education; biology *or* general science, another watered-down course, and so on). The cumulative effect of these test-based decisions through twelve years of schooling will either enhance or limit a child's future opportunities for education or a career. Unless you make an effort to understand what testing is all about, you may not even be aware of this process, let alone have a say in it.

The second lesson is that parents rarely ask enough questions about tests and tend to place too much faith both in test scores themselves and in their usefulness for making educational decisions. Says one critic of standardized tests: "The public's awe for numbers, and for anyone who can fling them about with an air of assurance, is at the root of this belief in the precision of test scores."

Many parents regard tests as having some near-magical power to predict a child's achievement or to ferret out his hidden talents. Tests have no such power. Often tests only *seem* to predict a child's ability to achieve because school people (who may have the best intentions) make test scores the basis for a self-fulfilling prophecy. An all-too-common example: On the basis of an IQ test and a couple of achievement tests, eight-year-old Dave is put in the low third-grade group. Children in the low group are considered "dumb," which affects their morale, and they are not taught as much or as rigorously as "average"-group children. When he is tested again in sixth grade, Dave's scores are below average. Did the third-grade tests predict Dave's sixth-grade performance, or did the way he was taught during the intervening years make his performance inevitable?

Knowing the respect parents have for test scores, school people frequently use them to justify school decisions and to silence parents' objections. Though test makers often warn that test scores alone should not be the basis for placing children in one group or another, they have been guilty of encouraging school people to hide behind tests. George Weber, a former official of the Council for Basic Education (CBE), tells of the teacher's manual for one reading-readiness test which notes that it is difficult for a teacher to tell a parent that in the teacher's judgment a first-grader is not "ready" to begin learning to read. The manual continues, "It is relatively easy, however, to say that a child has been given a test, the results of which indicate placement [in a class which will not be taught to read yet]. . . ."

It's worth noting how often school people say, "According to this test, your child . . .," when the tests support their views. Yet school people and others in the educational establishment are quick to disparage tests when results show that schools are not doing their job. "Quality of teaching is poorly indicated by performance on national tests," says Dr. Robert E. Stake, director of instructional research and curriculum in the college of education at the University of Illinois.

As everyone is aware, the trend on these large group tests has for twenty years or more been generally downward, with only a minuscule rise in the last several years. These national tests, as everyone is also aware, measure the academic achievement of very large groups of students. By definition, group tests are most suitable for measuring group performance.

It is ironic to hear educators object to results of group tests when these tests are being used as they were designed to be used—to measure the achievement of a large group of students, yielding results which enable us to spot trends and draw far-reaching conclusions about the adequacy of our schools. The irony arises because educators—your child's teacher, principal, or counselor—are frequently eager to use results of group tests as they were not designed to be used—to draw far-reaching conclusions about the learning capacity of an individual student. As psychologist Mitchell Lazarus notes in pointing out limitations of standardized testing, "Even the best tests available are suitable for only extremely broad and soft comparisons among students. Yet people who use test scores for making decisions routinely draw much finer distinctions. In a large fraction of cases, the decisions must rest on test error rather than on individual competence or ability [of the person tested]."

TESTING, TESTING: TERMS AND EXPLANATIONS
With all their flaws, tests are a fact of school life for your child. You'll be better able to discuss his scores with school people and to ask questions about decisions based on these scores if you understand these commonly used testing terms:

Cumulative record. A list of scores of all the standardized tests your child has taken since he started school.

Standardized tests. You have probably taken a number of these machine-scored tests, which present their questions in a printed booklet and require students to mark answers on a special sheet. Standardized tests differ in several ways from teacher-made classroom tests. A norm-referenced achievement test, the most commonly used type of standardized test, is designed to be taken by millions of students across the nation. These tests show how an individual or a group of students compares with other groups of students at the same grade level in such subjects as reading, math, or grammar.

The company which produces the test establishes the "norms" for scoring it by first trying out the questions on a sample group of students who are representative of all those who will eventually take the test. To compare students in their knowledge of a given subject, the test-maker must choose questions deliberately so that scores will cluster in a "bell-shaped" curve, with the largest number of the scores near the middle. Fewer high scores and low scores form the sloping sides of the "bell."

"Standardized" also means that all students taking the same test, no matter when and where it is given, should do so under the same (standard) conditions: with instructions given in the same way, with the same amount of time allowed for each person on each section of the test, and so on. A standardized norm-referenced test, then, has a predetermined distribution of scores and it should always be given under the same conditions.

In addition to achievement tests, your child will probably take at least two other types of standardized tests in school—intelligence (IQ) tests and (in high school) college entrance tests, the Scholastic Aptitude Test and the ACT Assessment, both discussed later in this chapter.

Keep in mind that the term "standardized" does not mean these tests are better than other types of tests. Standardized tests can and do contain poorly written questions—those which are ambiguous or just plain wrong.

Reliability. A reliable test agrees with itself. This means that if a group of students took the same test today and then took it again next week (and if we somehow made allowances for what they learned in the meantime), the overall scores would be very similar both times. An individual student, though, will probably give some different answers each time he takes the test. Before a test is put into use, test makers check its reliability by giving similar forms of the same test to the same group of students at different times. Questions on which students change their minds (decreasing the reliability of the test) are removed.

Validity. As one testing expert puts it, "Validity is the soul of a test." A valid or "true" test measures what it is supposed to measure. A test which fails to measure what it is supposed to measure is useless. (Worse, it can do great harm, as in the case of IQ tests, which we'll examine later.) Test makers trying to find out whether they have developed a test which measures what it purports to measure, competence in math, for example, may simply have an expert in math look over the test. If his opinion supports that of the test makers, they will say their test is a valid test of math competence. A test maker can also check the validity of his test by comparing students' performance on the test with their actual performance of the skill being tested. Neither of these methods, nor any other method of checking a test's validity, is ever completely foolproof, though. Some tests, therefore, may have no "soul."

Even if a test is reasonably valid when given under proper conditions, its validity is questionable or nonexistent under other conditions—if students are coached, for example. In a recent *New York Times* article, the director of admissions for one of a small but growing number of colleges which no longer require applicants to submit SAT scores notes that his school has "serious ethical questions about the Scholastic Aptitude Test, including concern about the growth of commercial 'coaching' courses that help students prepare for the standardized tests."

Another form of coaching occurs when elementary schools give students workbooks very similar to the tests. The added practice can result in higher test scores which don't reflect real gains in reading or other subjects, making the test useless.

Raw score. The raw score on a standardized test is simply the total number of correct answers; or, on some tests, the total number correct, minus the number wrong. By itself, a raw score doesn't mean much.

Grade-equivalent scores. A grade-equivalent score for a standardized test is an attempt to make the raw score meaningful by placing it at a grade level. The result can be misleading. Schools continue to use grade-equivalent scores, against the advice of testing companies. To illustrate the problems, Henry S. Dyer, a former vice president of the Educational Testing Service, gives this example: "If your seventh-grade child comes home with a GE of 12–7, you are asked to believe that his or her math performance is at the same level as that of students getting ready to graduate from high school, *even though the test may contain no math problems ordinarily dealt with in grades nine through twelve.*" If the teacher explains your child's test score as a grade-equivalent, ask to see the "percentile rank."

Percentile rank. While percentile is based on 100, it is not the same as percentage. A student's percentile rank on a test is figured from the percentage of students taking the test who get the same score or a lower score than his. Let's say that scores on a test taken by 300 students range from 15 to 25. Thirty students receive scores of 23 or above. Since thirty is 10 percent of 300, this means that the rest of the students, 90 percent of those who took the test, scored below 23. This puts any student with a score of 23, 24, or 25 at or above the 90th percentile. On the same test, 150 students scored 19 or above. An individual student with a score of 19 is therefore in the 50th percentile, because he scored above 50 percent of those who took the test. The 50th percentile separates the top half of the scores from the bottom half. Here is why parents were confused in that scene with the counselor at the beginning of this chapter:

An average IQ score is about 100. Parents who knew their children were of normal intelligence saw numbers like 50, 60, or 70 in the upper left corner of the sheet the counselor gave them. If IQ scores are ranked by percentiles, an average IQ lands in the 50th percentile, where we always find the average scores on any norm-referenced test. Scores a bit above average would be in the 60th or 70th percentiles, explaining those low numbers which the counselor told the parents were the actual IQ scores.

Test norm. This is the estimated average score that would be found if all students in a certain group (all U.S. children in fourth grade, for example) took a given test under the same conditions. A test norm is determined by averaging the scores of the norming group.

Keep in mind that in towns or suburbs with above-average levels of income and education the local norm (the average of scores of local students) on a standardized achievement test in any subject *should* be well above the national norm. Be sure to ask to see your child's percentile rank based on local norms, since this is apt to be far more meaningful than how his score compares with the national norm.

Norm-referenced tests. Most of the widely used standardized tests which measure children's achievement in reading, math, and other subjects are norm-referenced. On these tests a child's score does not depend on how many answers he has correct, but on how many answers he has correct *compared with* other children who take the test. Students are not being tested on an absolute standard of performance, but on their relative performance. On a norm-referenced test, a child may have an excellent score if he gets only 65 answers out of 100 correct, provided that most children get even fewer answers correct.

An important advantage of norm-referenced tests is that they allow us to see how groups of children compare with one another. Comparing performance of one fourth-grade class with another, or one school or district with another, we can draw conclusions about how well teachers and administrators are doing their jobs. And perhaps even more important for purposes of checking school performance, we can compare a school or district with itself over time. Looking at test results can help us to answer such questions as: "Is School District X doing a better or a worse job of teaching math now than it did five years ago?"

A serious shortcoming of norm-referenced tests is that they usually yield only a score, without showing why a child makes the mistakes he does and what can be done to help him improve. For example, if a child does poorly on the long-division section in math, we can't tell whether he is weak in multiplication or in subtraction, both of which are required in doing long-division problems. Knowing that he got a lot of answers wrong on this section doesn't tell the teacher what she can do to help him.

Re-normed test. Some norm-referenced standardized tests remain in use for as long as a decade or two. But school achievement in the U.S. as a whole has changed over time, dropping precipitously since the mid-'60s. Let's say the norm (average score) established for a given test written in 1965 was 53 answers correct out of 100 questions. Fewer children today will get 53 correct answers than was the case in 1966, which means fewer children today will score at or above the national norm set before the general drop in achievement. But the test can be "re-normed," by giving it to a representative sample of today's students, a new "norming group." Since the average student today makes a lower score, the new norm will be lower, say 49 correct out of 100 questions.

Naturally, if achievement is falling, school administrators would prefer to use re-normed tests, because students can get fewer answers right and still score at or above the lowered norm. This works both ways. If achievement has risen dramatically, students—and schools—would appear to better advantage if their scores were compared to norms established during a time of lower achievement. The cost of re-norming a test is high (probably $2 million or more), so test publishers don't do it too often. Still, parents, school board members, and citizens examining test scores to rate their school's performance should check to see whether a test was normed (or last re-normed) in a period of high or low achievement.

Criterion-referenced tests. There's much talk these days about using fewer norm-referenced tests to check achievement, and replacing them with criterion-referenced tests. It's important to understand that these two types of tests give us different types of information about how children are doing in school. As we saw above, norm-referenced tests answer questions like: "How does one child compare with others (or how does one group compare with another) in math computation in third grade?" Since the test makers write questions after suveying a large number of third-grade text-books and curriculum guides used by many schools, the test may include many questions which measure what third-graders need to learn in math. But in making up a norm-referenced test, the primary concern is to choose questions which will result in scores that form a bell-shaped curve.

.In making up a criterion-referenced test, on the other hand, a test maker's first concern is deciding what math skills children should have acquired in third grade. Then questions are made up to find out whether children have mastered these skills. In a criterion test, students are being checked against an absolute standard of skills which they *should* learn.

A distinct advantage of criterion-referenced tests is that they are more likely than norm-referenced tests to tell us whether a child has mastered essential skills. Those who show on a criterion test that they have not are more likely to get help, because they show the teacher where students need more work. Criterion-referenced tests "may even be more conducive [than norm-referenced tests] to the establishment of real standards of performance: minimum standards all can hope to achieve, higher standards that some can hope to achieve," according to the Council for Basic Education (CBE).

Test publisher. One expert estimates there are approximately 130 U.S. companies in the business of supplying school tests. These are among the fewer than ten that dominate the field: Educational Testing Service, Harcourt Brace Jovanovich, Science Research Associates, American College Testing Program, McGraw-Hill Publishers, Houghton Mifflin Co., and California Test Bureau. Testing is big business—between $200 and $300 million is spent every year for tests alone, not counting the cost of the personnel needed to administer them. Students in grades 1 through 12 take 300 million tests per year. Most test publishers are commercial, and even those who aren't, like the ETS, which can claim to be nonprofit, compete with the commercial publishers.

Test item. This is the test maker's term for "question." On standardized achievement tests, most questions are multiple choice, as you're probably aware. In a good multiple-choice question, one answer is clearly "best" or "right" and the rest are clearly wrong. Poorly written questions are a menace to the children who have to struggle through them and live with the test's judgment of their abilities.

When Edwin F. Taylor, who has edited the *American Journal of Physics* and served as a senior research associate at MIT, randomly chose five questions from what he considered the "least objectionable" elementary school science achievement test, he found every question flawed! He also culled thirty-two "worst," ambiguous, or just plain wrong questions from seven tests—an average of more than four questions per test. On a forty-item test, that's better than 10 percent, enough to make a decided difference in a child's science score.

Here is a question from Dr. Taylor's examples of actual multiple-choice questions for which *all* answers could be correct, though children were allowed only one answer:

When fish take water into their mouths they are

> eating
> drinking
> breathing
> tasting

Of these answers, only one will be marked correct. Yet no answer is clearly "right." The test makers may consider "eating" the correct choice, as larger fish eat smaller ones taken in with the water. But certainly eating must include "tasting." And taking in water is "drinking." "Breathing" shouldn't be the answer, since gills perform that function in fish. But the gills are located at the back of the mouth . . . Neither a nine-year-old who had studied fish for a week, nor a college zoology student could find the correct answer here.

If your child's school insists on giving these tests, don't take the scores too seriously. Make sure your child is not "grouped" for science learning on the basis of his score. Keep in mind that you are paying plenty to have your child take these tests. They should be good, or at least not diabolically ambiguous. You are also paying plenty in salaries to whoever chooses tests for your school. They should not spend your tax money to buy poorly conceived tests which contribute nothing to your child's education.

Truth in testing. Currently there's a movement to reduce the secrecy in which the testing business is conducted. New York passed a truth in testing law in 1979, requiring that each college entrance test (the Scholastic Aptitude Test [SAT] and ACT Assessment [ACT]) given in the state be published, along with correct answers, immediately after it is given. California has a similar law. Twenty-four other states have tried or are currently making efforts to pass truth in testing laws.

Efforts to pass a federal truth in testing law have not been successful, though Congress held fifteen days of hearings between 1979 and 1981 on proposed legislation. One result of these hearings has been that the Educational Testing Service, which lobbied strongly against the proposed laws, voluntarily agreed to extend the New York truth in testing guidelines on its college admissions tests to all states.

THE BATTERY OF TESTS:
KINDERGARTEN THROUGH GRADE 8

One expert estimates that by the time your child graduates from high school, he may have taken as many as twelve complete achievement test "batteries." Each test in the battery deals with a different subject—reading, math, social studies, and so on. In addition, your child will probably take IQ tests and reading-readiness tests, and possibly minimum-competency tests. (See chapter 10 for a discussion of problems connected with personality tests, which are also given in the elementary grades.) Here we'll look at each type of test roughly in the order children take them in school.

Actually, your child's testing could start *before* he enters school. State and federal laws require schools to run a screening program to find children with learning disabilities or other handicaps before they enter school. (See chapters 6 and 10 for more about special education.) Schools usually publicize these screenings, urging parents of preschoolers to bring them in for testing. However, parents are not required to have children tested. If your child has an obvious handicap, you may welcome the screening. If not, but you suspect a handicap of some sort, you may want to have him tested by a private agency, so that you will have more control in deciding whether he is placed in the school's special ed program.

IQ Tests (Also Called General Aptitude Tests)

As you probably know, "IQ" stands for "intelligence quotient," which is expressed as a number. But no two psychologists, and no two thoughtful people, for that matter, have ever been able to agree on a definition of intelligence.

Columnist Walter Lippman expressed his doubts about IQ testing emphatically more than sixty years ago: "If the impression takes root that these tests really measure intelligence, that they constitute a sort of last judgment on the child's capacity, that they reveal 'scientifically' his predestined ability, then it would be a thousand times better if all the intelligence testers and all their questionnaires were sunk without warning in the Sargasso Sea."

The worst of Mr. Lippman's fears have been realized. Too many people do think an IQ score is scientific. And too many educators are willing to use the score as if it did reveal a child's predestined ability. IQ tests are too often used to pigeonhole children and limit their further opportunities for learning, or as a convenient excuse for not teaching very enthusiastically. IQ tests have a pernicious relationship to failures in teaching reading. Like most group tests, they require a lot of reading. But what happens when a poor reader scores low on his IQ test? The school can say that the low score explains his failure to learn to read.

All this does not mean that there is no such thing as high or low intelligence, or that some people cannot learn more easily than others. But group IQ tests show what a child has learned, assuming, of course, that he reads well enough to take them in the first place. They do not test some innate, mysterious, unchanging intellectual ability, as psychologists once mistakenly believed and as too many people continue to believe. Most of us are probably smarter on some days than on others, just as we play tennis or bowl better on some days than we do on other days. It's well known that improving a child's opportunities to learn can often boost his IQ score, and that coaching for these tests works as well as coaching for other kinds of tests.

Henry S. Dyer writes: "Too many people forget—or have never realized—that the IQ, like any test score, *is nothing more than an index number that is useful for summarizing how a student has responded to a miscellaneous series of test questions*" (Dyer's italics).

Despite evidence that they are of limited use and can be abused, some schools go right on giving the tests. Let's assume that your school does use IQ tests, by whatever name, and that you need to be able to recognize them for what they are and make sure they aren't used to pigeonhole your child. These are among the more widely used group IQ tests: California Test of Mental Maturity, Lorge-Thorndike Intelligence Tests, Otis-Lennon Mental Ability Test, Short Form Test of Academic Aptitude. Most of the others have titles with such words as "mental maturity," "mental," "aptitude," or "academic aptitude," and so on. Three individual intelligence tests: Stanford-Binet IQ Test, Wechsler Intelligence Scale for Children, Wechsler Preschool & Primary Scale of Intelligence.

IQ tests—both types—give scores ranging from 40 to 160. The average is about 100, give or take 10 points. As is the case with achievement tests, some IQ tests are known for a tendency to yield higher or lower scores.

Some school people are as skeptical about IQ tests as they should be. You may talk to a teacher or someone else who is and feel reassured. But you can be sure if the school gives these tests, they will be in the record, and if they are in the record school people who are not so skeptical or who need a handy label for a child can see and use them.

Ask at school how IQ scores are used. You may hear a vague "Well, they are one of the measurement tools we use, one of the routine tests." Persist. Are they used for grouping? If they are used to tag children, then low score = low group = low expectations = less teaching = less achievement, as we saw earlier in this chapter. Find out what group your child is in and find out what part his IQ score played in putting him there. If the group is low and IQ scores were used for placement, have his reading checked. If it's not good, make sure he gets real help. You have a right to expect school people to direct their efforts at preparing him to do regular work at his grade level, not at tagging him.

Reading-Readiness Tests

Probably 80 percent of schools use these tests in kindergarten or first grade. Among skills tested are listening, following directions, recognizing letters, visual and motor coordination, matching, and word recognition. If a child's score indicates he isn't ready, instruction is delayed. Three readiness tests are the Gates-MacGinitie Readiness Skills Test, the Metropolitan Readiness Test, and the Murphy Durrell Reading Readiness Analysis. Others have similar titles.

Some educators point out that plenty of children have learned to read at home or in school without ever having been "proved" ready to learn. They also point out that after forty years of research on the effectiveness of these tests, the claims for these tests by their producers don't hold up.

One astute critic of tests, Dr. Banesh Hoffman, has noted that these are really reading "unreadiness" tests, since if educators wanted to find out who was ready to read, they would test as early as some children have actually learned to read—much earlier than the end of kindergarten. George Weber sums up the views of many who object to these tests: "It would be wiser to begin reading instruction, as some schools do, by attempting to teach all children the same things, without prejudging or predicting their success . . . First, it would give all children a better chance to respond to instruction and to allow factors other than those measured by a reading-readiness test to come into play. Secondly, it would shift the task of evaluation from a single test to the teacher, where it ought to be."

What can you do if your child's reading instruction is delayed because of his score on a readiness test? The vital thing to keep in mind is that these tests are if anything probably less "scientific" than IQ tests. The teacher may argue in favor of readiness tests simply because it's school policy or because her college professor believed in them. Still, you may be able to talk the school into letting your child begin reading anyway by pointing out that you're willing to help at home with "readiness." If the school refuses, you may be able to teach him at home yourself. (See chapters 6 and 9 on reading help.)

Achievement Tests

Your child will take more of these subject matter tests in his twelve or thirteen years of school than any other type of test. The aim, of course, is to find out what skills he's developed in math and reading, and what knowledge he has gained in other areas. As we've mentioned before, since these tests all have a multiple-choice format—no open-ended questions, nothing to write—they cannot measure writing achievement, no matter what the school or the test publishers claim. Here are some of the more widely used achievement tests: California Achievement Tests (CAT), Comprehensive Tests of Basic Skills (CTBS), Iowa Tests of Basic Skills (ITBS), Metropolitan Achievement Tests, Stanford Achievement Tests.

Like IQ tests, achievement tests are often used for grouping or tracking students. In other ways, too, they are very much like IQ tests—both contain math and reading. Choose a few questions from a math achievement test, from a reading achievement test, and from an IQ test and you will find it difficult to tell which ones came from the achievement test and which from the IQ test. As Dr. Judah Schwartz of MIT says of the similarity between the two tests: "The notion that you can construct an ability [IQ] test that will not be influenced by the child's experience [achievement] is not a thoughtful notion." This is why it's so difficult to understand the IQ/achievement score game which is played in so many schools. It goes like this: If your child scores high on an IQ test, and doesn't do so well on the achievement battery, he's called an "underachiever." If he scores average or a bit below on the IQ, but comes out looking good on the achievement battery, he's an "overachiever," which means that he has performed the marvelous, if somewhat paradoxical, feat of doing better than he can.

Why do school people get upset when results of achievement and IQ tests don't match? Probably because in a great many cases they do match. This makes it possible to claim that IQ tests predict school success, which is measured by achievement tests. Since both tests measure the same thing—what a child has learned—it's not surprising they agree in a large number of cases. For any number of reasons, though, a child can do well on one and poorly on another. Perhaps he's not feeling well, or he's worried about something when he takes the IQ test, so he does worse than he does on the achievement battery (overachiever). Maybe the reverse is true (underachiever). And as Dyer points out, the difference in scores could also be wholly a matter of chance, having more to do with statistical error in test scores than with the way your child answered the questions.

MINIMUM-COMPETENCY TESTS—GOOD OR BAD?

Minimum-competency testing—requiring students to prove mastery of certain skills before they move to the next grade or leave high school—is not a new idea, but it has been growing in popularity since the late '70s. More than forty states have passed laws requiring these tests. Parents and taxpayers feel schools must be held accountable, for two reasons. First, the drop in national test scores has been limited neither to specific areas nor to any one group. In some measures of achievement, including vocabulary, the decline has been greater for students of middle- and upper-middle-class background than for disadvantaged students. Second, employers and colleges have confirmed what test scores show: many students with high school diplomas do not have adequate training in reading, writing, and simple math.

Minimum-competency tests may be criterion-referenced—requiring demonstrated mastery of reading, writing, math computation—or norm-referenced—requiring only a relatively good score. You should ask several questions about minimum-competency testing in your schools.

Are they given at several levels or only as exit tests after eight or twelve years of schooling? Concerned educators and other observers agree that competency requirements should include frequent testing for mastery to make sure students are reaching appropriate goals each year. Though many states have adopted competency tests in the past several years, few deny diplomas to students who fail. In a 1983 Florida case, however, a federal judge ruled that schools do not have to give diplomas to students who fail the exit test. Those who say this is unfair forget that granting a diploma to students without adequate skills devalues the diploma for everyone else and absolves the school of its responsibility for teaching.

Will competency testing be used to discourage social promotion (the practice of moving students through the grades regardless of their achievement)? For example, the rule in a number of schools that use competency testing is that students who are two years or more below grade level in basic subjects be held back. Those who object to this practice argue that a child's self-esteem suffers if he is not promoted and that those most apt to be held back are minority children. But no child is helped by being pushed into the next grade without the skills he needs.

Will setting minimum requirements lower standards, as some have claimed? Since it's widely recognized that schools on the whole have not done a good job of meeting even minimum standards (teaching all students to read, for example), it seems sensible to work toward the minimum first. Later we can worry about maximizing the minimum. It's probably unrealistic to fear that students and teachers who now perform above the minimum will decide to reduce their efforts because competency tests are required.

Being held accountable will improve the performance of those schools, teachers, and students whose standards are far too low.

To find out about minimum-competency requirements in your school district, call the office of the school superintendent. Find out in what grades competency tests are given, whether they are criterion- or norm-referenced tests, and how the results will be used. To decide promotion? To give remedial help? Do students have more than one chance to pass the test? In some cases, the minimum requirements are set by the state; in others local districts have some discretion.

Keep in mind that minimum-competency tests are testing not only students, but teachers and schools as well. Many who fail these tests simply have not been properly taught. Poor readers are the most likely to fail. Yet many could have been taught to read well if teachers used the direct phonics method. (See chapter 6.) Students who fail competency tests need to have real remedial help, not just more of what didn't work the first time.

THE HIGH SCHOOL TEST MENU
Some years ago, a student who wanted to enroll in a ninth-grade algebra class was told she was not eligible. Her test score was too low. The principal had decided that to be admitted to the algebra class students must have a score of 45 or better on the algebra aptitude test, and this student's score was 17. Tearful pleading by the student failed to move the counselor and the assistant principal, who told her she would fail the course. Finally, after a visit by the girl's father, they decided to find a place for her in the algebra class anyway. Her father had insisted that she should have a right to try—and a right to fail. Describing the incident, the former assistant principal writes that he allowed the student to enroll in the class because, "I have always felt parents ought to have the last word on any assignment for *their* youngster!" But too often, tests do have the last word. Other students who scored below 45 on that test did not get into the algebra class. Their parents did not dispute the decision.

That low-scoring student placed high in the district math test a year or two later. She went on to major in math and physics in college and studied at MIT before beginning a successful career with NASA.

This story has three morals: Tests results can be wrong or misleading. Parents often know best. School people who base decisions on test scores may be reasonable enough to change their minds *if parents object.*

The experience of this student also illustrates an important lesson about test use and misuse. It is *always* a mistake to allow anyone to make a decision about your child's placement in a class or school program on the basis of a single test. Even if several tests are used, ask how the information supplied by each affects the decision about your child. If the counselor or the administrator can't give you a good explanation, there probably isn't one.

COLLEGE TESTS

In addition to the types of tests she's already familiar with, your child will have an opportunity to take several types of tests related to college entrance during her last two years of high school. Students may take these tests even if they don't plan to attend college. Information about test schedules and registration is usually available in the school guidance office. These are the principal college tests.

ACT Assessment (ACT) and Scholastic Aptitude Test (SAT)

These standardized college entrance tests are intended to measure high school achievement and general knowledge to help colleges and students predict how well they are apt to do on college work. Colleges may set a minimum ACT or SAT score students must earn to be considered for admission. The more selective colleges require higher scores. But even selective colleges rarely make test scores the sole criterion for admission. In some cases, high school grades weigh more heavily in the decision, and most colleges also consider other factors, such as extracurricular activities, in evaluating a student's qualifications. Which test a student takes depends on what colleges he plans to apply to. Schools in the northeast most frequently require the SAT, while midwestern and western colleges and universities are more apt to ask for ACT scores. Some schools accept either test. Many students take both if they're not sure which colleges they'll be applying to.

Both the SAT and the ACT are multiple-choice tests subject to the ambiguities and other flaws typical of this type of test. One criticism is that they penalize students who think deeply and favor those who have only superficial knowledge of the subjects on which test items are based. It is easier to make a good guess if you don't know all the possible ramifications of a question. At a recent conference of the National Consortium of Testing, attended by top people in test publishing and research, Dr. Judah Schwartz asked whether anyone present was willing to defend the multiple-choice test on intellectual grounds. Only one person said yes, and only if he could defend his answers and argue with the publisher afterwards.

A question frequently asked about the ACT and the SAT is whether coaching helps. It does. Test publishers don't like to admit it, but the existence of a flourishing commercial coaching business is convincing proof. In addition to taking a course, students can probably improve on the ACT and SAT by studying any one of a number of books that provide hundreds of practice questions, with answers, and tips for taking the tests. It also helps to take the SAT or ACT more than once, because only the highest scores need be submitted to colleges.

Achievement Tests

The publishers of the SAT also publish achievement tests in fourteen academic subjects ranging from English composition to Hebrew, chemistry, and physics. Some colleges may require some of these tests for admission in addition to the SAT. Others require students to take them to help in deciding how to place students in college courses in those subjects.

Advanced Placement (AP) Tests

Students who take advanced high school courses in some academic subjects, math and foreign languages for example, can receive college credit for this high school work if they earn a high enough score on the AP test in the subject area. A group of high school and college economics teachers are preparing to introduce an AP test in economics—the first in that subject—in the near future.

QUESTIONS TO ASK ABOUT YOUR SCHOOL TESTING PROGRAM

As a parent, you need to know more about how tests are used in your school because of their power to enhance or downgrade your child's education. As a taxpayer, you are entitled to know whether your school is spending wisely for tests and using them well. J. Parker Damon, a Massachusetts school administrator, has suggested that everyone concerned with testing—including parents—ask these questions about their school's testing program:

1. "How does the proposed standardized test supplement other forms of assessment and evaluation already in use?

2. "How much time will administering the tests involve? How much will it cost?

3. "How will students and parents be prepared for the testing?

4. "How will the test results be used and kept?

5. "How else might the same information be acquired?"

HELPING YOUR CHILD THROUGH THE TESTING MAZE

Being aware of the types and limitations of the tests your child may be asked to take is only the first step in making sure these tests work for him, rather than against him. The other two steps involve understanding your child's test-taking style, and, finally, understanding the scores as they're reported by the school.

The way your child approaches tests has a marked effect on how well he does. Chapter 5 lists test-taking techniques that can make a child more successful on teacher-made classroom tests. Most of those apply here. But there are additional factors that influence scores on standardized tests.

How does your child feel about taking the tests? Because they take so many standardized tests and because they know these tests won't directly affect their grade, some children don't try as hard as they might. Other children who are unduly upset by any tests are so anxious that their nervousness becomes a handicap. Depending on your child's attitude, you may be able to help him do better by explaining that the tests do affect his rating in school or by giving him the reassurance he needs to overcome his nervousness.

Is your child neat and careful? These skills are needed to make the best possible showing on standardized tests. Some children—not necessarily the "smartest"—are good at these things. Some aren't, so they have trouble filling in the bubbles or marking between the dots on the answer sheet. The scoring machine is unforgiving. You can help by reminding your child on testing day to mark carefully, and above all to *follow directions.*

Does your child work slowly and deliberately? If he's too slow, he'll be penalized because he won't answer as many questions as he could. Remind him not to dwell too long on questions (although most standardized tests contain more questions than anyone is expected to answer). Conversely, if your child works quickly and impulsively, he may not consider each question carefully enough. He needs a reminder to work carefully.

Is your child a reflective thinker, or unusually creative, able to see problems from several angles? These qualities, which nearly everyone agrees are attributes of real intellectual ability, can work against a student trying to answer multiple-choice questions. Take this simple grammar question, for example: Each of the boys gave. . . . oath. (a) his (b) their. A reasonably good grammar student would know that "Each" is singular, so it calls for a singular pronoun, and choose "his." A child who thinks about the question more deeply, though, might consider the possibility that "their" could refer to a club oath which is used by many in a group—a Boy Scout oath, for example. The Scouts have their oath, and each boy gave "their" oath. (B) is not clearly a wrong answer. It's a likely possibility if you consider that many children have probably not had much to do with oaths outside of a club. But no one can give reasons for his choice on a standardized test. In giving these tests teachers tell students "not to think too much." Your child may need such advice in this testing situation.

When the teacher or the counselor goes over your child's achievement tests with you, you should be looking for several things in addition to the score itself, as psychologist Stanley Klein points out in *Psychological Testing of Children:*

1. How does this year's work compare with last year's?

2. In what general areas does he seem to need help?

3. Since grade-equivalents are misleading, look at percentiles instead. Ask to see your child's percentile rank figured on the local norm (average scores for children in your district), not on the national norm (scores of all children who took the test). The most meaningful score will be the one that compares your child's per-

formance with that of other students with whom he has the most in common.

4. Are achievement test scores for more than one subject—reading and math, for example—added and then averaged? This lumping of two disparate subjects tells you nothing about his performance in either area. He can get a high average and still be extremely weak in one subject. Look at the scores separately to see how his performance in math compares with his performance in reading. This will tell you whether he needs special help in either area.

5. Keep in mind that if students are coached, the tests won't be a valid measure of real achievement in reading, math, or anything else.

DO WE REALLY NEED STANDARDIZED TESTS?

Standardized tests get things done. We use them to plan school programs, to rate schools, to admit students to college, and to allow students to "test out" of college courses (AP tests). These tests often exert such powerful and direct influence on the lives of people—not only students—and on institutions that it seems irresponsible to discuss standardized testing without acknowledging both the flaws in the tests themselves and their possible and actual misuse. Being aware of these issues will help you to put your child's experience with tests in perspective and to watch for possible misuse of tests by school people.

One unfortunate effect of standardized testing is its tendency to influence school curriculum. For example, some critics blame these tests for the failure of our schools to teach students to write. Even classroom teacher-made tests have become "multiple-guess," quick-scored affairs, which give students no chance to learn to think things through—and which relieve teachers of the work involved in evaluating students' thinking. From elementary school through high school, grammar workbooks teach students to put commas in other people's sentences and fill in the word in the blank space, à la standardized tests.

But standardized tests do not make this neglect of writing inevitable. Teachers who are conscientious and literate will teach students to write, regardless of how many standardized tests they take.

There is time to teach both writing—and thinking—and to make sure students learn what they need to know to do well on standardized tests. And with all their faults these tests do a reasonably good job of giving us the information we need to check the knowledge and skills of large groups of students in many academic areas. For example, choosing at random from sample copies of the ACT and the SAT, I find questions that require knowledge of the following facts and skills: the role of the Senate in foreign affairs, the behavior of gas molecules, formation of a coral reef, ability to recognize nonstandard English, ability to solve plane geometry and time and distance problems, ability to find the main idea of a paragraph.

These tests are far from perfect, but when we use them to measure performance of large groups, much of the chance error and ambiguity that makes them less than dependable measures of the performance of a single student on a given day tends to wash out.

At this point, we probably can't afford to do without standardized tests—given their role in evaluating the performance of those who run our schools. The best evidence that this is so comes from the educational establishment itself, which has continued to object to being judged by these tests ever since the decline in academic achievement became apparent. In the early '70s the National Education Association (NEA) passed a resolution calling for a moratorium on standardized testing. The Association for Supervision and Curriculum Development (ASCD) states, "ASCD should oppose use of SAT scores as a major barometer of school performance."

Useful as these tests may be for checking performance of large groups of students, keep in mind that it can be a grave mistake to let your child's score on a group test have the last word in any decision about his schooling. Think of it as a "testimate," merely one of the factors you should consider in planning for him.

5

LEARN THE BASICS OF HELPING WITH HOMEWORK

Research has shown what wise parents and good teachers have been pretty sure of all along: well-planned homework does boost children's learning in school. In addition, a well-known study by James Coleman found that students from private and Catholic high schools, who display higher achievement on the average, are more likely to spend over an hour doing homework every night than are public school students.

Consider the assignments your child brings home. You'll probably find nearly all of them are given for one of three reasons:

1.   Practice. This is vital in mastering new skills. For example, your child learns to understand how long division is done by listening to the teacher and by watching him do problems on the board. But she won't be able to do long division unless she tackles problems herself, making mistakes, learning how to correct them, and finally learning how to avoid them.

2.   Preparation. Beginning in the upper elementary grades, the teacher may expect your child to read ahead at home for work in class.

3.   Extension of knowledge. A fifth-grade teacher explains to the class how and why the pioneers moved west. For homework, they trace wagon trails on a map and list the obstacles the pioneers had

to overcome. "Traveling" the routes gives children new information and helps them to see the problems through the eyes of the pioneers.

Establish homework as a fact of life for your child. If you're not sure you know enough about teaching to help your child with homework, you'll be encouraged by a study at the Harvard University Graduate School of Education. After talking to parents and teachers and watching as parents helped children with a homework task, researchers concluded that parents and teachers use similar approaches and that parents are as helpful as teachers.

Everything I say here about homework assumes that the teacher collects homework, corrects it, and gives students credit for it while penalizing those who fail to do it. Some teachers don't check homework. Don't try to talk your child into doing homework if the teacher isn't doing her job. Talk to the teacher, and to the principal if necessary.

Now that you've decided homework is necessary, how to convince your child? A child with a homework emergency can turn sensible, loving parents into disagreeable wrecks. A child who needs constant prodding to get down to work can keep you edgy from dinner until bedtime—if you let him.

A few children, like Mary, a third-grader, are exceptions, self-starters from first grade on. After school she marches home, fixes herself a snack, and gets right down to work. Many other children are more like Ron, a fifth-grader, who drops his school books in a corner, rushes out to play, rushes in for dinner, and then heads for the television unless a parent points to the books.

Dad: You'd better start your homework.
Ron: Aw, not now. I don't have much. I just want to watch this one show first.
Dad: A half hour. That's it. Then I want you to get going.
Ron: (Forty minutes later) Where's the almanac? I have to look up four more states by tomorrow, and I have ten math problems to do. Somebody help me find the almanac!

Will Ron find the almanac? Will Dad keep his temper? Will Ron finish his math? Do you and your child suffer through scenes like this? You won't if you plan ahead.

SETTING THE SCENE

Since homework is your child's responsibility, he should do the planning, but he needs some guidance from you. Choose a time when there's no homework crisis and lay out guidelines.

Suggest that he choose a regular time for homework every day, a definite hour, not "after dinner" or "in the afternoon." Veto late evening, or any time that puts television first. Urge him to allow time to unwind or play outside after school before doing homework, but point out that once he sets a time, he should stick to it.

He needs a definite spot to work, one with good light and a place to keep papers, pencils, and a dictionary. If he doesn't have a room of his own, find a place away from television and other distractions. A seven- or eight-year-old may work well at a nearby table while you read the paper or get dinner, but as he gets older he should learn to study off by himself. Some children like a desk. Others prefer the floor or the bed and may appreciate a writing board or lap desk. Winston Churchill did his paperwork propped up in bed.

You and your child should agree in advance on how to deal with interruptions like phone calls that can wreck a good homework plan. You may want to let him accept one incoming call. Suggest that he tell his friends not to call during homework time.

What can you do when homework time interferes with a really good television program, a family outing, or some other special event? Explain to your child if he plans ahead—and does his work first—he can often fit everything in. He won't learn that work comes first if you let him sabotage the plan with spur-of-the-moment changes.

Give your child a notebook for writing down assignments. He may think he can remember them from seeing what's written on the board or hearing the teacher say which pages and what problems. Tell him most of us can't remember details like these after a full day of work or school.

Often there are good reasons for tackling homework assignments in a particular order. Talk these tips over with your child:

Do math first. It's the subject most difficult to deal with if you're tired.

Do rough drafts of writing assignments early. You can spot mistakes more easily in sentences written hours before than in those just finished.

Go through material to be memorized in several brief sessions; this is more effective than trying to learn it in one long session.

Look over homework assignments ahead of time to estimate how long it will take to read a chapter, or whether you should allow extra time for the math work.

Having a definite time for work and a definite place to do it takes some of struggle out of homework. For some types of children, though, even the best-laid plans need a special twist.

Barbara has music lessons, and Girl Scouts, and softball . . . The homework plan works well until she has to face the big recital, an unusually heavy load of school work, and the league playoffs all in one week. One mother of several busy children explains her method for dealing with the problem: "I tell them about 'corners of time' which they might waste otherwise—five minutes at lunch to study spelling words, time to read a few pages for a book report while waiting at the dentist's." She encourages older children to write down an hourly schedule on extra-busy days.

Some children actually manage everything better when they have a full schedule. Others flounder. If tension builds and homework slides despite a good plan, maybe it's time to say, "School comes first."

Then there's Harry, who invariably says there *isn't* any homework. Many children do this occasionally, tempted by a favorite television program or a long afternoon outdoors. If it happens only once in a while, let your child take the consequences of not having done his work: a lower grade, not knowing the answers, teacher's disapproval. Children who are usually responsible will get back on the track soon. If your child pulls this often, and you're sure there *is* homework, insist that he go to his regular work spot at the usual time anyway. Chronic homework hiding can signal other school problems. Talk with the teacher. Make sure he gets extra help if he needs it. It could be as simple as finding out from the teacher that he will always have math homework and signing the papers, a system that worked for one parent of a fifth-grade homework hider.

Sue, a fourth-grader, wends her way very slowly through each evening's homework. She may simply be one of those children who enjoy doing meticulous work. As long as she's not unhappy and makes good progress in school, there's no problem. But if Sue works at a snail's pace because writing down spelling words or copying math problems is a terrible struggle, see the teacher. Ask how long children should be spending on homework. Find out if Sue works too slowly in class. If her work pace is much slower than average and Sue is unhappy and doing poorly in school, you and the teacher should investigate.

Larry poses a problem as well. The sixth-grade science project is due tomorrow and he's starting it tonight. He wants you to rush him to the store for posterboard and colored pencils. "I forgot," says he when you ask him why he waited.

Protect yourself from homework emergencies like this by keeping up with what's going on at school. Find out from the teacher on Back to School Night what projects, reports, and notebooks she plans. But keep in mind that the responsibility is Larry's, not yours. The teacher has probably been reminding Larry's class about the project all along, so he had to do a lot of forgetting to create this emergency. Now you have two choices. You can get him what he needs to do the project. He can't do two weeks' work in one night, so he won't have a very good project. He won't learn much, either, but at least he won't get a zero. Or, tell him you can't help at the last minute. It was his job to work on the project right along and tell you what supplies he needed. He will get a zero, but he'll also learn something about responsibility. A zero now won't look nearly as bad as the grades he'll get later if "forgetting" becomes a habit.

WHEN TO HELP—AND HOW TO LISTEN

Children often need help, and you, as a parent, are there to give it. If your child's eraser tears an ugly gash in her book report, of course you'll help her tape it. But don't be too eager to help. If your fifth-grader opens his science book, flips pages, glances at a list of questions on the reading, and instantly wails, "I can't do these!" don't immediately rush to the rescue. He may actually be saying, "I don't want to," or "I don't know the answers right away," or "I wish you'd do it for me." From a safe distance, calmly suggest that you think he can answer the questions if he looks back over the reading. Leave it at that. Your child will become a homework leaner if you're too ready to help. Don't cooperate.

On the other hand, don't demean your child or his homework

by saying "That's easy!" or "You ought to be able to do that in five minutes." It's may *not* be easy for him. When you're having difficulty with something, does it make you feel better to hear that it's "really easy"? Chances are, you feel discouraged and resentful. What you—and your child—really want is a sympathetic listener. Be supportive and understanding: "I can see you really do have a lot of work." Don't criticize your child for complaining or the teacher for giving the homework. Then you can take credit for supporting them both.

Should you ever get directly involved in homework? Yes, if your child has been working hard on his own and is really stumped, and if you're sure you can help him to help himself as opposed to doing the work for him. Good teachers think assignments through carefully before giving them to the class, and they make it very clear what children are supposed to do and how they're supposed to do it.

Then, every once in a while, some child—yours or mine—comes home and acts as if no one ever taught him anything. Sometimes it doesn't occur to children to apply the guidelines they learned in class to the work they're supposed to do at home three hours later. Too often, they take short cuts, ignoring three of the most important homework rules: follow directions carefully, use your book properly, adjust your reading to the assignment. Here's how you can help:

Teach Your Child to Follow Directions

At the kitchen table nine-year-old Jim is hunched over a work sheet. He has read a paragraph about trees. In the blanks under the paragraph he is writing names of trees which lose their leaves in the fall. He tosses down his pencil and waves the paper at his mother. "It's all wrong! Four blanks and only three trees that lose their leaves. I don't get it."

Mother reads silently: "In the blanks below, write the names of the trees which do not lose their leaves in the fall."

What should she say as she gives the work sheet back to Jim?

(a) "You didn't read the directions right. The four blanks are for 'pine,' 'spruce,' 'cedar,' and 'hemlock,' trees that *don't* lose their leaves in the fall."

(b) "You read the directions wrong. You're supposed to fill in the blanks with trees that *don't* lose their leaves in the fall."

(c) "Read the directions again. I think you'll see why you couldn't find all the names you're supposed to have."

The last response, (c), is the one most likely to help a child learn from a mistake like this; (a) and (b) *tell* him that he misread the directions, while (c) nudges him to find his own mistake.

If your child rereads the directions once or twice and still "doesn't get it," tell him to read them aloud—a method that seldom fails.

If *you* can't understand the directions, they're probably unclear. Look closely at your child's workbooks and work sheets. Confusing directions are not uncommon in the workbooks (and mimeographed sheets copied from them) children get in school. If you find workbook items that don't make sense, let the teacher know. Teachers sometimes don't look closely enough until *after* children have struggled with senseless directions or useless exercises.

But most of the time a child who doesn't understand directions is simply not reading them carefully. Whether your child is in third grade or ninth, stress the importance of reading, understanding, and following directions. Carelessness here is a leading cause of homework problems, and of making mistakes on tests from first grade through college. In a high school or college class of twenty-five students taking an essay test, two or three students will invariably lose credit for answers because they haven't read directions carefully.

Help Your Child Learn to Use School Books Properly

Dave, the father of an eighth-grader, explains how he spent several evenings trying to help his son with grammar exercises in a workbook. "I felt he should have had a grammar book to look up the things he was having trouble with, but he said the workbook was all there was. I had decided to ask the teacher about it. Then he flipped open the workbook quite by accident and found a section called 'Handbook,' which had all the information he'd needed earlier in the week. Both of us learned a lesson!"

GLOSSARIES, TABLES, AND INDEXES

Children often aren't aware that their books have glossaries and other learning aids that could help with homework. Teachers may point out these features, but children have forgotten by the time they need to use them. Glance through your child's books occasionally. Make sure he realizes there's more to a textbook than the chapter he has to read for tomorrow.

Here are some textbook features your child should be able to use by the time he's in the middle elementary grades.

1. The table of contents gives a general outline of the book and sometimes includes chapter summaries and lists of topics.

2. The index is an alphabetized list of facts, names, places, substances, processes, specialized terms, and types of math problems included in the book, with page numbers. It's surprising how much time children will waste looking through the table of contents for a term like "mitosis" when they could find it in seconds in the index.

3. The glossary defines words or terms a student reading the chapters may have difficulty with.

4. Depending on the subject, textbooks may also contain charts, graphs, maps, lists, tables, verb conjugations, rules, formulas, or other back-of-the-book features useful in doing homework.

REFERENCE BOOKS

What reference books should you have on hand? Of course, a dictionary. Ask a children's librarian to recommend a dictionary for lower elementary children. By fifth or sixth grade your child can probably use an adult dictionary. If you can afford it, give him a dictionary of his own and in addition buy one of the large unabridged (complete) dictionaries. You can help your child *explore* and learn how to use these tomes. He'll find not only definitions and spellings, but a wealth of information not found in smaller dictionaries. In one unabridged dictionary, for example, the entry under "coin" is almost a full page and includes a table listing the names of foreign coins, their history, values, and metal content.

Almanacs are especially useful for geography, history, and statistical references. They are inexpensive, so you can buy an up-to-date edition every year or so. You may decide to buy one almanac for its wealth of statistical data, another for its detailed historical outline.

Talk to teachers and librarians before you buy an encyclopedia. Children outgrow junior editions quickly. Encyclopedias need constant updating in many subject areas, so this may be the most important feature to find out about before you invest.

When elementary teachers assign research papers without explaining what research is, children invariably copy verbatim from the encyclopedia. Help your child avoid this trap by seeing that he has fact-filled books on a variety of subjects—science, sports, pets, history—and knows how to find others at the library.

Remind Your Child to Adjust Her Reading to the Assignment

When they start school, children spend several years learning to read stories, with the emphasis on what characters do and say and what will happen next. Later they must make the switch from learning to read to reading to learn in such subjects as science and history. There's a lot more to grapple with on a page explaining how leaves manufacture food than there is on a page telling what happened to three children who dressed up as Halloween goblins. Teachers should remind students of the differences between reading for facts and reading stories. Your child may need reminding at home, too, that reading to understand and remember science, social studies, and other subjects is not the same as reading to find out how a story ends. These tips can help your child do better with fact-filled reading:

Read more slowly to concentrate on understanding processes and remembering facts. As textbook material becomes more difficult, it may be necessary to go over an assignment twice—a quick first reading to get a general idea of what must be learned, and a slower second reading to study specifics.

Read actively. Take notes or draw diagrams to aid in understanding a new process in science. Outline a history chapter by copying topic headings and jotting down the important names, events, and dates under each one.

Use the read-recall-review system. After reading, your child should try to recall important points. Then she should check back over the assignment for points she missed.

Whether your child is reading poems, stories, or a book for a report, encourage her to recall *before* she reads what the teacher said as he gave the assignment. Did he tell the class to look for the mood in a poem, a surprise ending in a story? If your child is reading a book for a report, will the teacher ask her to summarize the plot, or will she have to decide who is the most interesting character?

Once you've given your child a support system for doing a good job on homework, step back and let her work on her own. Don't hover. Don't check her papers unless she's asked for your help on a particular assignment, or unless you and the teacher are working together to help her with a problem.

Some well-meaning, conscientious parents, like Janie's, feel they must go over every bit of school work before she hands it in. Janie, a fifth-grader, does careful work on her own, and with parents double-checking she nearly always gets perfect papers. I suspect Janie knows her own work is very good and that she also knows it might not be perfect unless her parents did the final checking and told her to make those last small changes. Janie needs the satisfaction, and the responsibility, of perfecting her own work —and knowing it's truly her own.

HOMEWORK EMERGENCIES

According to most parents, math problems and writing assignments (when teachers do give writing assignments) are most likely to cause homework problems. Though good teachers give good guidelines for homework, some give guidelines that show more concern for the teacher's convenience than for the child's learning. For example, a teacher may insist that children circle the answers to math story problems on their paper. Yet he may not ask them to work out enough problems on the board in class to learn the importance of using a step-by-step approach for solving them. Teachers sometimes give writing assignments ("write a page about the pioneers") without giving children the guidelines they need. Poor teaching practices like these help to cause homework emergencies. You don't have to be a teacher, a math whiz, or a writer to guide your child over some of the rough spots in these subjects.

Math

New math has retreated from the classroom, but in some textbooks it left behind unnecessary theoretical terms like "additive inverse," which can confuse parents and students alike.

One thing hasn't changed, though. Students still have to copy numbers out of their books to do math problems. And they still make mistakes in copying those numbers. Tell your child to check his copying if he's stumped by a long-division problem that looks insoluble. Let him find his own mistake. Other careless errors that plague children doing math homework:

Trying to do too much figuring in their heads, instead of putting it down on paper, or trying to cram all their figuring in a space the size of a postage stamp. Insist that your child use scratch paper. If the teacher is a good one, she'll want students to show their work, anyway, and she'll make sure they have enough school-approved paper.

Not checking work. For example, in long division they can check work by multiplying the divisor times the quotient. If that answer equals the dividend, they have done the problem correctly.

```
QUOTIENT ───────→ 725   REMAINDER 32
DIVISOR ──→ 34)24682
DIVIDEND ───┐     238
                   88
                   68
                  202
                  170
                   32
```

CHECK:

```
    725   QUOTIENT
  × 34    DIVISOR
  2900
  2175
 24650
     32   ADD REMAINDER
 24682    ANSWER = DIVIDEND
```

Story problems cause students more trouble than any other kind of math. Their most common mistakes are not reading the problem carefully, not bothering to write down the information they need to find the solution, and not doing careful work and checking their arithmetic for careless mistakes.

The following story-problem example shows how students can

avoid these mistakes. Twenty Boy Scouts went on an outing to a theme park and then had a picnic. The bus ride cost a total of $60, tickets for the group totalled $250, and picnic supplies cost $30. How much must each Scout pay?

First, your child should read the problem at least twice. On the second reading, have him write down the facts as he goes along. If he doesn't understand the problem well enough to begin writing down facts after the first reading, he should read the problem aloud before trying to write down the facts.

The basic facts should be written:

> 20 Scouts sharing costs
> Costs—bus $60, tickets $250, picnic supplies $30

The next step is to determine how to use facts. In this case, find the total of the costs by adding them:

$250	tickets
60	bus
30	picnic supplies
$340	total costs

Find how much each Scout owes by dividing:

$$\begin{array}{r} 17 \\ 20\overline{)340} \\ \underline{20} \\ 140 \\ \underline{140} \\ 0 \end{array}$$

Check by multiplying quotient by divisor:

$$\begin{array}{r} 17 \\ \times\,20 \\ \hline 340 \end{array}$$

Thus, each Scout must pay $17.

Writing

Writing instruction in elementary school is usually neglected (see chapter 6). Your child is fortunate if he has a teacher who requires him to write. Make the most of every assignment, and compliment the teacher if she stresses writing—real writing, composing sentences and paragraphs—*not* grammar exercises.

Your sixth-grader comes home with an assignment to write a two-page paper about pioneers moving west, which the class has been learning about for several weeks. "We put a list of facts about the pioneers on the board and copied it down, but now I don't know what to write," he moans.

What can you do to help? Teach him the plan-write-revise system, a step-by-step approach that can help a child to do a better job with school papers, whether he's in fifth grade or high school.

PLAN

First, ask your child what other instructions the teacher gave. Perhaps she discussed the topic with the class, pointing out that they should narrow it down, instead of trying to write a hodgepodge of everything they know about the westward movement. A good teacher would have children write down instructions for doing the paper. Urge your child to look at his notes.

If he's still uncertain about what the teacher expects, try to help him narrow the topic by asking questions. Could he write about how pioneers prepared for the journey, about the routes they took, or some other aspect of the westward movement? Trying to cover too broad a subject in a short paper is one of the most common mistakes children make in school writing.

Once your child has narrowed his topic, encourage him to make a brief plan of what he wants to say. He doesn't need a formal outline unless the teacher requires one. Let's say he decides to write about the routes the pioneers took. His plan might look like this:

Getting to St. Louis [or Independence or Omaha]

National Road
Rivers, canals

West from Missouri and Nebraska

Oregon Trail
Santa Fe Trail
California Trail

Dangers and hardships

Destinations

If the teacher doesn't stress planning before writing, your child may balk at this step. Explain that it will save him time in the long run, because he's less apt to plunge off in the wrong direction, or get stumped halfway through by forgetting what he wants to say.

WRITE

Encourage your child to write a first draft without worrying about neatness. He shouldn't worry too much at this stage about mistakes in grammar and spelling, either. He'll make mistakes. Everyone does. Stopping to make sure every comma is in place will interrupt his thinking and make writing more difficult. A teacher and author of books for young people tells children that the first draft they write is the "magic draft," where all the good ideas will come out if you let them.

Your child must learn to make corrections in a final draft after the paper has taken shape. Teach your child that he should *expect* to do a second copy or draft and that this is not extra work or a penalty for mistakes he made in his first draft. It's a normal part of good writing.

REVISE

Urge your child to let his paper "rest" at least several hours, overnight if possible, before he tries to correct it. This will make it much easier for him to see what he needs to change in the second draft.

The best way for your child to spot mistakes in his writing is to read his paper *aloud* to himself or into a tape recorder, slowly. Hearing what he has written, instead of simply rereading it silently, will help him to spot many serious mistakes, including confusing, incomplete, or run-together sentences. For example, he may have written, "Because the desert is cold at night." Seeing it, he won't realize it's an incomplete sentence, because it begins with a capital and ends with a period. But hearing it he'll know right away that he has to add something to complete the thought.

While your child plays back the tape of his first draft, he can prepare to do a final copy by marking corrections on his paper. He can correct spelling and punctuation, cross out words, and add sentences at the top or bottom of the paper, drawing arrows to show where they belong.

Some children are horrified at the idea of "messing up" a paper this way, because they've been taught at school to overvalue neatness. Neatness does count—but *only* on the final copy. Should you offer to check his paper when it's finally ready? No. And don't become a walking dictionary, spelling every word he's unsure of as he revises his paper. He has a dictionary. Make sure he knows how to use it, and let him do the looking.

If he asks you to read his paper, don't concentrate on seeing what's wrong. Praise your child for what he's done well. Writing is hard work. Does his paper have a good title? Good sentences? An interesting conclusion? Praise what's good. Go easy on criticism. What if you spot a mistake—or several mistakes? Mention only one or two. Say, "I think there's a sentence that doesn't make sense in this paragraph." Let him find it.

KNOW WHEN TO GIVE UP

When you're trying to help your child, and he wails, "The teacher doesn't do it that way," retreat gracefully. It's not worth a ruined evening. If this happens often, though, let the teacher know that your child needs extra help from her. Make sure he gets it. One parent who was stumped by her son's math book did some homework of her own using the book after he was in bed, and managed to help him on her own. Another approach is to ask the teacher to coach you, so you can help your child.

A teacher in a small city in a western state gives parents her home telephone number and urges them to call for help with serious homework problems: "I know I may be able to save parents a ruined evening by answering a question or two. Children sleep better if everything's settled. And class goes better next day if I know what children need more work on . . . The school system does not encourage me to do this, but I feel it's important to be available to parents." She is disappointed that parents seldom call.

Parents in Philadelphia and a number of other cities have a different option—a telephone hot line called "Dial-a-Teacher." Eight teachers with expertise in various subject areas answer the phones, offering parents and pupils help with homework. The subject with the greatest number of calls is elementary mathematics, followed by English and elementary school language arts.

If there isn't a hot line in your area, you and other parents may want to ask the cooperation of the schools in getting one started.

TIPS ON CLASSROOM TESTS: HELPING YOUR CHILD PREPARE

Tracy: I have a spelling test tomorrow. Will you hear my words? (Eleven-year-old Tracy hands her father a study sheet with fifteen words underlined. The first word is "superstition." She misspells it. She also misses the second word, "occasion," and she spells the third word only after a wrong guess.)

Dad: (Patiently) I think you need some more work on these, Trace. They're not easy words. Maybe you should write them out a few times. Then come back and we'll go over them.

When they reach the upper elementary grades, children need to become aware that no one can study for them. It's a good idea to help your child check up on what he's learned. But don't waste your time or your child's by checking to see whether he can spell this week's words, or name the state capitals, or identify the parts of an ant unless he studies *first.*

Younger children, of course, may not be ready to study alone by looking at a book or work sheet. They can learn by talking the material over with you, by repeating the words as you say them, by pointing out places on the map as you look at it together.

Even after your child has learned to do a good job of studying on his own, some helpful tips from you can increase his chances of doing well on tests his teacher gives in math, social studies, English, or science. Suggest to your child that he ask the teacher what kind of a test the class will have. Students usually have to know material more thoroughly to do well on an essay test, where they must *recall* what they've learned and discuss it, than on multiple-choice or true-false tests where they need only *recognize* the answer when they see it.

If your child knows he'll have an essay test, suggest that he study first, then try to imagine essay questions the teacher might ask, and see how well he could answer them. (Too many teachers refuse to give essay tests. They don't want to grade the answers. If your child's teacher does, she's working hard to help children learn—and she's also giving them writing practice. Send her a note of appreciation.)

Here are suggestions for studying for short-answer tests from Bernard Feder's *The Complete Guide to Taking Tests:*

1. In completion tests, questions are sentences with a word or phrase left out for students to fill in. Study textbook and class notes, looking for key words and phrases.

2. In matching tests, students must choose items from one column that belong with those in a second column. Study by trying to connect likely "pairs" of terms in the textbook or class notes.

3. Multiple-choice tests ask students to pick the correct answer(s) from among several possible choices. Study by looking for groups of words, phrases, or ideas that seem to belong together, not by memorizing lone facts.

4. When taking a true-false test, remember that if any part of the statement is false, the entire statement is false.

These tips apply to all types of classroom tests:

Read directions carefully. Then reread the directions. Listen as the teacher explains how to go about taking the test. Ask questions if directions aren't clear. Even a careful teacher may write confusing directions or include a question which is ambiguous.

Don't rush through the test. Younger children often make this mistake and need to be reminded that they get no more credit for finishing first. Figure out when you first see the test how much time you can afford to spend on each question, or ask the teacher. Don't waste too much time on a question that puzzles you. Go on with the other questions and come back to that one. Pacing is extremely important on essay tests, since there will be fewer questions and more chance of losing many points if you don't have time to answer one of the questions.

Get a good night's sleep before a test. This is particularly important for math.

Many children get test jitters, which cause them to do less well than they otherwise might. If your child is overly nervous even about tests he's well prepared for, explain that nearly everyone feels nervous when they take tests and that being a little bit nervous may help him to do better. Don't add to his anxiety by over-emphasizing the importance of tests. Let him know you expect him to study and to do the best he can. No one can do more.

CHECK YOUR CHILD'S PROGRESS

Parent: What did you do in school today?

Third-Grader: I tripped over the wastebasket and Mrs. Watson looked mean at me.

Eighth-Grader: Nothing much.

How can you find out what's going on at school if your child doesn't seem to want to give out any information? Begin by listening patiently to whatever he has to say. The wastebasket incident above looms large in the third-grader's mind, because the whole class was watching and the teacher, who usually smiles at him, looked annoyed. As far as he's concerned, that *is* what happened in school today. Tomorrow, however, you may get more information by asking something specific: "What was the hardest thing you did in math [or the most interesting story in reading]?"

Specific questions will encourage older children to tell you about school too, but don't greet your child every evening with "How was school today?" Instead of asking what he did in class, you might say, "I'll bet everyone's excited about the play try-outs on Friday." If you show an interest in everything that goes on in school, talk about grades and classes will come more easily.

In this chapter we'll take a close look at the papers your child brings home from school, at report cards, and at how you can tell whether your child is learning what he should in class. But don't underestimate the importance of the information you can get—with patience—from your child's day-to-day comments. Says Dr. LeRoy Hay, a 1983 Teacher of the Year: "I make it a point to keep up with how my children are doing in school. I want to know how they're doing in reading and math, what they're studying in social studies. Sure, they try to shrug off questions, but I don't accept that all the time. I think parents have to know what's going on."

"LOOK WHAT I DID IN SCHOOL TODAY!"

One day I was visiting a neighbor when her daughter, a third-grader, came home from school proudly waving a paper. Across the top the teacher had written, "Very good. I liked reading about your shells."

Smiling, my neighbor began reading Chrissie's paper. Then she said, "I'm afraid you'd better read this over, dear. There's another mistake here. You spelled 'oyster' 'o-z-y-t-e-r.'"

Crestfallen, Chrissie stared at the paper. "But Mrs. Plunkettt said she liked my story."

"I'm sure she did. It's a nice story, but you have to spell every word right," said her mother.

Chrissie pushed the paper aside, and ran out to play.

"I can't imagine why a teacher wouldn't correct a mistake like that," my neighbor said, handing me the paper. "I hate to hurt Chrissie's feelings. But if no one tells her it's wrong, how will she learn?" I looked at the paper and saw that Chrissie had written good sentences and had spelled "mussel" and "scallop" correctly. The teacher had added a comma and a capital letter, but she probably let "ozyter" alone because seeing many red marks on a paper can discourage a small child. Chrissie's mother might have said, "You did a wonderful job of putting the names of all those shells in sentences!" Before pointing out a misspelled word, she could have praised Chrissie for getting so many hard words right. Of course, children need to learn to spell—and capitalize and punctuate—correctly. But they can't learn everything at once.

Whether you're looking at a math paper or a science report, remember the "compliments first" rule no matter what grade your child is in. Make your praise specific: "I'm glad to see you're being so careful about checking the arithmetic in these story problems." Or "After reading your report on solar energy, I understand why it couldn't heat a house in this climate." Avoid such meaningless comments as, "That's a nice paper." Such phrases tell your child that you see his hard work as a routine exercise.

Understand that as your child gets older, he may actually make more mistakes in his written work, at least temporarily, because he'll be including more information and ideas in his writing. In every subject, look for progress, not perfection. Keep your child's school papers in a folder, so he can look back and see what he has accomplished.

THE CONTROVERSY OVER GRADES

For decades many educators have been saying that if parents and teachers did a good enough job of motivating children to learn, report cards and grades would not be needed. Imagine a school where each child is a dedicated scholar, always eager to learn history, or multiplication tables, or French verbs, or the parts of an ant, without any thought of competing with anyone else or having to prove his knowledge on a test. In the real world, ignored by the theorists, it's different. Reporting on his visit to an extraordinarily successful inner-city school, Robert Benjamin quotes a teacher: "They know what level they're on. . . . Every day the top group comes up and checks their place on the chart and every night the others go home saying, 'I'm going to be in that top group.' "

Children obviously don't agree with the theorists, who frown on giving grades and achievement awards—though both observation and research show that most children will work harder for incentives like these. Louise Bates Ames of the Gesell Center for Child Development writes: "Many people speak as though competition is an evil thing, and as if it would never occur to children to be competitive if the school didn't encourage it. . . . Those children in a class who do less well than others should not be criticized . . . But competing is a perfectly natural and normal human drive."

Since it is necessary to rate student progress in some way, we must use report cards. But because the theorists have succeeded in convincing teachers and school administrators that grades shouldn't be competitive, a great many elementary schools, perhaps yours among them, switched to a reporting system that rates children on whether they are "working up to ability."

But no method yet devised by educators can tell the teacher or you precisely what your child's ability is. Here's one dilemma a teacher faces in trying to grade children on the "working up to ability" standard: According to his scores on aptitude (IQ) tests and what he says in class, Ms. C. has decided Ed is a very bright child. Kay has much lower test scores and impresses Ms. C. as being of about average intelligence. Kay does reasonably well on science tests. Ed does better than Kay, but not as well as Ms. C. thinks he could do. If Ms. C. grades strictly on whether these students are "working up to ability," Ed should get a lower grade in science than Kay, though he has done better than she did on the tests.

This system does not promote achievement, because it sends children confusing messages. To bright children it says, "Even if you do very well, it won't be good enough." To the majority of children it says: "Since you're just about average, mediocre performance is good enough."

It is impossible to come up with a wholly satisfactory reporting system. You can only hope for a report that's clear enough at least to tell you whether your child is learning what's taught in third grade or eighth grade well enough to succeed in fourth grade or ninth grade. If your child's report card does not give you this essential information, ask for it. You might say to the teacher, "I'm glad Jan is doing so well in math (or, I see Jan is not doing well in math). I'd like to know just what math skills the class has been working on and where Jan's strengths and weaknesses are."

What can you do if your child's report indicates that he's not doing well? Says a midwestern junior high teacher with over twenty years' experience: "Ask yourself whether you've given enough emphasis at home to the importance of school work. Try to discuss the report with your child calmly. If priorities are in order, and you have no reason to suspect your child has a special problem, check his homework daily, and make sure he has good study habits. Don't be afraid to assert your authority as a parent." Before you say anything to your child, remember that an angry outburst won't change the grade. More important, it may not change your child's attitude, either. Let your child know you expect him to do better and intend to help him. Skip the anger. Conversely, if your child knows he hasn't been working hard and you shrug off a poor grade, or let him get by with excuses, you're telling him that doing well in school isn't important.

News that your child is doing poorly in second-grade reading or fourth-grade math may be greater cause for concern than a low grade in fifth-grade art or seventh-grade social studies (unless the low social studies grade is caused by poor reading. Lack of reading and math skills can hinder his learning for years).

Be proud of your child if he always does well in school, but don't admire grades for their own sake. If you're upset by an occasional slip from "superior" to "good" or "average," you may be overemphasizing grades. What really counts is the learning a grade represents.

Now consider this scene between a sixth-grader and his father:

Dad: The math is barely passing, Jeff. I'm really concerned about that. It says here you haven't handed in all the homework.
Jeff: I guess I didn't. But the grade is mostly from the tests.
Dad: If you don't do the homework, you can't learn what you need to know for the tests, can you?
Jeff: Sometimes I don't understand the homework.
Dad: What can you do then?
Jeff: Ask you for help, or ask the teacher, I guess.
Dad: That's right. I think you'd better see the teacher after school tomorrow. And let's put math homework first. No ball practice until the math is done.
Jeff: No ball practice!
Dad: Not unless the math's finished. I'll ask the teacher to let us know how you're doing before the end of the month. Why don't you ask her at the end of next week how you're getting along? Then we'll see.

Notice that Jeff's father focuses on a solution, not on berating Jeff for the low grade, and he leads Jeff to face the cause of the problem—not doing homework and not asking for help. Then he sets up a plan. Suggesting that Jeff check with the teacher gives him some of the responsibility for finding out whether he's doing better.

FOLLOWING UP ON A BAD REPORT CARD
The reason for Jeff's bad report is obvious to both Jeff and his dad, but in many cases it takes a talk with the teacher to discover why a child's work isn't up to par. Since it's his progress you're talking about, you may want to include your child in the conference (un-

less he's too young or would hamper frank discussion between you and the teacher). Check with the teacher beforehand to see how she feels about a three-way talk. Make an appointment and decide ahead of time what you want to find out. These questions can help:

Does your child pay attention and answer questions in class?

Is she responsible about doing written work in class?

Would a seat change help? Some teachers allow close friends to sit together, though they keep each other from working. Good teachers avoid the problem or correct it swiftly. At one school, teachers and principal made deliberate plans before school opened to keep close friends from being in the same classroom.

Is your child spending enough time on homework? (Applies especially to children in upper elementary grades and beyond.)

If none of the above seems to be a possible cause of the problem, ask the teacher what she thinks the problem is. If she says your child has to work harder, tactfully insist that she come up with specifics, like a description of the problem. For example, if your child is having trouble in math, you need a statement like: "She's weak in subtraction facts." Having discovered the specific problem, ask the teacher for a plan for solving the problem. "Work at home with flash cards would help." Or "I'll put her in a different math group, so she'll get extra practice." Then make a definite date for another conference or phone call to check on your child's progress.

If the problem isn't too serious, you and the teacher working together can help your child to improve in a relatively short time. You can't afford to assume this will happen, though. Make sure she's getting the practice she needs in that other math group, and not just easier work. If you don't have solid evidence (papers that show more correct answers on class work or higher grades on arithmetic tests) of at least the beginning of real improvement in two weeks or so, your child may need more help or a different kind of help.

The teacher has a number of other children in class who need extra attention. A student who disrupts the class often claims more of the teacher's time than a well-behaved child who is doing poor school work—unless that child has an alert parent. If you see that your child isn't getting anywhere with the first plan, ask the teacher about other options. More help after school? Tutoring? Testing? Attendance at summer school (if the school year is nearly over)? Your child is far more likely to get real help if you press for action than if you sit back and leave everything to the teacher.

Louise Bates Ames writes: "People tend to coast all too long with their children's school problems, hoping, presumably that these problems will go away of their own accord. Few parents, if their child is physically ill, put off going to the doctor . . . Yet many do just that with school problems."

WHY YOU NEED TO LOOK BEYOND
REPORTS FROM SCHOOL

It's easy to concentrate so hard on whether a child gets a good or bad report from school that we forget that the report is not the important thing. The knowledge and skills a child gains are what really count. Does a report from the teacher that your child is making "excellent progress" mean that he's learning what he should be learning? What you're likely to learn from the grades or comments on your child's report card is how well the teacher thinks he has learned what he is being taught. The report seldom tells you much about what he *is* being taught. Even when the report lists skills— such as reading comprehension—you don't always know how comprehension is taught and tested. Your child may well get the same grades this year as last year, even if this year's class is being taught less than last year's.

The wide variety of grading systems in elementary schools makes comparison difficult, but a study of high-school grades has shown that as student scores on national standardized tests declined, teachers were actually giving students higher grades for class work in academic subjects.

No matter what grade your child is in, his reading assignments in science, social studies, and other subjects are probably easier than yours were. Says Dennis Gray, deputy director of the Council for Basic Education: "A major problem is what has happened to textbooks in the last fifteen years in response to the demands of school districts for lower reading levels." This is sometimes referred to as the "dumbing down" of textbooks. Instead of raising children's reading achievement, schools have given them easier books—without consulting or even informing parents. This has occurred not only in city schools, but in small-town and suburban districts all across the country.

Achievement tests, such as the California Achievement Test, the Iowa Tests of Basic Skills, and others, which most schools give annually, may in some cases give you a better estimate of what your child is really learning than report cards can. You should be aware, though, that these tests don't test everything that is taught in school. On the other hand, achievement tests can give parents the impression that the school is teaching what it is not teaching. Your child can do well in the language section of these tests even if he is not being taught to write, because writing is not tested.

You should also be aware that school districts often switch to a different achievement test periodically, perhaps every four or five years. Some of these tests are more difficult than others, tempting school districts with declining achievement to choose an easier test. Though most school people are honest, cheating does occur. Coaching students, preventing potential low scorers from taking the test, and altering and misreporting scores are among the tactics some teachers and schools have used to protect themselves. A CBE spokesperson says that parents too often tend to give "blind allegiance and excess weight to test scores in judging school performance or their child's achievement."

Stressing the need for parents to look beyond report cards and test scores to what is really going on in the classroom, a concerned educator tells what happened in a town not far from where she lives: "In X [an affluent suburb] parents never questioned the school program. As is usually the case in schools attended by students from privileged homes, X's test scores were higher than those in other schools in the area. Judging from this comparison, parents assumed their schools were excellent. Parents of 'top' students were shocked when college admissions people said, in effect, 'We've looked at your school program and compared your children with top achievers from schools in other states, and your children's training doesn't stack up.' "

At this point you may be wondering whether a parent with no special training in education really can judge the job his child's school is doing. Why not? In some school districts, including those in Salt Lake City, Utah, and South Carolina, parents now play a vital role in evaluating their children's schools. There's no sensible alternative. As we've noted before, leaving it all up to professional educators has not worked out very well. As an intelligent, concerned parent you can learn enough about education to decide whether your child is getting the solid foundation he needs.

HOW TO SPOT TROUBLE IN READING

Some children could learn to read standing on their heads in a dark room with a mouthful of bubblegum. If your child is one of these, you may not have given much thought to which method of reading instruction your school uses. But if you're not sure your child is as good a reader as he could be, here are some facts to help you decide what to do about it:

Reading Methods

Approximately 85 percent of our public schools teach reading from books which stress the memorization of whole words, with only incidental training in letter sounds (phonics), according to Mike Brunner, research associate at the National Institute of Education (NIE). This approach, called *indirect phonics,* puts major emphasis on teaching children whole words (look-say) and only slight emphasis on teaching the skills needed to "sound out" new words.

Critics point out that in *indirect* phonics, the teaching of letter sounds is not deliberate and systematic. Children learn to sound out words only after learning to recognize words by their shape and to guess at the meaning of words by their use in sentences. Instead of teaching all the letter sounds in the beginning, indirect phonics spreads this teaching over several years. Letter sounds are taught only indirectly.

Yet Dr. Jeanne Chall of Harvard, widely recognized authority on the teaching of reading, notes that primary school children learn best when teaching is direct. She also notes that children taught by the indirect method may have difficulty shifting their attention back and forth between whole words and letter sounds. Children learning by an indirect phonics method are usually not taught to blend sounds (tr-ai-n = train), which Chall reports is important for both early and later success in reading.

Critics of indirect phonics also point out that teachers using the indirect phonics method encourage children to guess at the meaning of new words by using such clues as the shape of the word or the meaning of the sentence, instead of working out the precise sounds of the word. Let's say a child reads this sentence in which he doesn't know the fifth word: "The boy found a paddle." He might guess "puddle" or "poodle" and become totally confused about what he's reading. Because the indirect phonics method requires children to memorize so many "sight" words and to guess at others, too many children become frustrated, inadequate readers. Some never learn to read.

A minority of our schools, 15 to 20 percent of them at most, according to Brunner, use the direct phonics approach. Direct phonics gives children early training in recognizing the printed letters and letter combinations that stand for the sounds of English. In direct teaching of phonics children learn at the very beginning—before they read stories—the sounds of printed letters and letter combinations and how to pronounce words made up of these sounds. They learn these sounds systematically. For example: consonant sounds (p, t, k, etc.), short vowel sounds (e as in "wet," a as in "bat"), long vowel sounds (i as in "fire"), and so on. Once they begin reading stories they are able to tackle new words by sounding them out. According to Dr. Chall, the research shows that all children learn to read better if they are taught direct phonics.

Your child's school may not use the terms "direct phonics" or "indirect phonics." To find out what's going on in school, you may have to do some translating: Other terms used for *direct phonics* are "code emphasis," "intensive phonics," "phonics first," or "synthetic phonics." Other terms that mean the same thing as *indirect phonics* are "meaning emphasis," "eclectic," "psycholinguistic," or "analytic phonics."

How Well Does Your Child Read?

This simple reading activity, suggested by Dr. S. Jay Samuels, co-editor of the *Reading Research Quarterly,* will help you to see for yourself whether your child has learned phonics skills well enough to understand reading material suited to his grade level. Keep this reading session as relaxed as if you were playing a game or simply reading with your child as usual. He shouldn't feel it's a test.

Find a book of stories appropriate to your child's grade level. The teacher, the school librarian, or a children's librarian will be able to suggest one. *Be certain your child has not read the book you choose.*

Read a story aloud to him. Choose a short one. You don't want his attention to wander. When you're finished, ask him to tell you what the story was about. Simply accept whatever he says. Don't correct him. If he has a reasonably good idea of what happened in the story, you know that your child is capable of understanding the stories in the book. Tell him what a good job he did.

Now ask him to choose another story from the same book and read it aloud to you. Tell him you'll want him to tell you about the story in his own words when he finishes. Don't interrupt as he reads. When he's through, ask him to tell you, without referring to the book, what happened in the second story. He should be able to tell you as much about this story as he told you about the one you read to him. If he can't do this, it means that he has not been taught letter sounds and blending (direct phonics) well enough to be able to concentrate on the meaning of what he reads, says Dr. Samuels.

He notes that children learning to read must get enough practice in sounding out words to be able to do it not only accurately, but also quickly and automatically. Children who haven't had enough practice may have difficulty reading aloud with expression, as well as understanding what they read.

This shorter activity will also help you to check your child's reading skills. Print up a short list of words taken from reading material at your child's level. Again, be sure to choose from books your child hasn't read. Include some short words (for example, *so, an, as, is, at, are, to, was, saw, on, no*). Children who haven't learned direct phonics often get these words confused because they're in the habit of guessing.

If your child can sound out unfamiliar words at his own level and if he reads short words without mixing them up, he's probably developing good reading skills. But if the only words he can read are the ones in the school reading book (which he may have memorized), he is not learning to read well—he's probably been taught with indirect phonics.

If your child (and perhaps others in his class) does poorly at sounding out words in these reading activities, Dr. Samuels suggests a talk with school people to find out why. You can find out which method is used to teach reading. Is it direct or indirect phonics? Working together with other parents, you can let school people know you want your children taught to read by the method shown by up-to-date research to be the more effective—direct phonics.

A first-grade teacher who switched to direct phonics after using another method for many years says, "We did nothing but sounds until December. Then we flew through the first few readers. I loved it! Every teacher [in other grades] in the school could spot the students who had been in those classes, they read so well."

Like this teacher, a number of others in schools which use indirect phonics reading books give their first-graders instruction in direct phonics before they start with the regular school readers. If your child has a teacher who does this, he's fortunate. More primary teachers would probably add direct phonics if they had not been misinformed by education professors, who told them that learning direct phonics makes it difficult for children to understand what they read. As I've said, research shows just the opposite. Children who have been taught to sound out words by the direct phonics method understand what they read better than children taught by indirect phonics, which stresses memorizing words. A study quoted by Dr. Chall states: "[W]e have yet to encounter a student who could decode [sound out words] fluently but failed to comprehend."

Reading Groups. Even in a homogeneous class (one made up of children of roughly the same ability), students will be grouped for reading according to how quickly the teacher expects them to learn, usually in a top, average, and low group. The levels are disguised by giving them names like "Bluebirds," "Cardinals," and "Eagles," to avoid upsetting children and parents. Children almost always know which group is which. Not all educators are convinced that grouping is wise. Says Charlotte F. Lockhart, former teacher and elementary school principal and the author of a direct phonics program: "Grouping is mainly for the convenience of the teacher. It doesn't help children—certainly not the ones you put in the slow group. What effect do you think it has on a child when you let him know right in the beginning that he's in the lowest group? That's no way to start a child in school. Let children know you expect all of them to learn, and then give them all the help they need."

Unless your school district is one in a thousand, though, you will find reading groups. It's important to know the level of your child's group. As we saw in chapter 3, teachers don't always volunteer this information. You must ask. Says an experienced elementary teacher: "Parents are sometimes told there's not much difference between one reading group and another, when there is actually a good deal of difference."

Once you've found out which group your child is in, you can find out the difference between reading groups by asking about grade-equivalent scores on reading achievement tests. As you'll recall from chapter 4, a third-grader with a grade-equivalent score of 6.2 (sixth grade, second month) is reading much better than the average third-grader, but he is *not* reading sixth-grade material. Remember, too, that it's common for the average grade-equivalent on achievement tests in a given school or class to be well above (or below) the national average. Let's say that the average grade-equivalent for students in your child's second-grade class is 3.5 (third grade, fifth month). If your child's score is 4.8, he will probably be placed in the high reading group. If his score is 2.4, he may be in the low group.

A child reading below the level of the rest of the class in his school is cause for concern, even if, for example, his score shows that he reads as well as the average U.S. second-grader. Why? That nationwide average includes many extremely poor readers. You want your child to read at least as well as the average student in his grade at your school. Even if the teacher says your child is "coming along nicely" in the low group, you need to find out all you can about the difficulties he's having and what's being done to correct them. Here are some questions to ask the teacher:

1. What errors does your child make in reading? Errors include mispronouncing words, adding words, omitting words, repeating words. Of course all children learning to read make errors in these areas once in a while. But frequent errors mean trouble. Can he sound out new words? Can he read aloud with expression?

2. What do his errors tell about his reading problems? For example, frequent omissions can mean, among other things, that your child is skipping words because he hasn't learned to sound them out.

3. How does the teacher help students in the low group to overcome problems like these? Be tactful here, but don't hesitate to ask for fear of sounding critical. You need information. If your child is

sick, and you ask the doctor to explain the treatment, you're not criticizing him. Your questions may make both you and the teacher a bit uncomfortable now. A reading problem will make your child permanently uncomfortable in school.

4. Is your child showing improvement? In what areas of reading? Does the teacher foresee a time when your child will be up to grade level, or reading as well as most other students in the class? When?

There's a Catch-22 in the low reading groups. Children who are having problems in reading get easier books, but if they aren't also taught the skills they need to tackle more difficult material, they can fall farther and farther behind. This is why you need to find out what goes on in the low group if your child is in it. You want to be a cooperative parent, but not so cooperative you let your child languish in the low group if he's getting nowhere. Dr. Chall shows that using the direct phonics method is especially important in teaching children who have trouble learning to read.

No matter which group your child is in (but especially if he's in the low group) find out how much time he spends doing workbook activities, compared with the amount of time he spends actually reading. Studies show that doing workbook exercises and "skill" sheets don't help children learn to read. "I don't need research to tell me that!" a Michigan parent of four said when she heard about this report. "At our house we've been calling them 'those damned dittos' for years. And now that I'm a teacher's aide and see kids having to work on those things in class, I'm more convinced than ever they're mostly busy work."

Unfortunately, some teachers assume that parents who ask why a child is in the low group are suffering primarily from a wounded ego. As patiently and as tactfully as you can, explain that you're worried about your child's reading not because he landed in the low group, but because he's headed for problems in school if he doesn't learn to read better. A good teacher will respect your concern and treat you as a partner in helping your child.

At some point during your talks with school people about your child's reading, they may suggest that you are damaging your child by "pushing" him or that an emotional problem is causing your child's reading problem. This can happen, but far more often it's the other way around. Children who haven't been taught to read properly develop emotional problems as a result. Says Peg Doctor, associate director of the Chicago's Reading Institute, which has been helping disabled readers for half a century: "It's extremely difficult for a student with a reading problem, particularly if he's intelligent, not to feel inadequate. Peers view him as inadequate. The teacher views him as inadequate. There's no doubt that poor reading skills cause emotional problems."

Get Help Quickly

If your child reads poorly (even if his test scores seem adequate or the teacher says he is "doing nicely"), don't wait before getting extra help for him. There are several sources of help:

1.   The school may recommend testing and a remedial class. Children often benefit from special attention in a small group setting, but whether your child gets lasting help in reading depends on the skill and training of the specialist in your school. Keep in mind that diagnosing reading problems is not an exact science. Dr. Samuels notes a study in which a number of reading experts asked to diagnose the same child's difficulties in reading showed almost total disagreement with one another as to the nature of the problem and what should be done to help the child. Studies have also shown that gains made in a remedial class may "wash out" when the help is discontinued.

Some reading specialists do a good job of correcting reading problems, but others have not been trained in the most effective methods. Any specialist who intends to help your child in reading should be able to discuss his problem in terms you can understand and explain what methods will be used to help him.

2.   If you are able to work well with your child at home, you can help him yourself. You can get direct phonics materials, including *Johnny Still Can't Read—But You Can Teach Him at Home,* by K. Diehl and G. K. Hodenfield ($2.50, plus postage), from the Reading Reform Foundation. (See the Glossary.) If the problem is a longstanding or very severe one, though, and your child is discouraged and antagonistic about reading, you may find it difficult to work with him.

3.   Hire a tutor who teaches direct phonics or take your child to a

well-established private reading clinic which uses this method. (There are a number of direct phonics programs. Among those which may be used in remedial work is one developed by Slingerland and another by Spalding and Spalding. The RRF can furnish a list of other direct phonics programs.)

Check the credentials of anyone you hire to help your child, and ask to talk to parents of other students who have used the tutor or the clinic. Then ask for an explanation of your child's problem and of what will be done to correct it.

When to Suspect Reading Trouble in Upper Elementary School

There's no guarantee that doing passably well in first-, second-, and third-grade readers—especially if the teacher has used the indirect phonics method, which stresses memorizing "sight" words—has prepared your child to deal with textbooks in the upper grades. At this level a child who is a poor reader, or even a mediocre reader, can find this weakness holding him back in all areas, even in math, where he may have trouble with story problems. What can you do if you suspect lack of reading skill is causing your child trouble in other subjects? Using short passages from your child's textbooks, do the reading activity suggested by Dr. Samuels. This will give you evidence to show the school people that your child needs help, if this is the case.

Be sure he gets real help and not just an easier textbook. And don't wait weeks for someone at school to "see what can be done." Push for a definite starting date. If school people don't move promptly, check the options listed above for getting extra reading help.

LITERACY MEANS READING *AND* WRITING

Only a few years ago, elementary schools were making almost no effort to teach children to write. In the past several years, there has been a move to add real writing instruction to the elementary curriculum. Unfortunately, no more than 5 percent of today's elementary school teachers have been trained to teach writing, according to Dr. Marcia Farr Whiteman, former team leader of writing research for the NIE. Some school districts have sent teachers to writing institutes so they can learn how to write themselves. These efforts are "filtering down into the classroom," in the words of Dr. Whiteman. But filtering can be a slow process. "Teachers need experience with writing themselves over time, and most don't have it," she says.

In many schools, underlining grammar terms and putting commas in workbook sentences still passes for writing instruction. Yet children learn to write only by writing their own sentences and paragraphs. Equally important, they learn to think by learning to write.

In the first three or four years of school, your child should be writing "stories," letters, and perhaps poems or a diary. The teacher should not zap his paper with red ink for every misspelling and punctuation error. Correct spelling and rules of punctuation can be taught separately, and children will learn gradually to incorporate them into their writing. The important thing at this point is that they learn to put their thoughts on paper. In his study of elementary-school writing, Dr. Donald Graves found that children begin to feel a need for correctness on their own by about third grade. (If the teacher overvalues neatness and won't allow children to erase or cross out as they write, they'll become discouraged; the teacher may need a tactful reminder that thinking isn't usually neat.)

In the upper elementary grades, children should be writing not only in language arts, but also in such subjects as social studies and science. They must learn how to organize factual reports and how to write answers to questions based on their reading. At this point, they can learn the plan-write-revise system and should be held to reasonable standards of correctness in spelling, punctuation, and sentence structure.

Watch out for teachers who stick to language-arts workbooks and say children "aren't ready to write yet." What these teachers mean is that they aren't willing to grade papers. If almost no writing goes on in your child's class, talk to the teacher. Ask what writing skills your child is supposed to master this year. If she can't answer this question, if she uses lack of time as an alibi, or if she talks about grammar and punctuation instead of real writing, you know there is no writing program. Get together with other parents and see the principal. Remind him that children need writing practice to be fully literate. If he says teachers aren't trained to teach writing, urge him to find one who is (surely there is one in the district) and invite him or her to run a workshop for other teachers.

If he says there isn't enough class time to teach writing, suggest that he gather up half of the workbooks in the school and lock them up. In many classrooms, children spend at least as much time in workbooks as with the teacher.

Junior high school students who don't write at least a page or two a week are not getting enough writing practice. If your seventh- or eighth-grader does little or no writing, talk to the principal. Explain that you want writing to be part of the school curriculum in all subjects, because it's a skill your child and others will need in college and on the job. Many educators think that computers and tapes have made writing an obsolete skill in the business world. Yet in surveying a varied group of business people on this question, I heard time after time that the schools have handicapped young people by neglecting writing. Pointing out an even more serious problem, George Orwell, author of *1984*, writes, "If people cannot write well, they cannot think well, and if they cannot think well, others will do their thinking for them."

How likely is your child to get good writing instruction in junior high school? The National Assessment of Educational Progress (NAEP) periodically tests thousands of U.S. school children in reading, math, and writing. The students who take these tests are carefully chosen to be a representative sample of *all* U.S. students their age. In the latest NAEP writing tests reported (1979), thirteen-year-olds were asked whether they routinely had writing assignments that required them to do a plan, write, and revise a paper. Only 3 percent answered "yes." Is your school doing better than this? If not, a group of parents can ask top administrators and the school board to add a strong writing program to the curriculum, beginning in the primary grades. (For information on dealing with the school board, see chapter 13.)

WHAT'S ELEMENTARY IN MATH?

How well does your child know subtraction? Can he do long division? Answering these questions is easier than finding out how well your child understands what he reads, or how well he writes sentences. In math the answer is either right or wrong. If your child is like many who took the latest NAEP math test, he can probably add, subtract, and multiply reasonably well. The NAEP report shows that students did poorly on long division, however. Seventy-five percent of the thirteen-year-olds got a wrong answer when asked to divide 1128 by 36.

Is your child learning how to use the arithmetic skills he knows to solve routine problems? If he's like many who took the NAEP tests, he may not do a very good job of applying these skills to problem solving. For example, in the most recent NAEP math test (1981–1982), 24.7 percent of the nine-year-olds were able to find the area of a rectangle, given two sides; 64 percent of thirteen-year-olds were able to do this problem. (These percentages show a decline from the 1978 NAEP tests, when 27.6 percent of the nine-year-olds and 70 percent of the thirteen-year-olds got the right answer.) When students take the NAEP tests, they show their work. On this question scorers noticed that a high percentage of students made the mistake of adding the sides, which gives the perimeter (distance around) the rectangle. To get the right answer for area, they should have multiplied the two sides.

Why the disappointing score on this relatively simple problem? Why is it that so many U.S. children—perhaps yours among them—are not learning to do problems like this in the middle elementary grades? Equally important, why are more than a third of the thirteen-year-olds still unable to do this simple problem in junior high?

Math educators offer several answers to these questions. Ann McAloon of the Educational Testing Service, a former curriculum coordinator who has also trained teachers, believes elementary teachers often don't put enough stress on problems like this because they themselves aren't comfortable with the concepts (in this case geometry) they had back in tenth grade. "Most know addition, subtraction, multiplication, division. That's it." She adds that most elementary teachers need and appreciate in-service math training, such as a brush-up in geometry.

John Saxon is an Oklahoma math teacher and the author of several math books which have helped students to make outstanding gains on national tests. He believes the fault lies not with classroom teachers but with the educators responsible for planning school math programs from first grade on: "They believed that if students were taught an overview of how numbers behaved and interrelated, then they would somehow have the understanding that would give them command of the other skills that they needed. The overview was stressed at the expense of fundamental skill building blocks. The children did not understand the overview and were denied the chance to learn the basics."

Saxon also notes that students have used books "filled with pictures of women in laboratory coats and full page pictures of 'function machines' but that devote insufficient time and space to the repetition of basic ideas."

Though new math has retreated, its foggy terms can live on in textbooks to confuse children needlessly. Take a careful look at your child's fourth-grade (or seventh-grade) math book. Would you enjoy studying from it? Is the language clear? Do lessons follow in logical sequence? If not, talk to other parents. Then ask the teacher and the principal whether they have evidence that this book really helps children to learn math.

According to the Council for Basic Education, these are some characteristics parents should look for in a good elementary math program:

1. Good coaching in class. Children need constant feedback from the teacher as they practice new skills. When learning subtraction, for example, a child shouldn't be turned loose to work problems—piling mistake on mistake—before someone checks to see whether he really understands how "borrowing" works. Sometimes students who have already mastered the skill can coach those who haven't. A recent report of observations in 1000 classrooms shows that teachers spend less than 3 percent of class time giving students corrective feedback.

2. A sensible plan for advancing from grade to grade. Children should be taught skills in a logical sequence which also stresses review and practice of skills learned earlier. Many more of those students taking the NAEP test would have done the rectangle problem correctly if their math program had included review and frequent practice in finding areas.

3. Appropriate emphasis on meaningful problem solving. In a CBE Publication, *Teaching Mathematics: What is Basic?*, Dr. Stephen S. Willoughby, director of mathematics education at New York University, points out that "unreal" story problems probably help to turn children against math, because they "give the learner the impression that mathematics is a way to make work rather than reduce or avoid work." For example, he offers this problem: "Mary took $5 to the circus. She spent $3.85. How much money did she have left?" This is an unrealistic problem, because a child who wanted to know how much money he had left wouldn't have to subtract. He could count what was in his pocket.

COULD YOUR CHILD HAVE A LEARNING DISABILITY?

If your child has difficulty with basic skills such as reading and writing, or if he has other problems in school, there is a growing possibility he could be labeled "learning disabled" (LD). The number of U.S. children said by school people to be "learning disabled" (LD) increased 100 percent between 1976–77 and 1983–84, despite a 10.9 percent drop in total school enrollment, according to figures from the U.S. Department of Education. Here are some facts you need to know:

"Learning disabled," first used in the late 1960s to describe children who have difficulty learning, is an umbrella term for a wide range of handicaps for which no cause has been positively determined. Learning disabled children are not mentally retarded, emotionally disturbed, brain damaged, or culturally disadvantaged.

Some children identified as learning disabled have such obviously severe problems as confusion about the location of the parts of their body or inability to understand what is said to them.

Some schools, however, may classify children as learning disabled if they fail to pay attention in class or fail to do their homework.

Barbara Kuczen, a professor of early childhood education, writes, "Social or emotional maladjustment, language difficulties, special types of deafness, and particularly reading disorders have been broadly included under this label . . . In fact, the same child could be classified in many different ways, depending on the state of residence." This confusion in classifying learning disabled children is not surprising, since there is no scientifically valid test for identifying anything called a "learning disability."

The vague definition of this handicap has led to a number of abuses in labeling children as learning disabled. "Nationwide, too many are being identified as LD. Some teachers can be too quick to shuffle children off to special ed," says an official of one state branch of the Association for Children with Learning Disabilities (ACLD). "Parents may resent the label and feel the classroom teacher should make a better effort to work with their child." But she adds, "If a teacher *has* made a real effort to work with a child and feels he does need special help, parents should agree to have a child evaluated. After all, if he isn't able to keep up with the class, he's apt to acquire a label, anyway. He should have special help if he needs it."

To cut unnecessary referrals, several states now require classroom teachers to list everything they have done and everyone they have consulted in trying to help a child before they suggest an evaluation for LD. In some states there have been charges that school districts mislabel or overlabel children in LD and other handicapped categories to qualify for more state and federal funds.

Yet there's no doubt that some children of normal ability do have trouble learning in school. The LD category includes children who are not learning well but who do not belong in any of the other handicap categories. Because many children classified as LD have reading problems, some concerned educators believe that many of these disabilities could be prevented by proper teaching in the regular classroom. In the case of a number of children said to be LD, the problem did not originate inside the child, but outside the child—in the way he has been taught. Writing in the January 1981 issue of *Journal of Learning Disabilities,* Charles M. Richardson, a former adjunct professor of special education, currently director of Learning Foundations, Dix Hills, New York, states: "Child study clinicians admit to devoting considerable time and effort to sorting out which clients' problems are innate, and which are the result of poor past teaching." His article concludes: "If the cause of some of the LD problem is poor teaching, and the remedy for all of it is good teaching, then we need to be spending (at least) equal time testing school systems for 'teaching disabilities.'"

If your child has trouble learning despite normal intelligence, regardless of the cause, you may have to become familiar with special ed procedures:

1. School districts screen children for learning disabilities before kindergarten. You are not obliged to take your child to such a screening. If in the course of a screening special education people suspect that a child has a learning disability, they ask parents for permission to evaluate him further. If your child is having difficulty in school, the teacher may suggest an evaluation, or you may request one yourself.

2. An evaluation to find out why your child has trouble learning and what might be done to help him cannot be done without your

written permission. If you do not want to have him evaluated, or if you have asked for an evaluation and the school refuses to do one, you or the school may request a due process a hearing before a hearing officer. If you disagree with the decision, you can appeal to the state department of education and to the courts.

If you have a doubt about the school's evaluation—or about the need for any evaluation—you may have your child tested by a qualified independent psychologist. Make sure the psychologist has the proper credentials for dealing with the schools.

3. School people, including special education professionals, and you as a parent will plan an Individualized Education Program (IEP) to deal with your child's learning problems. It is your right to approve or disapprove of plans suggested by the school for your child's IEP. If you feel the IEP or the special education class selected for your child doesn't meet his needs, you can appeal, just as in the evaluation stage above.

4. Once a child is classified as handicapped in order to get special ed help for a learning disability or any other disorder, he remains in this classification as long as he is in school—until he moves or graduates.

As you can see from this brief sketch, you'll need to learn a good deal about special education rights and procedures if your child is involved in a special ed program. You'll get information from your school district, but you need a reliable source of information outside the local district. Write to your state department of education. To make sure your child benefits from special education, you should monitor his program yourself. The Association for Children with Learning Disabilities publishes booklets and newsletters for parents and may furnish parent advocates for IEP meetings or hearings. For the name of the chapter in your area, write to the ACLD (see Glossary for address).

If either you or the teacher think your child should be evaluated for learning disability, you should take several steps.

First, ask the teacher what evidence of a learning problem your child shows in class. Insist on specifics and an explanation you can understand. For example, if your ten-year-old is writing letters backwards, ask her to explain how this could be related to his learning problem. Ask her to describe her efforts to help him—by varying her teaching method, after-class tutoring, and so on. If you feel the teacher has not made a satisfactory effort to help your child, speak to the principal.

Second, contact your state department of education for information about special ed and your rights under state and federal laws. Get in touch with the ACLD or another support group for parents of LD children.

Lastly, refer to the final item in the " 'Problem' Conferences" section of chapter 3 for help in preparing to discuss your child's learning difficulties with school people. Make sure you understand their explanation of his problem as they see it and how they propose to help him. If the explanation is not clear, ask questions until you get the answers you need.

PROGRAMS FOR GIFTED CHILDREN

School districts may set up special programs for children who show unusually high academic achievement or special achievement in the arts. You can find out from the superintendent's office whether your district has such a program and how children are selected for it. In most states, both state and federal money is available for these programs. In many cases the money available to schools for gifted programs may be discretionary, with local districts deciding whether to set up a program and apply for funds. You can get more information from your state department of education and from the National Association for Gifted Children (see Glossary for address).

COMPUTERS IN THE CLASSROOM: PROS AND CONS

Is your elementary school buying computers and the software to go with them? If so, exactly how will computers be used? Many schools plan to use them as teaching aids. In some cases this may be helpful—if enough well-designed software programs are available. A New England school district makes a small number of computers go a long way by transporting them from school to school in a van. Some high school students are taught the fundamentals of computer programming, a worthwhile effort for those who have the necessary math background to use a computer meaningfully. Computers have also been used to allow kindergarten children to type out words and sentences. Older children enjoy writing on a computer because they can write faster and correct mistakes with little effort.

Despite these advantages, there are signs that schools have not planned well before investing in computers. A recent newspaper article reported a shortage of science books in an affluent suburban school, which was nevertheless buying computers and software. The author, a businessman and former school board member, notes that when it comes to teaching students, especially elementary children, how to actually use computers, schools may simply be going through the motions—unless they can first teach students to understand the problems computers are designed to solve. Computers require educational dollars and classroom time that might better be spent in other areas.

Parents and taxpayers should ask school people two questions *before* they commit school time and school dollars to computers: Where is the research showing how well computers help children to learn? What are the strengths and weaknesses of the computer as a teaching aid? If school people can't give answers to these questions, backed up with solid evidence, they have not planned carefully and may not be ready to make the best use of computers.

Checking your child's progress in elementary school means far more than looking over a report card and talking to the teacher. You must pay careful attention not only to what your child is being taught, but also to how well he is mastering basic skills. You can't assume that your child will get the help he needs at school unless you as a parent understand what's available.

7

RECOGNIZING YOUR CHILD'S PEOPLE PROBLEMS

"Nobody likes me!" wails ten-year-old Joan.

"Of course they do. You must be imagining things," her father says.

"You just don't understand," murmurs Joan sadly and retreats to her room, where she spends Friday evening in tears because she was the only girl in her fifth-grade class not invited to the slumber party.

Joan's father understands she's unhappy and knows it has something to do with her not being very well liked at school. He can't change things, though, so he tries to reassure her by denying the problem. This makes Joan feel even lonelier, overwhelmed by a situation her father won't admit exists.

It's not easy to admit your child is miserable with a problem when you can't help. You can't change the social pecking order at school, but you can let your child know that you understand. "It's tough not to be invited. Want to talk about it?"

In this chapter we'll discuss some of children's more common social problems in school, ranging from shyness to difficulties in getting along with many different types of teachers. For some children there are special problems—the strain of adjusting to a new school, the extra effort required to develop a talent in addition to meeting the demands of school. You'll also find a brief section on drug problems.

PITFALLS FOR THE "HELPFUL" PARENT

While you can't make your child feel better by denying a particular problem, it's not wise to go to the other extreme, either. If he's usually the last to be chosen for a gym team or never included in any of the social groups in fifth grade, it's natural for him to feel devastated. You can be sympathetic and helpful without giving him the idea that the situation looks like the end of the world to you, too. If he senses you believe this, he may start to think there really *is* something wrong with him. It rarely helps to get directly involved, either. A young woman, Bonnie, describes how her mother unwittingly made things even more difficult for her when she was unhappy at school: "In those days I was really heavy, and the kids loved to make fun of me on the playground and at the bus stop, which was a couple of blocks from where we lived. Then the bus stop was moved to the corner right across from my house, and my mother found out about the teasing. Sometimes I'd see her standing at the window, watching. One morning she came dashing out of the house and yelled at the kids for teasing me. I know she wanted to help, but that only made it ten times worse. She didn't understand that. I wanted to die! I'd rather have been teased forever than have her open that front door. In sixth grade I lost weight and finally started making some friends. But there was always someone who knew about those mornings at the bus stop. 'Do you remember how her mother used to. . . .' "

Another pitfall in dealing with children's social problems is the temptation to make well-meaning comments that really add up to criticism: "You should act more friendly," or "You're just too shy." Labeling a child as shy won't help him, and it may make things worse.

If you're worried about a problem your child is having—in or out of school—it may seem natural to discuss it with grandparents or other relatives, or with your best friend. Before you do, ask yourself whether the person will keep it confidential and whether the friend or family member is apt to offer advice that could help your child. "There is such a thing as being too open," says Billie Reeder, an Oklahoma junior high teacher. "Sometimes I think discussing a child's problem outside the immediate family serves no real purpose, except as a catharsis for the parent. When aunts and uncles and grandparents and everyone else is told about the problem, it leaves a child so exposed."

TEACH YOUR CHILD PROBLEM SOLVING

As children get older, parents become less and less able to solve problems for them. Even if you could provide the solution, it's not always wise. What parents can do is treat a child with respect, acknowledge that a problem exists, and then help her to develop strategies for solving it on her own. For example, let's say your child complains her best friend won't speak to her. In *The Stress-proof Child*, Bonnie Remsberg and Antoinette Saunders suggest helping your child to see that she has several choices in dealing with such a situation: She can ask her friend why she's not talking; she can continue as she is now and do nothing; she can find a new friend. Have your child write down these options.

The next step is to help her anticipate the results of each course of action, say Remsberg and Saunders. Asking the friend why she's not talking may bring an unpleasant response, such as "I don't want to be friends with you anymore." Doing nothing will change nothing, but there's no risk of hearing an unpleasant truth. Finding a new friend could mean losing the old friend. Teaching your child a systematic approach to problem solving will help her to feel competent now and prepare her to deal with more complex problems later.

THE SHYNESS SYNDROME

Actually, chances are slight that feeling shy or left out at some point in school will cause your child permanent unhappiness. In *Shyness,* Dr. Philip Zimbardo notes that 40 percent of the people he surveyed reported they had once been shy but no longer were. Shy children may have more company than they realize. In a group of fourth-, fifth-, and sixth-graders, Dr. Zimbardo found that 42 percent were considered shy by classmates. By seventh and eighth grades, 54 percent were shy, with girls accounting for the increase.

Without belittling the problem, you may be able to think of a way to help your child see that things will probably get better. One mother reports that she gave her daughter a new perspective during an unhappy school year by recalling how several children in her own sixth-grade class sank to ordinary status as other children matured and moved up to take their places in junior high. If your child is old enough to understand, you might point out that shy people, because they are often more sensitive to the feelings of others, have an advantage over the nonshy in some situations. Another comforting note for the shy child is that everyone—even the most self-assured adults—occasionally feels shy and uncertain. Only 7 percent of the people in Dr. Zimbardo's shyness survey said they had never felt this way.

Encouraging a shy child to become more independent will help him to develop the assurance he needs. Here are ideas parents have used successfully to help children gain confidence.

When shopping, encourage your child to ask salespeople questions about colors, sizes, and styles of clothing, or ask when out-of-stock items will be available. One mother says children who aren't ready to do these things often can handle telephone inquiries—ordering from catalogues, checking before a shopping trip to find out whether a store stocks needed items.

Let your child give the family dinner order to the waitress in a restaurant, or ask directions when the family travels.

Even the youngest child can greet family guests at the door and take their coats, or pass food at parties.

Let your child speak for himself whenever possible. For example, with a little coaching beforehand, even young children can learn to describe their own symptoms to the doctor.

Try having a different member of the family responsible for suggesting a topic and leading the conversation at dinner each evening. Practice builds self-confidence.

Encourage your child to give his own party, planning food and entertainment, making introductions. Some children do better if they begin by co-hosting a party with a friend.

Dr. Zimbardo writes: "Shy children fear taking action because of their anxiety about failing or doing it wrong. Teach your child to take calculated risks and to handle failure. The message to get across is that the child's *attempts may fail* to get the desired goal, but *the child is never a failure.*"

Dr. Barbara Kuczen, a professor of early childhood education who also conducts parent training workshops, believes parents can go a step further in helping children to get along with others by offering them specific suggestions on how to be a good friend. When your child is in a receptive mood, offer him these tips:

1. "Remember how much you like it when someone listens to you. It makes you feel important. Listen to your friends and make them feel important.

2. "Share with your friends and treat them with courtesy.

3. "If your friends hurt your feelings or are mean to you, it is bad for their self-image and yours. Stand up for your rights or don't play with them, but don't let it bother you for long. . . . No one can hurt your feelings unless you let them."

Older children who feel friendless often keep quiet about it. They may say they hate school (even though they have no academic problems), spend their spare time moping around, and seem generally unhappy. If this description fits your child, offer help, but don't push. Try tactfully to get him to talk about the problem, and make it easy for him to entertain at home. You may be able to expand your child's social horizons by interesting him in Scouts, sports, or a church group.

Junior high and high school students in some areas can join clubs sponsored by adult service organizations and help out on community projects. For example, members of a high school Key Club (sponsored by the Kiwanis International) in one midwestern suburb regularly assist the fire department in conducting evacuation drills in retirement homes, serve as counselors at summer day camps for retarded children, and help to collect used eyeglasses for the needy in underdeveloped countries. Nothing builds confidence like giving real help to others. Watching competent, energetic teenagers at work, it's difficult to understand why relatively few communities take advantage of the contribution they can make.

ALLOWING FOR DIFFERENT SOCIAL STYLES
What do these two students have in common?

Marie, a bright, friendly girl in my eighth-grade history class, didn't have the shadow of a problem as far as I could see. She studied hard, played the piano beautifully, and was extremely popular with the other children. But during a conference, Marie's mother said, "I'm worried about her. There have been two dances this year, and she didn't go to either of them." I asked whether Marie was upset about not going. Her mother said, "No. That's really what worries me. She doesn't seem to have any interest at all.

You know how *serious* Marie can be sometimes. I'm afraid she'll just never be interested in boys or parties. . . ."

Everyone who saw Roberta T. with her mother was struck by the contrast. Mrs. T. was a svelte fashion model who drew admiring glances wherever she went and obviously enjoyed being the center of attention. Roberta was intelligent and friendly. She had a pleasant smile, but at fifteen her figure was thick and she moved clumsily. Watching them together it was easy to see that Mrs. T. was embarrassed by her inappropriate daughter, who could not help but be aware of her mother's attitude.

At this point, you've probably guessed that although these girls have very little in common, both do have parents who are not satisfied with their appearance or their attitude toward social life and friends. Disapproving of a child's legitimate interests and social style is a subtle form of parental lack of support. When parents send messages like these, a child begins to sense that no matter how hard he tries—and no matter how well he does—he is never doing things quite right. A child who feels this way may not develop the confidence he'll need later on to deal well with stress. You're more likely to send your child the right messages if you acknowledge that his temperament and social style may differ from yours without being "wrong."

A teacher with long experience in a junior high school in an upper-middle-class suburb says: "I get the feeling that some parents are perhaps too concerned about their child's social development, even at the expense of academic development. And a few parents try to improve their own social status by pressuring their children to associate with the 'right' kids."

"I HATE THE TEACHER!"

About the only thing you can be sure of if your child seems unhappy with the teacher is that you should find out more, particularly if he complains habitually. Your child may "hate" the teacher temporarily on a day when things don't go right at school. Maybe he didn't do as well on a test as he expected to. Perhaps there's more homework than he wants to do. If your child is used to teachers of the "let's-make-kids-feel-good-instead-of-worrying-about-whether-they-learn-anything" variety, he may find it hard to adjust to a more demanding teacher.

"This is Rich's father. He says you kept him after school yesterday. To clean out his notebook. Is that right?" The voice on the telephone was angry.

"Yes, I did. You see—"

"Well, I don't think that's your job. How he keeps his notebook is none of your business!"

Before I could say anything else, Rich's father hung up.

I suppose that Rich, who naturally didn't want to stay after school, complained to his father that I was a mean teacher. I had made him stay after school just because I didn't like the way he put his paper in his notebook.

If Rich's father had asked a few questions, though, he would have learned the whole story. I was teaching eighth-graders how to take notes in history class, and more often than not, Rich couldn't find his notebook, or a blank sheet of paper, or the outline we were following. He was too busy rummaging through his books and papers to get much out of what was said in class. Naturally, all the paper rustling and notebook flapping disturbed other students, too. When reminders didn't help, I asked Rich to spend a few minutes after school putting his notebook in order, so he could start doing the work he was supposed to do. I doubt that Rich explained all this to his father.

It may take careful questioning to find out why your child is unhappy with the teacher. What does she do or say that he doesn't like? Have a talk with the teacher to explore the problem. You can be tactful but honest: "Jerry seems to have the idea you're picking on him. I thought we should get together and try to figure out why he feels that way." Teachers seldom have time to single out children and pick on them, but if a child feels this is the case, a talk with the teacher may clear the air.

While you don't want to ignore a problem with the teacher that makes your child really unhappy over a long period, you don't want to be known as a fussy, overprotective parent, either. If you rush over to school every time your child is slightly upset, you may give him the idea you feel he can't cope on his own. Children sometimes complain that a teacher is unfair, or favors boys over girls, or vice versa. Unfairness does exist, but it's not easy to prove. Whether the situation is real or imagined, your child will probably have to learn to live with it. Sometimes you may be able to suggest a possible solution and let your child take it from there: "Maybe you girls could choose someone as a spokesperson and go in a group to talk with the teacher."

Children can gain confidence dealing with some teacher problems on their own, once someone helps them to see the possibilities. Twelve-year-old Cliff often came home from school upset because he felt the teacher blamed him unjustly for talking in class. He wanted to set the record straight, but as he told his father, "I guess I just wouldn't dare go right up to Mrs. F. and try to make her believe me." His father suggested Cliff write a note. Here's what he wrote:

> Dear Mrs. F.,
> I think you were mad with me yesterday because you thought I was talking when you were explaining a problem on the board. I really was listening to what you were saying. I wasn't talking.
>
> > Respectfully,
> > Cliff Arnold

SPECIAL PROBLEMS

Every child yearns to be "just like the other kids." Yet many children must grow up under conditions other than the sought-after "normal." Some change schools several times, forging a new place for themselves with each move. Others have physical problems. Even something as minor as a mild allergy can curtail activities in gym class or keep a child off the track team. And of course, many children must wrestle with physical handicaps far more severe. A few children stand out as different because of their commitment to develop a talent. While theirs may be "happy problems," these children must deal with lessons, practice, and recitals, in addition to the usual strains of growing up and going to school. Often children who are very different from "the other kids" cope extremely well, thanks to parents who know when—and how—to help.

Moving

American families are increasingly on the move, and it's highly probable that your child will have to change schools at least once

114

before he graduates from high school. Moving does put a child under special stress for the obvious reason that he must leave one set of friends and school surroundings and adjust to new ones.

What can you do to help? First of all, examine your own feelings about moving. Do you see having to make a new home in a new area as an unfortunate change or as a challenge? If you see the move as an opportunity to grow, your child will absorb your attitude and find it easier to deal with. Moving, like other changes, can be viewed as adding richness and challenge to life, or as a threatening disruption. The attitude of parents helps determine how well a child deals with present changes and with future stress.

As a rule, the younger your child is, the more easily he'll adjust to new surroundings and the less difficulty he'll have leaving friends. On the other hand, children who change schools during the first few years stand a greater chance of missing out on developing solid reading or math skills. Having to switch from one book to another or from one method of teaching to another can cause problems. If you plan a move when your child is in the primary grades, find out whether methods used in the new school are compatible with those used in the other school. Discuss with the new teacher the possibility of giving your child extra help at home to prevent a gap in reading or math learning. (See chapters 6 and 9 for information on helping your child at home.)

A midwestern parent of five children who have changed schools several times because of family moves outlines her two-step plan for finding out whether the schools in a new community will suit the children: "First I talk to real estate people—not just one, but several. I've found that if they can't answer my questions, they usually know someone who can. This is a good way to find which school districts in the area are better and which ones to avoid. Real estate people can tell you how the public schools compare with private or church schools in the same community, too. Once I get this information, I'm ready to do some research on my own. I sit in on the classes the children would be in if we moved into the district, and I talk to the teachers. This gives me a feeling for the atmosphere of the school and what goes on in the classroom. I also ask about sports and activities. The last time we moved, we chose one school over another equally good one, because I found out they were starting a soccer team. One of my older boys wanted to learn soccer, and this was an ideal setup. He learned with everyone else and made the team. Most of the battle of moving is won if the kids are happy in school."

A change of schools is probably easiest on a child, both socially and academically, if it comes between elementary and junior high or at the beginning of high school. Making new friends and getting used to a new school is easier if the other children are making similar adjustments. Some parents put off moving the whole family until a child reaches one of these break-off points.

You can help your child make the switch to a new school by keeping these points in mind when you're planning a move:

1. Write ahead to get information from a number of schools in the general area where you plan to settle. You can ask about methods used to teach reading, programs available in math, foreign language, sports, and after-school activities—whatever is important to your child. Comparing answers from several schools may help you decide on a district.

2. Ask realtors, friends, and co-workers who live in the area for information about the schools. Naturally, you'll want to check things out yourself, but you can gain valuable insights from their opinions.

3. Make your child aware of the advantages of going to a new school—a chance to make new friends, build a new image, discard old habits, develop new interests.

4. Sympathize with her when she complains about leaving old friends or seems anxious about entering a new school. At the same time, let her know you feel sure she'll do a good job of making the adjustment.

5. Consider the possibility that living near the new school may make the transition easier for your child. A house close to school often becomes a natural gathering place for friends or a meeting spot for Cub Scouts or Brownies. If locating close to school isn't practical, choose a neighborhood which includes potential friends for your child.

6. Once you know which school your child will attend, take him for a visit before he actually enrolls. Note how children dress, whether they buy or carry lunches to school, what school supplies

seem standard. Have your child spend a few hours on his own in the new school.

7. Don't expect instant adjustment. Unless he's unusually gregarious, it may be some time before your child feels completely at home in the new school. He'll have ups and downs as he feels his way and begins building new friendships.

8. Don't walk or drive him to school. Let him go on the bus or walk with the other children.

9. Don't encourage your child to stay home, even if he's shy and feels ill at ease in new surroundings. Shielding him from having to make the adjustment won't help in the long run.

Physical Problems

Avoiding overprotectiveness applies just as well to helping children cope with a physical problem, as wise parents like Len's have discovered. When I knew him, Len was a tall, blond eleven-year-old in the sixth grade. He wore glasses and always looked cheerful. He appeared quite normal, even to those who knew he suffered from epilepsy. Some marveled at his cheerfulness, knowing that at any time—sitting in class, playing at recess, riding the school bus—he could suffer a seizure. It didn't happen often, but the possibility was always there. I realize now that Len must have been discouraged or frightened sometimes, but he never showed it.

Len's parents decided that despite his illness, he should have a chance to grow up as normally as possible. The teacher knew of Len's problem, but had been asked not to treat him as "special." His parents discussed with Len and his friends what should be done to look after him if he had a seizure away from home. Len bicycled with his friends on streets that weren't too busy, always riding ahead so someone would see immediately if his bike began to waver. On Scout hikes and overnights, someone was assigned to keep an eye on him. Everyone, including Len, took these arrangements in stride.

Happy Problems

Children with happy problems need help from parents, too, according to Kathy, a petite, curly-haired sixteen-year-old who is an honor student and professional ballerina: "The most important thing my parents do is encourage me. They don't expect perfection. They know I expect it too much sometimes, and they remind me that with all I'm doing, perfection just isn't possible. They know when I'm discouraged, too, and they help me to get through those moods. I don't get home from ballet class until ten at night. Then I may have homework to finish. Most of it, though, I do in the car or on the train going back and forth to lessons downtown. I have to use every minute. I have weekend nights and all day Sunday to catch up on sleep, homework, and social life. My friends are always understanding. I've known them since junior high. They know what I have to do. When I need them, they're there, but they don't pressure me when I don't have enough time. Once I considered going to an arts high school in the city. In some ways that would make life easier, but I'd hate leaving my friends."

DRUG USE

Nearly all public high schools today share a drug problem to some degree. Drug use may begin in seventh and eighth grade, or even earlier in some areas. Marijuana and alcohol are the most widely abused drugs. Several years ago a survey showed that approximately 90 percent of all high school students had used alcohol in the past year and at least 50 percent had used marijuana at least once. Percentages for the use of other drugs (stimulants, sedatives, tranquilizers, opiates, hallucinogens) are far smaller, but cocaine use is increasing.

Some young people who go to school where drugs are very much in evidence "never touch the stuff," while others seek out drugs and become heavy users. "Peer pressure, personality, circumstances all play a part," says Dr. Robert Buckley, a clinical psychologist who specializes in treating teenagers. He points out two attractions drugs may have for a teenager. First, they may provide "instant group," an entrée into a circle of friends who have drugs in common. Second, drug usage immediately reduces anxiety about a teenager's school or family problems.

There is not space here for a full discussion of drug problems. For detailed information about drug abuse, consult one of the many current books on the subject. The following signs and symptoms of drug use come from "Kids and Drugs: A Youth Leader's Handbook," produced by ACTION, a federal volunteer agency:

Physical symptoms: acting intoxicated, bloodshot eyes or droopy eyelids, imprecise eye movement, wearing sunglasses at inappropriate times, abnormal pallor, change in speech and vocabulary patterns, frequent and persistent illness, sniffles, cough, insomnia, napping at inappropriate times, repressed physical development, sudden appetite (especially for sweets), unexplained weight or appetite loss, neglect of personal appearance or grooming.

Behavioral changes: unexplained moodiness, depression, anxiety, irritability, hypersensitivity or hostility, decreased interaction and communication with others, preoccupation with self, loss of motivation and loss of interest in sports and hobbies, drop in grades, reduced short-term memory and attention span, stealing money or valuables, lethargy, need for instant gratification, changes in values and beliefs, change in friends and unwillingness to introduce friends.

Physical evidence: odor of marijuana (like burned rope), incense or room deodorizers, eyedrops, mouthwash, marijuana cigarettes (rolled and twisted at each end), butt or "roach" (end of marijuana cigarettes), roach clips, powders, seeds, leaves, plants, mushrooms, capsules or tablets, cigarette papers, pipes, pipe filters, screens, strainers, "bongs" (water pipes), scales, testing kits, hemostats, small spoons, straws, razor blades, mirrors (for cocaine), stash cans (soft drink, beer, deodorant and other cans that unscrew at top or bottom), unfamiliar small containers or locked boxes, plastic baggies, small glass vials.

Teachers may be able to verify a parent's suspicions about drug abuse by reporting changes in a child's behavior or other symptoms. Keep in mind, though, that the school is not a drug treatment center. A teacher who sees as many as 125 students a day may be too busy teaching to notice any but pronounced signs of drug abuse. To protect the majority of students, who usually are not chronic drug users, school administrators should deal promptly and firmly with offenders.

If you suspect drugs, don't hesitate to check a teenager's room, purse, or car. Protecting your child from drugs is more important than respecting his privacy. If you find that your child is using drugs, you can check with your church, community service agency, or with a school counselor for suggestions about where to get help. You can also seek help from a licensed private counselor who specializes in treating adolescents.

FIRST AID FOR POOR COMMUNICATION

What if you're eager to talk to your child and he just isn't saying much? Every parent experiences this sooner or later, especially with older children. Two parents—a father in Florida and a mother of three in California—mentioned that drives in the car can be great opportunities to talk things out with a child. "I think of it as rolling therapy," the California woman said. "Actually, it was the kids' idea, not mine. I just noticed that whenever one of them was alone in the car with me, she was apt to talk about all kinds of things she otherwise wouldn't, especially with the other two children around. After a while, I learned to invent 'errands' and invite a child to hop in the car if I thought she was troubled or needed time alone with me."

The Florida man, father of a teenaged son, tells a similar story. "He and I were not getting along—which is putting it mildly. He had taken up with an irresponsible bunch of kids, and he was beginning to act the same way himself. One night when he got in late after being out with these friends, I ordered him to get in the car with me. We drove the rest of the night, mostly in silence. Then we started talking, and we both got good and mad. I found a park and pulled in. We had a shouting match that finally got things settled between us. Afterwards, we stopped for breakfast and turned around and drove home. It was a spur-of-the-moment plan, but it worked. We never could have had it out that way in the family room at home."

Another father found that it's often easier to talk to children on the phone than in person: "They open up more over the phone, problem or no problem. I discovered this when my older son was visiting his grandparents. It worked later, too, when he was away at school. When he called, the words would just pour out. It was a lot different from trying to get him to tell me what was on his mind when we were in the same house."

KEEPING "EXPERT" ADVICE IN PERSPECTIVE

Like many parents, you probably find that hearing what the experts have to say about child rearing can sometimes help you to develop guidelines for dealing with your children. Listening to the experts is not without risk, however. Being exposed to an overdose of advice from psychologists and others who are seen as authorities on children has led far too many parents to mistrust their own common sense in handling children's problems.

Teachers, the authorities parents have most contact with, are not psychologists, but elementary teachers in particular hear a good deal during their training about educating "the whole child." As a result, some become overly concerned about psychological adjustment. They can be all too eager to pass this exaggerated concern on to parents in the form of facile, pseudo-psychological explanations for children's behavior. For example, this is the off-the-cuff analysis one parent, a news reporter, heard from a fifth-grade teacher when he asked about his daughter's carelessly written sentences during a conference: "Her writing certainly doesn't show her true ability. I suppose having a parent who writes makes her feel terribly insecure about her own writing, so she just doesn't try as hard as she should. I think she's unconsciously afraid of competing with you."

Whether you see this as the teacher's alibi for not requiring this student to work harder or simply as laughably inept amateur psychology, it points up a trend. No matter what aspect of your child's behavior you're concerned about—anything from shyness to sentence structure—you won't have to look far for an expert who's eager to explain the "real" meaning of the behavior in question. Be sure to weigh all explanations against your own common-sense judgment, and maintain a healthy skepticism about any explanation that sends you on a parental guilt trip. As Jeane Westin writes in *The Coming Parent Revolution*: "The greater the influence of psychologists and social healers, the greater has been parental guilt and the need for family-counseling services."

In trying to deal with a child's social problems, it's not always easy to tread the fine line between being helpful and getting too involved or making the problem worse. Fortunately, though children do need our support, they're often better able to withstand stress than we think.

8

HELP YOUR CHILD MAKE THE MOST OF HIGH SCHOOL

> Just when kids are most vulnerable, parents often say, 'I've gotten you through elementary school and junior high school. Now you're in high school, and you're on your own. You have to grow up.' At age fourteen kids are scared to death of being on their own.
>
> —A high school principal

High school presents a bewildering array of choices—courses, activities, programs, and sports. At fourteen, most children have developed at least a few definite ideas about what classes they do and do not want to take in high school. Nearly every school has counselors to help students with their plans.

How well qualified is a parent to give advice about courses or credits or school activities? As a parent, you have the single most important qualification for giving your child good advice—you know him well. You can find out what you need to know about courses and all the rest far more easily than anyone at school can get to know your child. Wise school people encourage parents to play an active role in high school planning. The principal above, who spent many years as a guidance counselor, says, "A parent can *learn* about the curriculum, and he already knows his expectations for his child. He ought to be able to say to the counselor, 'Here's what we need,' or 'What can the school do for my child?' Not enough parents do this. I think in part it's a carryover from elementary school—where parents are not treated as informed adults."

Helping your child make decisions about high school planning can be complicated, as the parents of Tim, who had taken algebra in an advanced eighth-grade class, discovered. "The teacher called to say she wasn't sure whether to recommend Tim for geometry, which is what he expected to take the year after finishing algebra. She explained that although Tim had done well in algebra, most of the other advanced math students had done a good deal better. She thought I ought to decide, since Tim was 'on the fence.' If he didn't go on into geometry, he would take algebra again, the usual high school freshman math course. I appreciated the teacher's talking it over with me, but I wasn't sure what to do. I hated to tell Tim to repeat algebra and make it seem as if his hard work had been for nothing. On the other hand, if he did have trouble with geometry, it would make his adjustment to high school that much more difficult. Recalling how faithful he'd been about doing his homework and getting extra help when he needed it, I decided to leave the decision up to him. Tim chose to go ahead with geometry, and it worked out well. He's pleased that he'll be able to take an extra math course his senior year."

In this chapter you'll learn what a guidance counselor can—and cannot—do for your child, how tracking works, the value of extracurricular activities, the pros and cons of mixing an outside job with school, and tips on helping your child find out about careers and colleges.

HOW TO WORK WITH THE GUIDANCE COUNSELOR

Ninety-five percent of school counselors have a teaching background, plus a master's degree in counseling. Dr. Frank Burtnett, an assistant executive director of the American Association for Counseling and Development (AACD), estimates there are approximately 45,000 high school counselors—one for every 350 to 400 high school students—nationwide. In more lavishly funded schools the ratio may be 250 to 300 students for each counselor.

As is the case with teachers, the training and competence of guidance counselors varies widely. This, plus the necessity for counselors to serve large numbers of students, means that very few of these students will get real counseling in planning their programs at school. Dr. Burtnett points out an additional problem: "Counselors are apt to be used by administrators as high-paid clerks."

How can you work with the counselor to do the best possible planning for your child? First, take advantage of the planning sessions many high schools offer for parents and students. Often these are held in the evening. They will give you a chance to hear about general requirements, to look over the high school course book or class schedule, and ask the counselor questions. If your school doesn't offer parents this opportunity to learn about the high school program, you can urge school officials or the parents' group to consider such a project.

The second thing you can do to help your child is to sit down with him before his freshman year and go over the course book and the list of high school requirements together. You may not know all the answers, but you can learn enough to help him rough out a four-year plan of courses. This probably will change as he moves through high school, but it's important to see an overall plan to make sure he meets requirements and can fit into his schedule all the classes you and he feel it's important for him to have. Ask the counselor about course sequences, graduation or college entrance requirements, or anything else that isn't clear to you.

Keep these points in mind when you and your child work out a high school program with the counselor:

Counselors can give you the facts about courses and programs, including the following: scheduling, graduation requirements, content of courses, and course prerequisites (other work which must be completed before a student enrolls in a course). They should be able to answer such questions as, "Will the science course my child plans to take fulfill the science requirement for most colleges (or for a particular college)?"

The advice the counselor gives your child may not be any better than the program offered by your school. For example, if your high school allows students to satisfy graduation requirements in social studies by taking trivial courses, a good many students who are capable of and would benefit from more substantial work will waste time in them.

In addition to their training and their knowledge of school policy, scheduling, and courses, counselors bring to the job their own personal views, which influence the advice they give your child. Theodore Sizer writes of a guidance counselor who never directed poor or working-class children who were academically talented to any private colleges or competitive public colleges. Her view was that these children might meet the children of the wealthy there and as a result be disloyal and uncomfortable in their own neighborhoods. Many parents might have protested that this counselor was using a double standard in planning for their children—if they had been aware of what she was doing.

Always weigh the counselor's advice carefully, but don't feel that you must follow it in planning for your child. Counselors can't read parents' minds. They may go along with a student's unwise choice because parents don't make clear what *they* think is best. Let's say your child is trying to decide between "Ghosts and Goblins," a course that involves reading short stories, seeing movies, and no writing; and "Nineteenth-Century American Literature," which involves reading novels and writing papers. If both count toward graduation, whether your child takes the more worthwhile course may depend on the point of view of the counselor, or on which class has more space available, or on a number of other considerations which have little to do with what's best for your child—unless you have some input.

No matter who does the planning—you, the counselor, or your child—avoid closing off his options too soon. Taking less demanding courses, general math, for example, instead of algebra, will limit his choices before he's ready to make final decisions about college or a career. Urge your child to plan a high school program that touches all bases—math, English, science, social studies, foreign language—even if he isn't planning on college or plans to attend one with liberal entrance requirements. Plans change. Also, in many states there is now a move toward upgrading entrance requirements for state universities.

A recurrent theme in advice offered to high school students by career counselors, professors, employers, and college students (some of whom had learned the hard way): Taking just enough math or writing courses to fulfill high school graduation requirements is a mistake. Get as much training in math and writing as you can.

You may have to watch carefully to make sure your child gets enough writing instruction. Many high school English teachers avoid having to grade papers by teaching mainly literature and grammar, pretending to students, parents, and administrators (who should know better) that students can learn to write without doing much actual writing. The majority of teachers in other subjects avoid having students write (that's the English teacher's job) or they undercut their few writing assignments (and escape responsibility for having to grade them carefully) by saying, "All I care about is the information." There are usually a few teachers, though, who understand that writing is a vital part of learning. Urge your child to take their courses. He'll have to work harder than he would for "short-answer" teachers, but he won't be a handicapped writer in college or on the job.

HIGH SCHOOL ON THE FAST (OR MEDIUM OR SLOW) TRACK

You're probably familiar with the theory behind tracking (ability grouping). Put the brightest students in the same classes and give them challenging work and tough assignments. Likewise, you put the average learners together and tailor the work to their ability. You do the same with the below-average learners. Everyone is challenged at his own level, and no one is discouraged by being asked to do work that's too difficult.

There is more than one type of ability grouping. In one system, students may be placed in tracks labeled "academic," "general," or "vocational." Students in each track sometimes take almost entirely different courses. Under another grouping system, all students choose from among the same courses, but these are taught at several different levels—"college preparatory," "average," and "essential," for example. There may be a trend away from the first type of ability grouping, according to Dr. Janice Adkisson of the Association for Supervision and Curriculum Development. She believes the efforts to upgrade high schools scholastically will make the class level system more popular.

Regardless of the system used in your school, what's important to you as a parent—and to your child—is the degree of choice you have in deciding what his level will be. If you feel your child is being advised to take courses at a less challenging level than he should or to close off options too soon, discuss it with the counselor. If you and other parents feel you have too little say in making decisions about the level of courses your children take, point this problem out to the board of education in your district. See the final chapter for information on working with the board.

It's especially important for you to have a say in such choices, since evidence suggests that ability grouping is not always in the best interest of the majority of students. One problem is the attitude of teachers, conscious or unconscious, that often goes along with tracking and other types of ability grouping. High teacher expectations for top-track students pay off. Students usually work harder and learn more in these classes. Occasionally, though, top-track teachers shift too much of the responsibility for learning to students, assuming that such requirements as daily homework and recitation are unnecessary in teaching an above-average class. This is unfortunate, since students—even the most able—who are required to do less work usually learn less as a result.

Students in the average track have different problems, the most serious being that they may not be expected to do extremely good work, because, after all, they aren't in a top class. The message is that mediocrity is good enough.

The low-track classes often suffer from low teacher expectations and from the presence of disruptive students who make it difficult for a conscientious teacher to give other students the help they need. In some cases, low-track students earn graduation credits simply by showing up for class and being reasonably well behaved.

Does tracking meet the needs of students—or the needs of teachers and administrators? A teacher with extensive experience both in schools which put students of all abilities in the same classes and in schools which use ability grouping says: "When all abilities are in the same class, teaching is a lot harder than it is with tracking. When you track kids, though, they're isolated in their own ability groups. Students in the low or medium track never have a chance to hear the better students answer questions or give a talk in class."

In *A Study of Schooling,* a report on eight years of systematic classroom observations, researchers led by John I. Goodlad, former dean of the graduate school of education at the University of California at Los Angeles, advised that tracking be abolished. Among the reasons: "Ability grouping and tracking appear not to produce the expected gains in students' achievement. . . . Students of average and especially low achievement tend to do less well when placed in middle or low than in mixed groups. . . . The conventional wisdom . . . is that teachers will tend to direct their teaching to the lowest achievers, thus disadvantaging or slowing down the higher achievers. Our data challenge this assumption—most of the mixed classes resembled high- more than low-track classes in nearly all of the areas studied."

Despite the defects of tracking, your child can use the system to his advantage. Even if he usually enrolls in average classes, don't discourage your child from trying a top-level class in a required course, English or U.S. history, for example, if your high school allows students a choice of levels. As Goodlad points out, students in top classes usually get far better teaching, as well as more challenging material, than those at other levels.

Students who have a choice sometimes hesitate to take top-level classes because they would prefer an "A" in an average class to a "C" in a top-level class. Some schools solve this problem by weighting grades, so that a "B" or a "C" in a top-level class may be worth as many points as an "A" in an average-level class. Keep in mind that whether or not a high school weights grades, colleges are usually more impressed by good grades in top-track courses than by excellent grades in lower-level classes. One selective college states in its brochure: "Evidence that students have taken the most challenging courses available to them is an important criterion for admission."

Investigate carefully before your child enrolls in or is placed in a low-level course, particularly in a required subject, English for example. Why does he or someone at school think he needs to be in the low group? Get an answer to this from the counselor. If your child has average (or even slightly below average) academic ability, he should be able to do at least passing work in a midlevel course, where he will learn far more than in the low level. A student who has trouble with high school work of average difficulty does need help. But you can't assume switching to the lowest level is the solution. Ask questions. If your child has a specific problem—poor reading, for example—will he get specific help in the low-track class, or will he simply be allowed to fall farther and farther behind? For far too many lower-track students, the latter is a real possibility.

Ability grouping is "definitely subject to abuse," according to Robert Abbott, a special education supervisor. "Too many children get locked in, particularly at the secondary [high school] level." He also notes that in many high schools students placed in low-track classes or special education classes are automatically barred from some courses which could help them to prepare for jobs or further education—microcomputer courses, study skills, or typing, for example.

Your child's best bet may be sticking it out in the midlevel class and getting whatever help he needs from a tutor or a remedial teacher, either in or out of school.

EXTRACURRICULAR ACTIVITIES— IN AND OUT OF SCHOOL

School activities like debate, playing on or managing a sports team, working for the newspaper, or helping to produce the class play can add a valuable dimension to your child's experience in high school. A high school teacher recalls that his own interest in doing well academically followed success in extracurricular activities. "The recognition I got for managing the team made me more enthusiastic about school. I gained confidence and found I wanted to do well in class, too. As a coach and as a teacher I've seen the same thing happen with other kids. Any activity or sport that interests them is worthwhile, because it can lead them to become more involved in academic work."

Your child knows what interests him, but a little guidance from you can help him to make the right choices. Consider these points in offering advice:

1. Freshmen sometimes miss out on extracurricular activities because they don't know what's available or because they're shy about signing up. Make sure your child gets the information he needs by reading the catalogue, talking to the counselor, and attending Activity Night, if your high school sponsors one for incoming freshmen.

2. In many activities—team sports and the school newspaper, for example—it's important for students to start off as freshmen to gain experience. If your high school freshman seems interested in an activity but hesitates to sign up because he's not sure it's the thing for him, or because he's not sure he'll have the time, encourage him to try it anyway. He can drop out if he finds he can't handle it. Signing up later may be more difficult.

3. Occasionally, it's worth carrying a lighter class load to make time for activities—as long as they don't interfere with doing well in serious courses like math, English, science, history. Extracurricular activities may offer students more worthwhile learning than some nonessential courses for which they receive credit. For example, your child is likely to learn more by managing ticket sales for the school musical than by taking a class in ice skating, even if the latter counts toward graduation.

4. Colleges do look favorably on applicants who have taken part in high school activities, but students shouldn't become joiners to impress college admissions people. They would rather see high school students show a real commitment to two or three activities than take part briefly in eight or ten.

Outside Jobs

"Dear Abby" published a recent letter from a high school teacher, which reads in part: "A message to business people: Stop hiring teen-age students to work during school hours. And please stop hiring teen-age students to work after 8 P.M. on evenings before a school day. They need time to study and to get a good night's sleep for school the next day."

Many other teachers and many parents agree with the writer of this letter. Yet there are clever, well-organized teenagers who can handle challenging school work and a job, too. The outstanding science student in one large high school was also a talented athlete and the head busboy in a popular restaurant. Other students, however, may reduce their own expectations for themselves, using work as an excuse for sliding through school with hastily done assignments. As is often the case, it is a question of balance. Talking with parents whose teenagers work, I found that most establish a simple rule: "Keep your grades up if you want to keep the job."

SHOULD YOUR CHILD GET JOB TRAINING IN HIGH SCHOOL?

One way to begin answering this question is by making a list of the jobs your high school is equipped to train students for. Probably there's typing (or word processing), shorthand, and bookkeeping to train them for office work. For students who want to become auto mechanics, there may be auto shop courses. Perhaps there are also wood and metal shop courses, computer courses, and facilities for teaching hairdressing. The courses vary from school to school, but the number of jobs students can be trained for will be only a small fraction of those available to high school graduates. Consider this partial list of jobs that will be in demand, compiled by the U.S. Department of Labor: medical insurance clerks, cashiers, surveyor helpers, machine tool operators, dental assistants, merchandise displayers and window trimmers, extruder operators, automotive painters.

Even if your school offered a good many more vocational courses than it now does, it could not afford to keep those courses current. In many schools, equipment for teaching job skills is obsolete as well as limited. Classes may be teaching skills which are obsolete or nearly so, more to protect teachers' jobs than to serve students.

Speaking from outside the educational establishment, Frank Armbruster, Director of Interdisciplinary Studies at the Hudson Institute, writes of even more important reasons why students may be short-changed in vocational education: "Strong evidence over the recent past reveals that children in these [vocational education] programs are often neglected as far as the basic skills are concerned. . . .Children in high school do not know, nor do their parents, what they will be doing later in life. If an opportunity should arise for them to go higher by means of advanced education or positions that require better education of the classical type, these children should not be denied that right because of the failure of schools to insist that they learn the fundamentals in the traditional academic areas in primary and secondary school."

When I surveyed employers to find out what skills they wanted high school–trained entry-level employees to have, not one mentioned any specific job skills. A New England manufacturing executive wrote a three-page letter that included this appraisal of the preparation of high school graduates for the world of work: "One third lack adequate writing skills. Probably two thirds lack adequate basic arithmetic skills. Probably nine tenths lack a balanced view of the world around them and probably nine tenths regard 'profit' as an inherently bad concept."

This doesn't mean your child won't find some worthwhile job-related high school courses. Cooperative work-study programs, a promising trend in vocational education, combine in-school classes with on-the-job experience in the community. But it is important to make sure your child is not sidetracked into learning narrow skills at the expense of acquiring the basic academic training he'll need in order to do well in a wide range of jobs and to take advantage of future opportunities.

WHAT DO YOU WANT TO BE . . .?

One day early in her junior year in high school, my daughter came home from school upset about a college-planning talk she'd had with the counselor. "She kept asking what kind of a job I'm interested in, and I don't know what I want to do. Does that mean I can't choose a college until I decide on a career?"

I assured her that few people know at age fifteen what their life's work will be. Then I explained that the counselor was probably using the opportunity to get her started thinking about the decisions she would have to make in the not-so-distant future. As for choosing a college, it is easier if you have at least a rough idea of the type of work you want to prepare for. Still, a large percentage of college freshmen have no definite idea what kind of job they want to aim for. And colleges and universities are usually noted for strengths in more than one area.

By sponsoring a Career Day, a school tries to bridge the gap between what students know about and what's actually there. However, these career sessions sometimes put major emphasis on occupations students are already aware of—architects, police officers, dentists, fashion models, bank tellers.

One way to help your child become aware of a broader range of occupations than he can see for himself is by talking about your own job and the jobs of friends. Discuss your own work in a way teenagers can understand. Define terms like "back order," "overrun," "profit margin," "commission." What does an insurance agent do? A foreman? A store department manager? A manufacturers' representative? Encourage your child to ask questions, and encourage talk at home about how things the family uses every day are manufactured, distributed, and sold. Discuss news stories and magazine articles about new types of work, and talk about the training needed for these jobs. Call your child's attention to the major businesses and industries in areas you visit on vacation trips. If you pass your own job knowledge on to your child and stimulate his interest in finding out more about possible careers, he'll be giant steps ahead of his peers who have to rely on what they can see and what they learn at school.

One high school career counselor who gave students an opportunity to get a firsthand view of the world of work learned that many knew even less about careers than he suspected. A student who wanted to be a dietician was indignant when she was taken to spend a day on the job with a hospital dietician and discovered that the work kept her in the kitchen the whole time.

The school counselor can't give your child definite answers about which career he should aim for, but talking over his interests and academic strengths with the counselor—and learning about job possibilities from you—can prepare your child to make his own decision. In addition, he can take tests which may help him to see his own abilities and interests more clearly.

A test which shows whether a person has some of the specific abilities needed to succeed in various occupations is called a vocational aptitude test. Interest tests may show whether a student's interests match those of people who are successful in various lines of work. Two such tests are the Kuder Preference Record and the Strong Vocational Interest Blank. Aptitude and interest tests should serve only as guidelines. In *Psychological Testing of Children,* Dr. Stanley Klein points out that not all aptitude tests are based on sound research. He also notes that a teenager's interests are in the process of changing, so results of tests could change from year to year.

Employment demand in a chosen field is another factor your child must consider in choosing a career. Training for a field that's popular today doesn't guarantee a permanently successful career. Changing careers, or at least getting additional training to meet new demands in the job market, is fast becoming the rule rather than the exception. This underscores the need for your child to get a good general education in high school.

CHOOSING A COLLEGE WITH YOUR CHILD

With 3000 colleges and universities to choose from, you do need a good deal of information, plus a workable system, to make a wise choice. A counselor can be helpful here, but you must be ready to supply her with information about your child's needs and interests and be willing to do some digging on your own, too. Counselors vary widely in their knowledge about colleges and in their skill in matching students and learning institutions.

Junior year in high school is the time to begin looking seriously at specific colleges and applying for admission. You don't have to wait until your child's junior year, though, to take these steps which can make choosing a college and applying for admission easier when the time comes:

1.   Make sure your child takes high school courses that will give him the broadest possible choice of colleges. One college counselor reports that parents sometimes urge their children to take high school courses in such subjects as existentialism or Eastern thought in order to impress colleges. He says, "It's best to stick to 'meat and potatoes' courses in high school. That's what most colleges want to see on the record."

2.   Since many four-year colleges require students to take either the Scholastic Aptitude Test (SAT) or the ACT Assessment (ACT), find out when they will be given in your school. Your child may benefit from taking these tests several times, since he can choose which score will be sent to colleges. He can also take the Preliminary Scholastic Aptitude Test (PSAT) as a sophomore. The results of this test will be sent to him, along with his answers, his test booklet, and a list of correct answers, so he can see his strengths and weaknesses and better prepare to take the SAT later.

3.   Read books about choosing a college and encourage your child to read them. Most bookstores have a large selection of these books.

4.   Send for course catalogues and brochures and inquire about costs of any schools your child might be interested in. Asking about fees and reading a catalogue puts you under no obligation, and it will give you valuable information to file for future reference. Books and catalogues will show you how colleges compare in size, costs, and programs.

5. Try to arrange to visit a college or two, perhaps during a family trip. Let the admissions office know ahead of time that you'd like to see the campus so they can arrange for a guide. There's no substitute for having been there when the time comes for your child to decide where he wants to apply.

Even if your child hasn't reached the application stage, you probably have general questions.

Will We Be Able to Handle the Costs?

The good news is that financial aid is available in the form of grants and loans from both federal and state governments and from colleges and universities themselves. Even better news is that your child does not have to have straight "A"s or top test scores to qualify for this help, nor does family income have to be at the poverty level. Nearly every family—including those in the upper-middle and even some in the upper income brackets—is eligible for some financial aid.

The size of the loan you qualify for depends on the cost of the college your child attends and on what is determined to be a "fair family contribution" from you, based on your income. To find out how much you will be expected to contribute, you fill out a Financial Aid Form (FAF), available from the school counselor, and send it to the College Scholarship Service in Princeton, New Jersey, or the American College Testing Program in Iowa City, Iowa. When your child is admitted to a college, you are eligible for financial aid to make up the difference between college costs and your fair contribution. For example, let's say you are expected to contribute $4500. If your child's college costs are $6500, you will qualify for $2000. If college costs are $9500, you qualify for $5000 in aid, perhaps a combination of loans, grants, and part-time work for your child. At one prestigious college, 65 percent of the students hold campus jobs and 30 percent receive scholarship aid. At some top private colleges and universities 75 percent of the students receive aid.

Are My Child's Grades High Enough?

If he has a high school diploma, your child can get into more than one third of the nation's colleges and universities. If he has a "C" average, that proportion jumps to two thirds. Granted, he will not be admitted to Yale or Stanford, or any other highly selective colleges or universities with so-so grades, but many good private colleges have liberalized entrance requirements because they could not fill their freshman classes otherwise. The pool of high school graduates will decrease every year into the early 1990s. But some state schools are beginning to raise their entrance requirements. What this means is that you can't go on hearsay when you try to figure your child's chances of admission. You won't know until he talks to a knowledgeable counselor and sends in an application. Most counselors advise applying to four or five colleges and universities, including at least one where your child is almost certain to be admitted and one or two where he just might make it.

Which Is Better, a Large School or a Small One?

The right one for your child depends on his needs and on his aims in going to college. A large school offers more choices than a small school in programs of study and activities, which can be extremely important. Facilities like laboratories, libraries, stadiums, and auditoriums are more elaborate and varied on a big campus. On the other hand, a small school can offer personal attention, both in and out of class, and more of a chance to take part in campus activities. At a large university, undergraduate students are usually taught by teaching assistants who are graduate students. At a small school professors, who are interested in teaching rather than in doing research, run most of the classes. Only your child can decide which features are more likely to suit her.

What If College Is out of the Question?

One possibility is a two-year community college; admission requirements are liberal, and costs are low because students live at home. Many community colleges have both two-year programs that are complete in themselves and courses that can prepare students to continue their education at four-year degree-granting colleges. Check first to make sure community college courses will be accepted for credit at the four-year school your child wants to attend.

Of the approximately 250 jobs listed in a recent U.S. Department of Labor publication, 100 require more than a high school education and less than a degree from a four-year college. Students can prepare for some of these jobs in a community college program, in technical schools, or in classes run by employers. Some examples: Community colleges frequently train dental assistants and offer courses that help real estate agents to prepare for licensing exams. Electricians train in two-year community college technical programs or in technical schools. Insurance firms train their own claim adjusters; the government trains construction inspectors. The most successful trainees in all of these fields are those who have acquired a broad base of general knowledge in high school, including proficiency in reading, writing, and math.

WITH A LITTLE HELP FROM MY PARENTS

Based on the information you have read in this chapter, you can take the following four steps to help your child make the most of high school:

1. Listen to what your child has to say.

2. Discuss your child's test scores with the counselor and learn about high school programs.

3. Look over your child's school record. Consider his strengths and weaknesses, academic and otherwise. Is he enthusiastic about school? Does he need remedial help in any subject to make the most of high school? What are his interests? How much are they apt to change during four years in high school?

4. Take his strengths, weaknesses, and interests into consideration when you help him to make the choices about courses and levels. Use the counselor as a resource person in helping you to advise your child. Be sure that both you and your child understand what the consequences of his high school choices will be four years from now.

9

BETWEEN PARENT AND TEACHER

How can I help my child to do his best? What do teachers really expect? As a parent you've probably wanted to ask your child's teacher questions like these, but perhaps the time never seemed right—or you may have hesitated, uncertain of how the teacher would react. Here, five experienced teachers speak about what parents can do to help a child succeed in school.

A midwestern elementary-school teacher with twenty-five years' experience in a middle-class community says, "When their child is in first grade, parents always seem enthusiastic about school. They almost never miss a conference or a parents' night. By the time a child gets to fourth or fifth grade, though, they often say, 'I'm too busy to come.' Why give up on a child so quickly? Certainly I'm not speaking of all parents. Over the years, I've found that most parents are eager, enthusiastic, and cooperative. . . . Every year is new; each teacher-student relationship is new. It might be in fifth grade that a child really hits it off and wonderful things happen. I also wish parents would read to their children more. You'd be shocked at the number who don't know nursery rhymes. I know more parents are working, but even a little reading at bedtime can mean so much."

A fifth-grade teacher from a college town in the southwest also speaks of parental attitudes: "I've taught in districts where parents don't think school is all that important. Some feel skiing is more important, or that taking a round-the-world trip is more educational than being in the classroom. I can't deny that those things are educational. But there's a sequence of learning that's important to the child, and he may miss all the necessary steps in math, science, and reading. Even gifted kids can't skip them. . . . Parents can help by making sure children aren't too busy. They sometimes have aerobics today, soccer tomorrow, and piano the next day. They've already been in school for six or seven hours and they'll be in class another hour or two [counting music lessons, etc.]; then if you give homework, it's a longer day than the parents have had. Children who are too tired and stressed can't respond to what's going on in school."

A teacher who has taught elementary-school children for twenty-six years suggests honesty between parent and teacher: "A parent's being honest with the teacher about previous problems is important when a child is having trouble at school. Far too many times parents will say, 'This child never had a problem until he had Mrs. X.' or 'Last year, he got all A's and B's.' I can't figure out why they say this when it's so easy to check. Parents and teachers must be co-workers. I've always encouraged parents to call me with questions, or send notes to school. . . . Back to School Night is the most important night of the year. I try to let parents know exactly what's expected and what they can expect of me."

A junior high teacher with more than twenty years' experience in an upper-middle-class suburb in the midwest says, "A parent with a seventh- or eighth-grade child can sometimes be very concerned that he be ready to go to a certain college in five years, and the youngster is still at the stage of trying to remember what to bring to class. The parent has leaped over the problems we have to deal with right now. Quite often in conferences, we hear a parent say, 'He's thirteen now. He's in eighth grade. Why should I check to make sure that he's doing his homework?' The answer is that age doesn't necessarily indicate maturity."

A former Teacher of the Year, who heads the English department in a New England high school, says, "Today's parents can have a supportive partnership with the school, which means a constant awareness of how the child is doing in school, and communication with the teacher. Being supportive also means that you don't allow flimsy excuses for missing school. It's not uncommon for kids to miss school to stand in line to buy concert tickets, or to go Christmas shopping, with parental knowledge. This is much more of a problem than it used to be all across the country. I think parents should always take their concerns to the school—about a child's progress, the content of a course, why the class is reading a particular book. Very often there's a good solid reason. But without an explanation, that question continues in the back of a parent's mind as a source of weakness in that school."

A CLOSE LOOK AT A CLASSROOM

"I can't stand Mrs. H.!" my daughter said about her junior high math teacher at least once a week. But I noticed she always did her math homework first, and her math had definitely improved.

Visiting the class, I found Mrs. H. and her students too engrossed in their work to notice me. They were checking homework. Books were open, homework papers out on the desk. Mrs. H. was writing the problems on the board. "What's the next step here?" she asked, pointing to the first problem. Several students raised their hands and she nodded at one, who gave the correct answer.

Mrs. H. finished the problem, and turned back to the class. "How many have this answer?" Hands went up, heads nodded. Five or six students looked baffled, a fact that didn't escape Mrs. H. as she glanced around the room. "This one was tricky. I'm glad so many of you got it. Now who can tell us what the catch was in this problem?" Silence. "Why was it easy to make a mistake?" A few hands went up, then a few more. "Dave?"

"I think it was easy to skip the second step. I almost did."

"That's not it!" several students chorused.

Mrs. H. called on a slender girl near the window, who explained that you had to set up equations to show the relation between the items to be found before you could start the second step. The rest of the homework went more quickly, since most students had it right.

When the homework had been checked, Mrs. H. paused to let students record their homework scores in their folders. The rest of the class period was spent introducing new material and having students work at their seats, doing three problems from the book. Finally, Mrs. H. gave the homework assignment, putting one of the new problems on the board with step-by-step input from students.

Before I had been there long it occurred to me that I had seldom seen a group of people so sure of what they were supposed to be doing and so intent on doing it. The work was challenging for eighth-graders. It owed its success to Mrs. H.'s conviction that her job was to teach, and that theirs was to learn. She gave assignments and required students to do them. She set goals and let students know she expected them to reach those goals.

Perhaps you feel that this is overstating the obvious, that anyone knows a teacher is supposed to do this. Unfortunately, it is not always obvious to the educators in charge of training the teachers who run our public school classrooms. Some of them would disapprove of Mrs. H.'s approach. They say that before planning a lesson, teachers should survey all their students to discover their individual learning styles. For example, an article in the journal *Educational Leadership,* co-authored by a professor of education and a school superintendent, tells teachers to take into account as many as eighteen "elements of learning style" in planning to teach a single class. Among these "elements" are whether individual children prefer bright lights or "softly lit" areas, whether they prefer cooler or warmer room temperature, whether children like hard or soft chairs, whether they are "peer-oriented," whether they feel they could learn better if they "move from area to area" (walk around the room).

The article also suggests that the teacher tape-record what goes on in class so that students who don't feel like learning at the time the lesson is taught can listen to it later. Perhaps intensely "peer-oriented" students, whose preferred "learning style" is talking among themselves instead of paying attention to Mrs. H.'s morning math lesson, can take a cassette home.

This article is more or less typical of many that have appeared in dozens of educational journals over the past five or ten years. As a parent you ought to be aware of some of the outlandish ideas your child's teacher may have been exposed to in the course of his training and in some of the journals he reads. The theorists in colleges of education are usually not required to test their ideas in an actual classroom where they are primarily responsible for teaching twenty or thirty average children math or reading.

While a highly skilled teacher working with a small class of able, cooperative students can make individualized learning work, few teachers either have the skill or work under such ideal conditions. A six-year study concluded in 1984 shows that when a teacher tries to work separately with individual children and groups in the same classroom, individual students actually spend less time with the teacher than if the class were taught as a whole.

A good many teachers ignore educational theorists who urge them to try schemes that show little promise of succeeding in a regular class. Unfortunately, some teachers ignore the obvious practical problems and try to make the schemes work, anyway. One second-grade teacher gave each child in the reading group a different book, in effect wiping out the learning advantage of having children listen to one another read. A high school math teacher told the class (made up of students of the same general ability) that each student would be allowed to go through the book and do the problems at his own pace. At the end of the year 15 to 20 percent of the class had failed to finish the last three or four chapters—material they had to master before going on to the next course.

GOOD TEACHERS HELP THE WHOLE CLASS

Unfortunately, what is supposed to be "individualized" or "self-paced" learning often turns out to be individualized nonlearning for many students. In contrast, Mrs. H. uses the class setting to advantage. She sends students to the board, so the rest can watch as they do the problems. The whole class benefits from hearing the questions and answers of individual students. And Mrs. H. takes the responsibility for deciding how fast students should cover the material. Students who need it can get truly individualized instruction by seeing her after school.

Mrs. H. doesn't simply tell students she wants them to work hard. She sets an example. Class begins on time, and she follows a routine. She stands to conduct the class. Standing makes it easier to scan the class for signs that students are having difficulty understanding, and "stand-up" teachers are more apt to use that important visual aid, the chalkboard. Most important, teachers who stand send children an enthusiastic message. "This subject is worthwhile. Your learning is important to me. We're all going to work hard." And Mrs. H. lets students know they must do the work. As she explains to parents on Back to School Night, "I tell the class that if they don't turn in their homework, I feel they need help in finding time to get it done. I ask them to come in after school to catch up."

When conscientious, common-sense teachers like Mrs. H. set up a plan like this, they need support from parents to carry it out. Yet elementary-school teachers from several different parts of the country told me they sometimes hear from parents that a child couldn't do his homework because of a shopping trip, a ballgame, or because the family went out to dinner. If your child is lucky enough to have a teacher like Mrs. H., give her all the support you can, and urge other parents to do the same.

Why did my daughter say she didn't like Mrs. H.? Probably because she made students work harder and she ran a tighter ship than many other teachers. Recalling Mrs. H. a year later, though, my daughter said, "She really made sure you learned math." That is the whole point of teaching, most would agree.

But not everyone does agree. Many professors of education who train teachers for our classrooms believe that helping children learn reading or writing or math is not the whole point. According to these educators, how a teacher affects a child's feelings and values is more important than what she teaches him. Many observers believe that this attitude on the part of too many educators is primarily responsible for the current academic decline in our schools. A team of researchers from several universities conducted a six-year study to find out why school children in Taiwan and Japan do better in math and reading than children in American schools. Researchers discovered that teachers in the other two countries are convinced that their sole mission is to teach knowledge and skills. Another finding of this study, which included careful observations of how teachers manage classrooms in the United States, Japan, and Taiwan, was that classrooms in the other two countries are highly structured, with strict discipline. In American classrooms children waste time walking around and talking with classmates, and often work on their own without guidance from the teacher.

CHECK THE TEACHING IN YOUR CHILD'S CLASSROOM

If you live in an area with a reputation for having good schools, perhaps you've assumed there's no need to check on the quality of instruction in your child's class. Perhaps you've also assumed that all the poor teaching (and only poor teaching) takes place in inner-city schools. Neither assumption is correct. Dr. Robert E. Nichols of Purdue University, who visited a number of schools in the course of developing a language arts program for inner-city children, offers a close-up view of inner-city classrooms. "What surprised me was the variety of teaching. In one class the teacher finally managed to get everyone settled down by nagging them constantly in a whiny, irritating voice. 'No whispering. Stay in your seat. Get your work done.' I think if I were a child in that class, I'd want to get as far away from school as possible. Another class was chaotic—the teacher had no control at all. The kids were throwing books, lifting up the furniture. If I hadn't settled things down, I think they would have torn the room apart.

"But one of the most inspiring classroom performances I ever saw was in an inner-city fourth-grade class where there was unusual rapport between teacher and students. The teacher's good nature spilled over into her classroom performance, which included clever use of dramatic techniques. She obviously loved language and was able to transmit this love to her students. She was asking questions, using the Socratic method, and those children loved it. They were interested, answering, paying attention."

Lucky class! Any child in any school would be fortunate to have such a teacher. Note the variation among teachers working under the same difficult conditions: the gifted fourth-grade teacher, the whiny, but perhaps adequate teacher, and the one whose class was out of control. The teachers in your child's school probably work under far better conditions, which makes it possible for them to do a better job than many inner-city teachers. But in *any* school there is apt to be a wide variety of teaching performance: a few top-notch teachers, a far greater number who range from good to barely adequate, and some with classes so poorly managed that children can't learn.

The best way to find out about the quality of teaching in your child's class is to take advantage of parents' visiting day or to visit on a regular school day. If your state is not among the twenty-one states that allow parents to visit a child's class at any time (see chapter 10), check with the school superintendent's office to find out what arrangements you have to make.

Regardless of where you live or how your schools are rated, you can check on what's happening in your child's class not only by visiting, but also by paying attention to several clues.

First, listen to your child's comments.

a) "If we finish our math early, he helps us do special problems on the board."

144

b) "I draw on my paper because there's nothing else to do after I finish the workbook."

a) "We have a quiz twice a week, and we correct our mistakes the next day."

b) "We do three dittos every day, and we never get our papers back."

a) "The teacher reads us a story out of a real good book every Friday."

b) "We always have movies on Monday. It gets boring, and kids in the back start humming."

As you've probably guessed, the first comment in each pair suggests good teaching. In interpreting comments that suggest poor teaching, keep in mind that children occasionally exaggerate or misinterpret what goes on in school. But much of the time they do report accurately. "Listen to your child," says a parent and former guidance counselor. "Teachers are only human. Often they will do what is most convenient." Find out whether your child is often left with nothing to do after finishing his work. If the teacher never hands back those ditto sheets, your child is probably doing busy work.

Try to decide whether comments like these suggest an occasional slip up by the teacher or habitually slipshod teaching that results in less learning for your child. If it's the latter, talk to the teacher about it, tactfully: "Rick keeps saying he finishes his math [or reading or workbook pages] early and then has nothing to do. I thought I should check with you to find out whether there are really other things he should be working on." Knowing you're aware of the situation, the teacher may make an effort to see that your child does not continue to mark time. Nothing will change if you don't speak up.

Second, listen to the teacher's comments—not only about your child, but about the class in general. Is she enthusiastic about her students and her plans for helping them learn, or is she discouraged and pessimistic? A statement like this suggests possible problems: "We have several children this year who constantly disrupt things." No two classes are the same—some are lively and eager, others are more placid, and still others contain more than their quota of "talkers." It's not the teacher's fault if she gets a group with several disruptive students. A good teacher won't allow them to interfere with everyone else's learning, though. Listen to your child's comments and question him to find out whether troublemakers are stealing time from the rest of the class.

Another teacher comment which suggests a problem: "These children are not as able as most third-grade classes I've had." This may be true. Again, it's how the teacher handles it that counts. I once heard a sixth-grade teacher say the class wouldn't have writing assignments because the students "got all tangled up in their sentences." These children got no instruction in a vital skill because their teacher's expectations were unforgivably low. (Or perhaps he didn't want to grade their papers.) In contrast, listen as this primary teacher talks about working with first-graders in a suburban school serving a disadvantaged area: "Many of those children are really not ready for first grade; you can tell from their tests and from the way they act in class. You really have to cheer them on . . . make them believe they can do it. I've always found that makes a big difference in how well they learn to read. Sometimes they really do surprise you!

"I remember one teacher who used to work her head off with her first-grade kids. She always planned lots of interesting things for them to do. But she never really thought they were capable, and she didn't push them in reading. Her class never did accomplish much."

The experience of many good teachers underscores the decisive influence teacher expectations can have on how well children learn. Bonnie Bracey, a Virginia teacher, reports that though her class was labeled "gifted and talented," not all students were actually in this category, according to test scores. "I made no distinction between those who were identified as gifted and talented and those who weren't," she says. "I told the class, 'Everyone has different talents and abilities. I don't know what all of yours are, but we're all going to work hard to discover them.'" The children who were *not* identified as gifted and talented, but who had been taught as if they were, made the biggest gains in achievement during the year.

Seeing your child's teacher in action, listening to your child's comments, and talking with the teacher herself should give you a reasonably good picture of what goes on in class. If you see a pattern of conscientious, effective teaching, let the teacher know you're pleased. Write a note and be specific. "I'm glad to see that you require the children to write weekly papers and correct them. I think this has helped Joan to be more careful about her written work." Later in this chapter we'll discuss what you can do about a major classroom problem, or a teacher who refuses to deal reasonably with complaints.

THE VIEW FROM THE CHALKBOARD

No description of how teachers work is complete without a view of their problems as they see them.

"Helplessness. I think that's the main problem for teachers. We're not in control of what we're doing. Some things are just as important as pay—having a say in curriculum, for example," says a fifth-grade teacher from the southwest.

A high school teacher says: "The profession doesn't offer much for an experienced teacher. I'm more interested in the quality of my teaching day than in the pay. Things like sabbaticals could help, but in our district you're not allowed to study in your own subject area. You have to take courses in teaching reading or computers— something to bring glory to the district."

An elementary-school teacher from the south says, "Parents think there are only principals and teachers in the school building, but there are so many other people here besides the ones who teach in the classroom. It seems that every time I turn around, a counselor or someone else is asking me to count how many white children, how many black children, how many Asian children. I just see children. I wish all these people would let me alone so I could do what I'm supposed to do—teach!"

"Administrators and textbook publishers make all the decisions and we have to carry them out," says a midwestern teacher. "It would be a threat to administrators to allow us to make decisions. This paternalistic attitude is frustrating to teachers."

Good administrators are keenly aware of teachers' problems and respect them as professionals. Says Dr. Douglas McGugan, an Illinois administrator who recently retired after more than thirty years as a teacher, principal, and superintendent: "It's frightening to look over an elementary teacher's lesson plans—I'm talking now about competent, well-prepared teachers. Do you have any idea how much they have to know to do a good job? And I don't think people realize how much energy it takes to teach twenty-five or thirty eight-year-olds for six hours a day."

You can help alleviate teachers' problems. As a parent who values competent teaching, you can look for opportunities to give good teachers the support they need, support that is all too often lacking within the school.

CAN YOU CHOOSE YOUR CHILD'S TEACHER?

If you go about it in the right way, you can sometimes choose your child's teacher. Other parents have. Of course, schools can't allow parents to choose their children's teachers very often, because the classrooms of the dedicated, effective teachers would be overflowing with students, leaving some teachers with nearly empty classrooms. That would be administratively untidy, not to mention in violation of the teachers' union contract.

But your first concern is your child. Why not try to get the teacher who seems right for him? Laura, a Maine mother whose children attended a small neighborhood school, was told that her daughter would be assigned to an accelerated fourth-grade class the following year. Laura knew the teacher of this class treated children like miniature college students, and she didn't feel this was good for nine-year-olds. As diplomatically as she could, Laura explained her views to the teacher who had recommended that her daughter be placed in this class. With the teacher's help, Laura managed to get her daughter into the other fourth-grade class.

Let's say your son or daughter is going into fifth grade next year, and you're convinced that one of the three fifth-grade teachers in your school, Mr. W., would be an ideal choice for your child. There are no guarantees, but here's an approach that may work: Make sure you have good reasons for requesting Mr. W. and get them across to the principal. A veteran school administrator says parents making such a request sometimes ruin their case by failing to think things through ahead of time, or by downgrading another teacher. Saying "I hope you plan to put my child in Mr. W.'s class, because I've heard awful things about Mrs. Z.'s" obviously won't help much. Approach the principal with well-thought-out, *positive* reasons:

Parent: I'd like to talk to you about Jill, who's going into fifth grade this year. As you're probably aware, she does very well sometimes, but I'm afraid she doesn't always work as hard as she should. I know Mr. W. has a reputation for working unusually well with children like Jill. Do you think there's any possibility of putting Jill in her class?

Principal: Well, now, I don't know. We're still working on the class lists . . . I'm sure Jill would do very well with any of our fifth-grade teachers. [Principals feel they have to point out to parents that all teachers are equally good, even if they know otherwise.]

Parent: Of course. But as I said, I feel Jill would do especially well with Mr. W. I hope you'll keep us in mind. We'll appreciate whatever you can do . . .

This parent presents a solid argument that sounds sincere, since she levels with the principal. She acknowledges they're both aware that Jill's work isn't consistent. And there's no criticism of other teachers in this appeal.

Watch your timing. Talk to the principal before children are assigned to teachers. Late changes would involve explanations and juggling students to equalize class size. Jill's mother spoke to the principal before class lists were final, making it easier for the principal to agree to the request. Find out from the superintendent's office when principals begin preparation for the opening of school and make your request then.

Let the principal know you consider your request and his time important by making an appointment to see him. A principal who is about to rush off to a meeting won't be in the right frame of mind to do a favor for a parent who drops in unannounced. One principal told me parents so often expect him to be instantaneously available that he's extremely flattered when they're considerate enough to call ahead.

NEVER UNDERESTIMATE THE POWER OF A PRINCIPAL

Unless you have a special request, you may not pay much attention to the principal in your child's school. Yet his (or her) role can be crucial in determining how well children learn.

Critics say principals often make the mistake of spending too much time on administrative details, meetings, and public relations, and almost none overseeing what goes on in the classrooms, where the real work of the school takes place.

Research backs up the critics. Several Michigan schools where children's achievement in basic subjects had improved over several years were compared with similar schools in which achievement declined. Among the findings: High achieving schools were led by principals who stressed academic achievement. Principals in low achieving schools were not good instructional leaders. It is difficult to understand why research is needed to establish the obvious— and far more difficult to understand why the public must pay for this research when the schools so often ignore it.

To find out how concerned the principal is about learning in your child's school, ask your child when the principal last visited his class. If your child is in high school, ask how often the heads of departments (English, math, science, etc.) visit classes. Principals and department heads can't supervise instruction if they don't see teachers in action. What goes on in class is the whole point of having a school. Administrators and department chairmen who rarely set foot in classrooms are saying to parents, to teachers—and to children: "Teaching and learning are not important to me."

A superintendent of a unified school district in a small New England city sends a different message to teachers and students in the schools he supervises. Instead of simply visiting classes, he teaches one—freshman history in the high school. To students, teachers, and parents, this says: "Teaching is important. Learning is important."

PROTECT YOUR CHILD FROM
INCOMPETENT TEACHERS

You're visiting your child's sixth-grade class. You walk down a clean, bright corridor, wondering where all the noise is coming from. The sixth-grade teacher, Mr. L., greets you at the classroom door with a ditto sheet. "We're having math groups now. Maybe you'd like to try a few of the problems." At least this seems to be what he is saying, speaking above the babble of sixth-grade voices that sounds more appropriate for the playground than for learning math.

Two or three students are actually concentrating on math. The rest are talking and laughing, glancing now and then at their work. Gradually you become aware of an adult voice talking about math. It's not Mr. L., who is in the back of the room. It's a tape recorder. You hear a second adult voice saying something about math— another tape recorder. During breaks in the kids' chatter, you—and they—hear two different math lessons broadcast simultaneously.

How can you save your child from months of noneducation in Mr. L.'s class? Getting your child switched to another teacher is the answer, unless the principal is willing and able to get Mr. L. to do a better job. We'll discuss how you can deal with the teacher and the principal after a closer look at some other signs of incompetency in the classroom.

Try to be objective—admittedly not an easy task when your child is involved. Don't decide a teacher is incompetent because he or she gives your child a low grade or reprimands your child for misbehavior, or because your child doesn't like the teacher. At some point a child has to understand that he can learn from a teacher he's not particularly fond of. A truly incapable teacher will be a disaster for everyone in the class—not just for your child.

Four Signs of Teacher Incompetence

1. Inability to manage students and direct learning—a leading cause of teacher failure. Some otherwise well-qualified teachers simply can't deal with a group of children. In poorly managed classrooms, children may talk at will, wander around the room and in general waste time instead of learning.

2. Failure to instruct. Not assigning or grading work, or habitually failing to grant students' reasonable requests for help. Keeping children entertained instead of teaching them.

3. Lack of self-control. Bizarre behavior or frequent fits of temper, which may include flagrant verbal abuse of students or physical abuse.

If your child's teacher is physically abusive, or if the class is so wild that children are likely to be hurt, insist that the principal take immediate action. If he fails, go to the school board. Following up is vital. The NCCE reports a case in which a teacher was shutting kindergartners in a closet. The principal promised parents it wouldn't happen again. It did. Parents took turns sitting in the classroom until an aide was hired to watch the teacher. Not knowing the outcome, we can only hope the principal and teacher were fired and run out of town.

4. Ignorance of subject matter or of the basic skills of reading, writing, and arithmetic. Colleges of education far too often grant bachelor's and even master's degrees to teachers and administrators deficient in the basic skills.

Steps You Can Take

What can you do if your child lands in a classroom presided over by a teacher who can't—or won't—do his job? Let's say it's a third- or fourth-grade class. Judging from what your child says, you suspect little learning is taking place. Take action. Visit the class. Without being too obvious, jot down notes on what you see and hear. They'll come in handy later. A capable teacher allows a few minutes for settling down at the beginning of a learning period, and most children respect limits the teacher has set.

In a poorly managed class, either the teacher sets no limits, or children ignore them. In a situation like this, you don't need a teaching certificate or a college degree to see that children are not learning the skills and facts they need. They may enjoy themselves some of the time, they may like the teacher, but they are being cheated—and so are you.

Next, make an appointment to see the teacher. Don't hesitate for fear you'll cause a problem for your child; the problem is already there.

Begin your meeting with something positive—a comment about the attractive bulletin board or the science table. Bring up the classroom problem by asking how many students are in the class, and then add "I know it must be difficult to get that many children this age to quiet down, but Jan has told me several times she has trouble hearing directions because of the talking. I felt I should mention it to you because I'm worried that she's not getting much done."

The teacher won't be pleased to hear this, but she should be grateful you spoke with her first instead of going to the principal. She may complain about the poor behavior of the class or of today's children in general. Says one school administrator of long experience: "Teachers sometimes say kids are different today, but most aren't much different from me or my brothers and sisters when we were young. Kids need discipline. If it's lax, they'll take advantage of the situation."

After your talk with the teacher, wait a week or so to see whether there's a change. Your visit may prod her into working out a better plan for managing the class. A meeting with the teacher can accomplish several things: You'll have let the teacher know—as tactfully as the situation allows—that you are aware of and concerned about the problem; you'll have given her a chance to make a needed change without having a complaint go further; and if you do have to see the principal, you'll have strengthened your case by talking to the teacher first.

Sometimes a visit to the teacher may not accomplish much in the way of change, but it will give you more information about a serious problem. Let's say your child has a seventh-grade social studies teacher who doesn't seem to have much intention of teaching history or geography. There is rarely any homework, and it appears the teacher fills class time with movies and slides, followed by oral questions or discussions; descriptions of his bicycle tours of Europe; having children design national flags or copy English translations of European popular songs. (There's nothing wrong with occasional use of such activities for enrichment, but too many teachers go overboard, using so much enrichment that children get little solid content.) During your meeting, you might say something like, "Sue never brings her book home to read. She tells me reading isn't required. I know she enjoys the movies and the class discussions, but I don't see how she can learn all this material without taking tests or reading." The teacher may say students can get all the information from an outline handed out in class. I've heard teachers justify teaching very little factual material on the grounds that students don't like to learn names and dates, or that they'll just forget it all, anyway. Though a good many teachers don't share this philosophy, others think children can gain "understanding" about the world without learning facts.

TALK TO THE PRINCIPAL

You can't tell the social studies teacher how to do his job, any more than you can order the third-grade teacher to manage her class and teach children the skills they need. But you do have a right, if not a responsibility, to let the principal know you think children are being short-changed in the classroom. Make an appointment to see him. Tell him what you observed in your visit to the classroom, and mention your visit with the teacher. Refer to your notes during your talk. This will show that your complaint is documented and enhance your image as an objective, determined parent. Remember to say something positive about the school. Better still, remind the principal of a complimentary note you've written about a good teacher or school program (if you have done this; see chapter 11).

What can you say, for example, about the social studies class?

Ask exactly what students are supposed to learn in seventh-grade social studies. This is one way parents can let the schools know they expect their children to be taught solid content. The principal ought to be able to tell you in plain English what the curriculum is (what nations, historical periods, geographical regions, etc., will be studied) and what children are expected to know at the end of the year. If he can't tell you, don't let him shunt you back to the teacher. Ask to see the curriculum guide, a written plan of what children are supposed to learn in each subject. You may be able to find out what seventh-graders in your district are supposed to learn in social studies by talking to someone from another school before you see the principal.

Armed with this information, you can tell the principal why you don't think this material is being taught in your child's class. A sample question: "How much can children learn about the natural resources, climate, government, and trade of Western Europe by watching movies, filling in blanks, and hearing about bicycle trips?" Add a couple of clinchers, based on what you heard from the teacher: "They don't use the book" or "They've had only one test since the beginning of the year."

As you talk to the principal, keep the following guidelines in mind:

Be cordial, but make it plain that you're not there merely to air a complaint. You want the principal to work with the teacher so things will improve. A good principal doesn't want bad teaching in his school; a lax principal doesn't want such flagrantly bad teaching that a parent makes an issue of it—especially one like you, who can present a complaint effectively.

When the principal agrees to "see what he can do," improvement may be on the way. But you need to set a deadline to make sure he's willing to act promptly. Make plans for another talk before you leave. Setting up another meeting lets both the principal and the teacher know you'll be keeping an eye on things, and it minimizes the possibility of anyone treating your child badly as a result of your complaint.

Be prepared for the platitudes and putoffs some principals use to handle parents and to avoid discussing the problem. A few samples: Kids are harder to discipline today; sometimes children give parents a one-sided picture of what goes on in class; you have to realize that teaching methods have changed a lot since you and I were in school; all of our teachers are experienced professionals.

Listen politely and ignore such statements. There's no need to discuss who's to blame for an out-of-control class, or whether children really can learn as much by watching movies and discussing them as they can by reading and writing. Calmly restate the problem: The third-grade class is so noisy and disorganized that children can't learn. The social studies class is being entertained instead of learning history and geography. You want the principal to bring about a change for the better as soon as possible. You're worried that your child and others are losing valuable learning time. Make sure the principal understands that you're aware that the whole class, not just your child, is losing out on learning.

The principal will probably not admit to you that the teacher could be doing a poor job, even if he knows she's a loser. A capable principal, however, will investigate reasonable complaints and press for improvements.

If you're persistent enough, chances are the principal will persuade the teacher to make changes in the classroom or suggest a change of teachers for your child, assuming there is another teacher available. If he doesn't, you can. Many principals consider a change of teachers only after you and he have tried other alternatives—and only after he's convinced a parent is determined to get a child into a class where the teaching is at least adequate. If the principal is helpful, send a note thanking him.

Don't ask for another teacher after the school year is under way unless the one your child has really is a disaster. If you make the request this year when it isn't absolutely necessary, you may be left with no options later on, when it is. If the teacher switch does take place, watch to see whether the official reason given for the switch to another class is "personality conflict" between your child and the incompetent teacher. This implies that your child is partly to blame, since it takes two to conflict. The principal and the teacher don't want to admit the real reason for the switch—that parents wouldn't put up with poor teaching, or no teaching. The official reason goes in the record. Make sure written statements don't reflect unfavorably on your child; it's your right to have such comments removed (see chapter 10).

HOW TO WORK WITH OTHER PARENTS

Often it pays to get other parents involved. A show of parent strength gives administrators real incentive to make a change. This approach worked well for California high school students who couldn't understand the algebra teacher's broken English. Worse, the teacher didn't answer their questions. When they didn't understand the way he presented a problem, he simply restated it and went on, leaving students confused.

Ten parents of students in the class met and decided that no teaching was taking place because the math was not being explained. They chose a spokesperson to meet with the head of the math department and the principal. As a result, a teacher's aide was put into the class to help with explanations, and students were offered in-school tutoring by the math department. But many still had problems, so parents again talked to the math chairman and the principal. A month later the class had a new teacher.

Involve other parents at the beginning if you sense that the principal will be uncooperative, or if you think the problem is too big to handle alone. But if you feel you may be able to get your child into another class, there's no point in working with a group.

Having the support of other parents is an asset—in many cases essential—if you decide to take the problem to the superintendent or the board of education. (For information on dealing with the board, see chapter 13.) If you do work with a group, follow the example of the California high school parents: choose a spokesperson and be persistent.

MAKING THE BEST OF A BAD DEAL

What if there's no other teacher available and little hope of improving the one your child faces every day in class? It's up to you to fill in the learning gaps and give your child the emotional support he needs. Children always lose when teachers aren't capable. The loss is most serious in the primary grades, when children are learning basic reading and math and forming attitudes about school that will be with them for years.

Mrs. B., the mother of Sue, a first-grader in a midwestern

school, found that the teacher, a pleasant older woman, had trouble communicating with children and was not teaching them to read. Mrs. B. talked to the principal, who was new to the school. He sympathized but told her he couldn't replace the teacher, who would retire at the end of the year. He promised to make sure that Sue would have an excellent teacher the following year.

A neighbor introduced Mrs. B. to a primary-school teacher from another school who lived nearby. This woman gave her reading materials and instructions for teaching her daughter direct (intensive) phonics. Mrs. B. helped Sue to learn phonics during the summer. Thanks to this training, and to a second-grade teacher who turned out to be as good as promised, Sue did become a capable reader.

If your primary child has a teacher who is not doing the job, you too can give her the help she needs at home. Concentrate on reading if your child is in first grade, or if she is in any other grade and not doing well in reading. (Recall the tests given in chapter 6 to check your child's reading.) By giving her phonics training at home, you will help her to improve her reading, regardless of which reading book she uses at school. To find out where you can get reading materials for home use, write to the Reading Reform Foundation (see Glossary for address).

A first step to helping your child with math is getting the math textbook and other materials used in his class. Ask the teacher. No need to explain beyond saying you want to reinforce what she's doing in class. If you can't ask the teacher, try the principal or another teacher at school. It's best to use the same math book he has in class. If you can't get it, ask the school librarian for help in finding a similar book. With more and more families teaching their children at home, many bookstores now stock a wide variety of materials for parents to choose from. Among the books that give helpful instructions for teaching children elementary reading, math, and cursive writing, along with drills and exercises, is *How to Tutor,* by Samuel L. Blumenfeld.

For supplementary learning games and other educational activities for home use, write to the Home and School Institute (see Glossary).

Is there danger of confusing your child if you don't use the same book the teacher does? Possibly, but the question you may have to consider is this: Isn't your child in even greater danger of being confused if he's in a no-learn situation in class and gets no help at home, either?

Carolyn Hillebrand, an Illinois teacher noted for her skill and enthusiasm in working with primary children, offers two suggestions for parents who want to help children at home. First, be consistent. Work with your child at the same time every day in a quiet spot where you won't be disturbed. Don't skip it "just for tonight," and don't let phone calls, television, or a trip to the supermarket interfere. Having a standing appointment lets your child know how important his learning is. Sticking to a schedule also helps him to develop a sense of responsibility. Second, keep sessions short—not more than fifteen minutes or so—for first-, second-, and third-graders. Less is more when it comes to tutoring younger children, whose attention span is short. Your child won't learn if you keep at it too long and tire him out. If your child balks at daily reading or math sessions, suggest that he invite a friend to learn along with him.

Another possibility is hiring a professional tutor, usually an experienced teacher, who will teach your child reading, math, or both for an hourly fee. You may be able to get the name of a good tutor from your school district office or from a college or university in your area. Other parents who have hired tutors may be able to recommend someone. You can also find ads for private tutors and tutoring services in the newspaper. Before you hire anyone to help your child, make sure they can deliver the help they promise. Ask how long they have been in business. Check their credentials, and get the names of several former clients who can tell you about the tutor or the service.

Since tutoring is costly, you may want to try hiring a tutor to work with several children. Parents in one midwestern town used this approach when their children needed extra help in an advanced junior high math class. Students took turns hosting the tutoring sessions. Nancy Berla of the NCCE suggests compiling a list of reputable tutors as a possible project for local school parents' groups.

OUSTING A BAD TEACHER

The responsibility for putting a semiliterate or otherwise unfit teacher in the classroom lies with the local board of education and with the superintendent who does the hiring. But it is the school principal who supervises a new teacher for the first two or three years and decides whether the teacher should *stay* in the classroom. The principal's evaluation is crucial. A teacher may pass a written test and yet be unable to teach children. A principal who lets an incompetent teacher gain tenure will eventually be responsible for miseducating hundreds of children.

Mr. L., the sixth-grade teacher with the tape recorders, was a pal to his students, though he didn't teach them much. Many incompetent teachers cause children real grief, though. Teenagers who have to endure poor teaching resent being cheated. A third-grader in a chaotic class won't know he's missing out on math or reading, but he will be upset spending five or six hours in a noisy, unsettled class. He may worry about not being able to finish his work or be irritable after a day in school. Make sure he has time to unwind in the afternoon, and don't overdo talk about school.

Sometimes the problem is less obvious than noise and disorder in the classroom. Nancy, the mother of a second-grader, reports that her daughter's teacher told the children to write a research paper and gave so little direction the class floundered. Parents who inquired about the assignment got no help from the teacher. They hunted frantically for "research" material second-graders could read. Assignments like this kept students in a state of crisis, unsure of what the teacher wanted and afraid to ask. Nancy's daughter developed headaches that disappeared at the end of the school year. She also developed a feeling that she was a "dummy" (which lasted longer), thanks to the teacher's lack of direction. Nancy and other parents talked to the principal, who kept close track of the teacher's class the following year. The teacher resigned shortly thereafter.

You may wonder whether in this case talking to the principal was worthwhile, since Nancy's child and others still had to put up with the teacher, and so did a second-grade class the next year. But even in a situation like this, complaining is vital. Elementary-school teachers are often moved from grade to grade. By speaking up now, you may protect your child or a younger brother or sister from getting the same teacher in a year or two. And parental pressure lets principals know parents blame them for bad teaching.

So many parents complained about Mr. L. of the tape-recorded math lessons that the principal had to act. He transferred Mr. L. to another school in the district. In some school districts, really rotten teachers rotate. This is only a band-aid solution, but it is better than none. If your district is large, your youngest child may graduate before Mr. L. returns. Parents in one elementary district, fed up with an incompetent teacher who had been rotating through their schools for years, stopped the teacher in mid-whirl. They organized and took turns sitting in his classroom until he resigned.

Another official ploy for dealing with an incompetent teacher who gets too much flack from parents is to give him or her a nonteaching job, which means in effect that parents and other citizens must pay to keep a teacher out of their children's classrooms. In high school, incompetent teachers may be scheduled to teach required courses so their classrooms won't be as empty as they should be.

Why do incompetent teachers rate so much protection? Teachers' union contracts have job-security provisions that make firing teachers extremely difficult. In addition, teachers are protected by state laws giving them tenure of position (virtually a lifetime contract) after two or three years in many states. To fire an incompetent or otherwise unfit teacher, a principal must show carefully documented evidence that the teacher has violated the state's standards for ethics or job performance and that remediation (efforts to help the teacher improve) have failed.

Parents can be crucial in building a case against a teacher. Albert C. Jurenas, who served as principal fifteen years in an elementary school district and now heads a university laboratory school, says: "To help a good principal, keep it [evidence of teaching incompetence] objective and frequent, and put it in writing. If parents give me records like this, I can do the job. I don't like to have a parent say, 'I didn't tell you last year when Johnny was in her class, because I was afraid he'd get a bad grade.' A teacher who is being criticized would be really stupid to pick on a student. That would be pretty obvious."

Intervention and Other Reforms

Recently developed plans for eliminating poor teachers or requiring them to do a better job include a program called "intervention" set up by the Toledo (Ohio) Federation of Teachers in 1981. Teachers identify fellow teachers who have difficulty in the classroom and "teacher consultants" are assigned to help them improve. Those who don't, may lose their jobs. As of 1984, twenty-four teachers had been recommended for intervention. At the time of this writing, seven of these teachers have been fired or persuaded to resign, five improved their performance, and the rest are still in intervention. In the five-year period before intervention went into effect, no experienced teachers were fired. Under the school-based management plan in Salt Lake City, Utah, parents can request a council of teachers, administrators, and principals to review a teacher's performance.

California is among the states which have passed laws to make it easier to dismiss incompetent teachers. "Principals can spend time in the classroom. We need to go after it [the incompetent teacher problem] wholesale," says State Superintendent of Public Instruction William Honig. Many states have passed or proposed laws to raise standards for certification of teachers, to require evaluation of working teachers and to supervise beginning teachers more closely. Although unions oppose measures like these, many teachers support changes that promise to upgrade the profession. You can encourage higher teaching standards in your state by writing to your state legislators. (See chapter 13 for information on how to go about it.)

Dismissal Procedures

Armed with evidence from parents and results of his own investigation, a good administrator can insist that a teacher improve or face possible dismissal procedure. What can happen when a principal has built a strong case against an incompetent teacher is a process called "counselling out"—a forced resignation. If the teacher refuses to be counselled out and fights the dismissal, there will be a hearing before an official appointed by the state board of education. If the principal has been conscientious in gathering evidence against the teacher, the local board of education will be able to present a solid case for dismissal. Nevertheless, the union will defend the teacher, and the decision of the hearing officer can be appealed in the courts. Rather than pay for a court battle, the board may decide to pay the teacher to resign.

Unless children are being physically abused or are tearing up the classroom—or parents unite and take a firm stand against bad teaching—principals usually won't admit that an incompetent teacher could have slipped in the schoolroom door. "There's a tacit acceptance by principals of poor teaching, because principals move vertically [to more important administrative jobs], while teachers can only go horizontally [from school to school]," says Daniel Safran, founder of the Center for the Study of Parent Involvement in Oakland, California.

When asked what she considered the most serious problem of the teaching profession as a whole, an experienced teacher, the wife of a principal, said, "Weak principals are our biggest problem. Please quote me on that. Strong principals could help to solve the bad teacher problem, but so many just don't do it."

3

Parents' Rights and Parent Action

10

LEARN YOUR RIGHTS *BEFORE* ANYTHING GOES WRONG

"Sit back, and agencies and experts *will* make decisions about your family. But speak up on behalf of your children and you can begin to gain the confidence, skills, and power to control more of the quality of life your children have."

—A publication of the Children's Defense Fund

"I was worried about Dave's work in fifth-grade math. When the teacher showed me his scores on the achievement tests, I thought the scores looked low, but I'm never sure what all those numbers mean," says Sharon, a registered nurse. "When I asked the teacher to explain the test scores, she told me I didn't need to know all the statistics. She said that when Dave settled down to do his work, he understood the math well enough. I asked how the rest of the children in Dave's class did on the achievement test, but she told me she couldn't discuss other children's scores. I went home feeling upset, not sure what I should do. . . ."

Dave's mother had reason to be upset. Not only was the teacher being uncooperative in refusing to give a reasonable explanation, but she was also failing to comply with the law. And like too many other parents—even those who are otherwise well informed—Sharon was unaware that she had a legal right to insist on having the information she needed to understand her son's progress.

Fortunately for Dave, the family moved several months later and he entered a different school, where he was retested. His new fifth-grade teacher willingly explained Dave's scores, including where he stood in comparison with the rest of the class. (Teachers can't discuss individual scores of children with other parents, but they can discuss class norms or averages.)

But you don't have to trust to luck—or to the good will of any teacher or administrator—to find out what your child's test scores mean. You are entitled to explanations of test scores and other official school records under the Family Educational Rights and Privacy Act (FERPA) of 1974, also known as the Buckley Amendment. Here are several of the important rights this law gives you as a parent or guardian:

You can examine and have explained to you *all* of your child's *official* school records, including standardized test scores. You may get copies of these records by paying a small copying cost. (Note to divorced parents: Many noncustodial parents wrongly assume they have lost their right to see their children's school reports and other records. Even if you do not have custody of your child, you still have this right—unless the school is informed of a law or court order to the contrary. By supplying stamped self-addressed envelopes, you can make it easier for your child's school to send you copies of his reports and other records.)

If the records contain errors or information you feel would reflect unfavorably on your child—for example, comments that label him as a "problem"—you can ask that these be removed. If school officials refuse your request, you may ask for a hearing. You are entitled to put your own letter of correction and explanation in your child's permanent record.

You have a right to refuse unauthorized persons access to your child's records. The school can't disclose them to anyone outside the school without your written consent, or without your child's consent once he reaches legal age.

The school should notify you and all other parents annually of your rights under FERPA. A school which willfully violates parents' rights under this act is liable to lose federal funds. If you want more information about FERPA, or if you think your rights under this law have been violated, you can contact the FERPA office in Washington. See the Glossary for the address.

A number of states have school records laws similar to FERPA. In Virginia parents have immediate access to children's school records. Under FERPA and laws in many other states, the school must give parents access to school records within a reasonable time, ranging from several days to several weeks following the request. It's wise to communicate with the school in writing when asking to see records or making other important requests. Keep a copy so that you can prove you did make the request if the school later denies it.

FERPA and similar state laws help to put you on an equal footing with teachers and other school people in overseeing your child's education. These people use school records, including test scores, to communicate among themselves about your child and to make decisions about his education—decisions you may not always agree with. For example, Dave's first teacher, who felt he was doing "well enough" in math, though he lagged far behind most of the class, did not indicate he needed extra help. When his mother fully understood his test scores, she thought otherwise.

HOW TO INSIST ON EXAMINING SCHOOL RECORDS

Of course, there are many teachers who are eager to help parents understand everything about their children's learning, including test scores. At the other extreme are the teachers and principals who answer parents' questions grudgingly or not at all. From them you may hear, "Those records aren't available now. Maybe if you can come back when we've had time to look them up . . ." or "I guess it takes special training to understand all those test statistics, anyway." If you do encounter a teacher or anyone else at school who refuses to give you the records, or the test scores, or the explanation you need to help your child, try the approach suggested by parent education expert Sadie Hofstein: Calmly repeat your request with increasing firmness. Say first, "I want this information because it will help me in planning for my child." Next, say, "I know it's my right to have this information." Finally, "If you can't give it to me, I'll go 'upstairs' to get it."

When it comes to school records, you can't assume "everything is in order" unless you've seen for yourself, as the parent of a student in a New England elementary school found out.

Will had trouble in school almost from the beginning: poor grades, low-normal scores on IQ (aptitude) tests, and a reputation for acting up in class. But the summer after Will finished fifth grade, life began to look more promising. Medical tests showed he suffered from a previously unsuspected physical disorder. With treatment, the doctor was certain Will would do much better in school, since it was likely that his physical condition had caused his poor showing on tests and perhaps the poor behavior, too. In September, when Will started sixth grade, his parents attached the new medical reports and doctor's comments to the required form for the school nurse, along with a note asking her to give the information to Will's teacher. Several months later, during a conference with the sixth-grade teacher, Will's father glanced through his son's record folder. He found the familiar low aptitude (IQ) test scores from previous years, the reading and math achievement scores (also low), and copies of previous report cards (including complaints about classroom behavior). But there was nothing about Will's physical condition, the treatment, or the doctor's comments about the changes he expected in Will.

Will's father says, "As far as the teacher's record was concerned, he was still a student from whom she could expect low performance and poor behavior. No one knew about the probable connection between Will's medical condition and his school work. The note had never reached the nurse, who would have passed it on to the teacher. They finally found it buried in a file in the superintendent's office."

An attorney who has dealt with many aspects of school law advises parents to review children's records often and to be sure to do so when a child goes from one level of schooling to another, from elementary school to junior high, for example. Ask to see records kept by the counselor and the nurse, as well as test scores and reports from teachers. Find out whether any records are kept on microfiche, microfilm, or in computer data bases. You have a right to examine these also. Check the comments written about your child by teachers and other school people.

"Look for insights into your child's attitudes and behavior in what teachers have written in the records," says a psychologist who is a former school guidance director. "If you find a note such as 'Child is uncooperative,' discuss it calmly with the teacher who wrote it. Find out specifics. Even if you feel the teacher is right, get the comment out of the record. It can supply the next teacher with a negative mindset toward your child. Remember, kids do change. Point this out to the teacher who wrote the damaging note and to the principal if necessary. Tell them the negative comment is educationally unconstructive."

LAWS ALONE CAN'T PROTECT YOUR RIGHTS

At this point you may wonder why it may be necessary to resort to what Sadie Hofstein terms "appropriate aggressiveness" to get information you're entitled to, and why you have to check your child's records to make sure they're handled properly and don't contain damaging comments. Aren't school people trying to help children? Aren't parents and schools supposed to trust each other? Well, yes—much of the time. At other times, you will be trying to do what is best for your child, while the school acts in its own best interests as a bureaucracy. Says Illinois attorney Jerry Lambert, a former teacher who has dealt with many aspects of school law, "We are living in an adversarial society. If you don't stand up for your rights—and your child's—no one else will."

Most school people are not actively trying to deprive you of your rights as a parent, but for a number of reasons, they may discourage you from exercising these rights:

1. Many teachers and administrators developed their strategy for dealing with parents years before passage of FERPA and other laws which protect parents' rights; habit dies hard. School people find little in these laws to benefit them.

2. The people in charge of schools, like those in charge of other bureaucracies, dislike explaining procedures or records, let alone changing them to meet the needs of the people they serve.

3. Though top administrators are informed about laws protecting parents' rights, some teachers and other school staff people may not fully understand these rights.

4. The many parents still unaware of their rights make it easy for schools to ignore them. Local parents' groups could educate mem-

bers about their rights as parents by sponsoring workshops led by attorneys with special knowledge in this field.

We have discussed in detail the federal law dealing with school records, FERPA, because you really can't be an effective advocate for your child unless you have access to his records and understand them.

PARENTS' RIGHTS IN YOUR STATE

Since education is largely state-controlled, many of your important rights as a parent are spelled out by the laws of your state. Here is a general look at the rights of parents granted by the states, as summarized from the "Parent Rights Card," published in 1982 by the National Committee for Citizens in Education. (To get a Rights Card, which lists specific rights for each state, send a self-addressed stamped envelope and 25 cents to the NCCE. Please see Glossary for address.):

1. Student instruction. In twenty-one states and the District of Columbia, parents can visit a child's class at any time during the school day, after first notifying the school office. The states include Alabama, Arkansas, Arizona, Florida, Indiana, Iowa, Louisiana*, Maryland, Maine, North Carolina, North Dakota, New Hampshire, New Mexico, Nevada, New York*, Ohio, Oklahoma, South Carolina*, Texas, Utah*, Virginia*. In some states parents are guaranteed a minimum number of conferences with a child's teacher. Thirty-nine states and the District of Columbia allow parents to educate children at home if they meet standards and conditions set by the state.

2. Student discipline. No matter where you live, you have the right to take legal action against a school official who uses "excessive or unreasonable" physical force to discipline your child. You have the right to appeal the suspension of your child from school in the District of Columbia and in all states except Kansas, Utah, and Wisconsin. You can also appeal a decision to place your child in a class for students labeled "disruptive," unless you live in Georgia, Kentucky, Michigan, Missouri, North Dakota, South Carolina, Utah, Vermont, Washington, or Wisconsin.

*Local policies may prevail in some states.

3.   Other rights. No matter where you live, you have the right to look at all official school policies in your district. All citizens also have the right to look at the budget—it is a matter of public record. In twenty-nine states parents and other citizens have the right to speak at all public meetings of their local school board. In twenty-seven states any parent or citizen group has the right to organize and be heard by school officials.

4.   The rights of handicapped children. If your child is said to be learning disabled or otherwise handicapped, federal law (the Rehabilitation Act of 1973 and the Handicapped Act of 1975), as well as state law, requires that he have an "appropriate" public school education. Your written consent is required before your child can be tested to determine his special education needs. The law states that you must be notified by letter and invited to the meeting at which his program is discussed. Your written consent is also required to place your child in such a program. You may refuse to consent to the final decision. (For more about LD children, see chapter 6.) You can get copies of the laws and regulations pertaining to special ed by writing to your state department of education.

For a detailed study of the legal side of dealing with the schools, see *The Rights of Parents in the Education of Their Children,* by David Schimmel and Louis Fischer. But keep in mind that federal and state laws and local rulings change. You may be able to get a satisfactory answer to questions about your rights from local school officials. If not, consult the legal advisor in the office of your county school superintendent. Your state department of education is another source of information on parents' rights.

Loss of Local Control Limits Parents' Rights

School administrators and teachers, acting under the authority of local school boards, have the responsibility for educating children, keeping records, and seeing that parents are informed. In recent years, however, local policy makers and school administrators have lost much control to other powers—state and federal laws and court decisions, and teachers' unions. These state, federal, and union rulings often severely limit your right as a parent to oversee your child's education. For example, many parents object to court-ordered busing, which takes children to schools miles from home, in effect disrupting and lengthening the school day without increasing real learning time. State requirements mandating local school districts to teach specific courses (health, drivers' education, etc.) can limit time and money which local schools might otherwise use to strengthen academic programs. Teachers' union collective bargaining agreements often contain provisions (those affecting class size, for example) that restrict a school board's decision-making power. For example, let's say your school board wants to save money by increasing the size of every class from twenty-five to thirty. They plan to use the money saved to start a new science course. If the teachers' union agreement states that no teacher can have more than twenty-five students in class, the board can't cut costs—and may have to do without the new science course. Your school board is not free to make a decision that could improve your child's education. In this way a union can usurp power that rightfully belongs to you and your elected representatives.

In some states the courts have made it more difficult for teachers' unions to dictate school policy. In Pennsylvania, for example, parents can challenge a collective bargaining agreement if its effect is to give the union policy-making power that rightfully belongs to the school board. William Rioux of the NCCE believes parents should form their own unions and insist on having a say in contract bargaining. In chapter 13, you will learn how you and other parents and citizens can work for more control of education through your elected representatives.

Some Rights Can Be a Double-Edged Sword

Laws and court rulings have given you and other parents the right to protest disciplinary action taken against your child in school, and you also have the right (except in Kansas, Wisconsin, and Utah) to protest his suspension or expulsion from school. These restrictions have protected students from abuse and unjust treatment by teachers and school authorities.

But laws and decisions protecting students' rights have also encouraged troublemakers to flout the teacher's authority, disrupt classes, and prevent the majority of well-behaved students from learning. This exaggerated concern for students' rights can undermine authority of all good teachers and school administrators. In addition, laws designed to protect students' rights have at times provided administrators with an alibi for failing to solve school disciplinary problems.

A recent (January 1985) Supreme Court decision will make it easier to discourage student lawbreakers and to keep schools safe for the majority of students. The ruling gives teachers and school authorities more leeway in searching students for drugs and weapons or other evidence that they are violating the law or school regulations.

SCHOOL INVASIONS OF PRIVACY: GRAY AREAS

The daughter of a good friend of mine came home from school upset one day when she was in fifth grade. "One of the ladies at school [my friend later discovered it was a social worker] took some of the kids out of class and asked them questions about boys and dates and things like that. I hope she isn't going to ask *me* any of those things."

My friend's reaction—and mine—was outrage that children had been taken out of class and put on the spot by being asked to reveal their feelings about private matters. This incident made us both aware of how easy it is for adults to catch children off-guard—especially in a school setting. It's important to teach children to defend themselves against school invasions of privacy in what I heard one attorney refer to as the "gray area" of personal values and feelings. First, if you haven't already, talk with your child about your views on revealing private business (such as family income) or personal feelings (moral values, sexual matters, religious or political beliefs) to outsiders. Next, help children plan how to cope if they're asked questions that pry or make them uncomfortable.

To a child under ten, make it plain that he doesn't have to answer questions from teachers or other school people about personal matters. Teach him a simple response: "I don't think I can answer that. Maybe you should talk to my parents." To an older child, explain that while school people deserve his respect, he doesn't have to answer their questions about his private thoughts and feelings. Encourage him to think beforehand how he would respond if someone asked him a prying question. If pressed, he too can refer the questioner to you.

A former school guidance director advises parents who suspect an emotional problem and want their child tested to use a psychologist not connected with the school. "This protects the privacy of the child and the parents, and they can have the results entered in the school record only if they feel it would be in the child's best interests," she says.

School-administered personality tests—or any test which deals with children's feelings and emotions—pose another threat to children's privacy in school and are not apt to make a positive contribution to academic learning. Tests or attitude scales may ask a child questions about his feelings toward himself, his family and religion, his values, or the world in general. Children may be told that there are no right or wrong answers and that they can answer honestly, "because no one at school will show the papers to their parents." Yet children's answers to these personal questions will be on file for school people to see and use.

Dr. Harold M. Voth, senior psychiatrist and psychoanalyst at the Menninger Foundation and professor of psychiatry at the University of Kansas College of Medicine, writes: "The personality . . . of the pupil should be off limits to educators. How a child develops psychologically is the sole responsibility of the parents." Commenting on the attempts of teachers or school counselors to deal with such issues as suicide, he says, "They may be well-meaning, but they are opening up problems they are ill-equipped to deal with." He refers to a case in which a boy killed himself immediately after taking part in a group discussion of suicide.

Suicide among teenagers is increasing. Observers point out that the pessimistic views sometimes presented to students in science and social studies materials and the growing classroom use of such powerful psychological techniques as psychodrama, sociodrama, and role playing may be in part responsible, since they leave vulnerable teen-agers with feelings of despair and helplessness.

In the past decade or so, many schools have introduced into their regular programs a number of controversial and experimental classroom activities almost certain to invade children's privacy, in addition to wasting valuable learning time. In "Magic Circle" younger children are encouraged to discuss their parents, home life, friends, fears, and conflicts. "Values clarification" or behavior modification exercises may urge students to answer questions like these: "Reveal who in your family brings you the greatest sadness and why" *or* "Tell where you stand on the topic of masturbation." Students may be asked to decide under what conditions lying, stealing, or cheating are permissible, or to play games like "Lifeboat," in which one person must be sacrificed to save the rest.

Some educators claim values training helps students to develop their own method of making decisions about right and wrong, instead of relying on ready-made value systems. Critics point out that values clarification exercises and psychological probing disturb students and undermine parents' efforts to teach children moral and religious values at home. Dr. Voth writes that values clarification tells the young "to reject all values on a grand scale and suggests that the young mind possesses the inherent wisdom to discover truth. This is utter nonsense, and it is highly destructive to the young person. Young people need a frame of reference by which to order their lives."

What can you do if you don't want your child subjected to values clarification, sensitivity training, or other psychological techniques in the classroom? The first step is finding out whether these psychological programs are used in your school. They may be included in elementary or high school as part of the class work not only in health and home economics, but also in English (or language arts), social studies, or science. Programs designed to change children's attitudes or moral values may have such neutral-sounding labels and titles as "decision making," "critical thinking," "futuristics," *Facing History and Ourselves, Teaching Individuals Positive Solutions,* and *Me-Me Drug Prevention Program,* among others. Often the only way to find out about such programs is to pay close attention to children's comments about class activities and to read the materials they bring home.

PUPIL RIGHTS AMENDMENT

Next, you need to know how the school program in question was developed and how it is funded. If federal money is used and the program meets certain other conditions, the school must by law ask for written permission from parents before a child may take part. Under the 1984 regulations of the Hatch Act (Pupil Rights Amendment) no student is required as part of a federal research or experimental program "to submit without prior consent [of parent or guardian] to psychiatric examination, testing, or treatment, or psychological examination, testing or treatment, in which the primary purpose is to reveal information" about the following: political affiliations, mental or psychological problems, sex behavior, illegal, antisocial, or self-incriminating behavior, critical appraisals of family members, or income. In addition, the Hatch regulations give parents the right to *examine* all teaching materials used in such programs. (To get a copy of the Hatch regulations, ask your local library to order *Federal Register,* vol. 49, no. 174, Sept. 6, 1984, pp. 35321–35322, or write to the Hatch Act office, listed in the Glossary.)

You can tell by looking at the school budget whether the program you're concerned about is federally funded. Even if it is not currently financed with federal money, the Hatch regulations could apply, since many of these school psychological programs were developed at least in part with federal funds.

If you believe the Hatch Act does apply, and you have not given consent for your child to take part in the program, you can first protest to local school people. If they don't comply voluntarily, you can appeal to the state board of education or to the courts, and finally to the Hatch Act office. At this writing, six cases are pending in that office under the new regulations.

If the program or class you object to is paid for with state or local funds, you can ask school officials in your district to excuse your child from participating. In more than half of the states parents can request that a child be excused from studying subjects or taking part in school activities they object to on religious, moral, or other reasonable grounds.

Laws in Oklahoma and California protect the privacy of school children involved in state research or experimental programs, and several other states are considering similar laws. Some school districts have used Hatch guidelines locally. In Salt Lake City, Utah, parental consent is required for any school program which relates to students' private life. Superintendent M. Donald Thomas believes this has helped to cut down on the intrusion of college research in the classroom, according to a report in *Network* (May 1984), an NCCE publication. If you and other parents in your district favor such a parental consent regulation, you may suggest that the local school board consider enacting one. (See chapter 13 on working with the school board.)

A final word about laws: Necessary as they are, it would be a mistake to think that simply passing laws can guarantee any child a good education. In fact, a blizzard of new school laws might well have the opposite effect—by giving us a false sense of security.

Federal and state laws are not the only source of rights for you as a parent. By banding together, parents in some school districts have gained the right to be informed about and to participate in such vital aspects of education as curriculum. For example, the United Parents Associations, Inc. of New York City insisted that the schools issue a curriculum outline to parents showing what would be taught grade by grade, giving parents one criterion for checking whether their children's teachers are covering the required material. In Salt Lake City parents are members of school councils which deal with curriculum, and in a Minnesota school district, parents are part of a committee to spot weaknesses in curriculum and decide on improvements.

The premise throughout this book is that no commission or law or expert can do more to improve education for your child right now than you and other informed parents can by acting on your own good judgment and concern as parents. Your most valuable assets are your knowledge of your child and your right to speak up—to ask for improvements—when things aren't right at school.

ASKING FOR CHANGES: WHAT YOU NEED TO KNOW

At one time or another most of us have made the mistake of waiting too long to act when confronted with a problem at school. Common refrains I heard from parents were "I wish I had done something sooner," or "I know I should have complained, but I let it go. . . ."

You have a right to ask for needed changes at school because you are responsible for overseeing your child's education, and because your taxes pay the people hired to supervise your schools and teach in your child's classrooms. Here are four fears that cause too many parents to "wait and see" instead of speaking up:

1. The school will take it out on my child.

If something is really wrong at school—if your child isn't safe, if he isn't learning—the school is already "taking it out" on your child. Trying to solve the problem isn't likely to make matters worse. Weigh the risk against the possible benefit. Should you fail to point out a serious classroom problem for fear the fifth-grade teacher may give your daughter a grade of "good," instead of "very good"?

Many parents I talked to echoed the decidedly positive view of a mother of six: "I've never hesitated to ask questions or comment—even critically—when I thought it was necessary. I feel my children have been treated better as a result, because school people know I keep an eye on things."

2. The educators know more than I do.

This may be true in some cases, but that doesn't always mean they're doing their job well or acting in your child's best interests. Don't let your respect for experts overcome your common sense if things aren't right at school. Since the teacher is the first person you're likely to speak to when you request a change, keep in mind that part of her job is to carry out the rules of the institution. She may not have the authority to do what you want done. On the other hand, some teachers deal with requests they don't like by stalling, hoping you lack the confidence or determination to go higher. Says one parent advocate: "Never take a low-level 'no.' "

3. School people will say I'm overprotective and not capable of being objective about my child.

A parent who is also a psychologist has a ready answer for this. "I often say to the teacher or whoever I'm discussing the problem with, 'Maybe I'm not being objective. I'm making assumptions based on [whatever the evidence seems to be]. If I'm not being objective, help me by giving me *facts* about my child. Please be specific.' "

4. Speaking up won't do any good.

Read on for cases where it *did* work.

Jimmy, a third-grader in a small New England city, complained that his math book was the same one he'd used the year before in the school's second-grade accelerated program. The teacher told Jimmy's mother: "He'll just be reviewing for a while. Then we'll see." Weeks passed with no change and Jimmy told his mother: "I did all this stuff last year. Now I'm doing it over and over. I hate it!"

Jimmy's mother talked to the teacher, but instead of changing his book, she tried to make him the class pet, which Jimmy hated. His mother talked to the principal, who did nothing. Finally she went to the superintendent. Says Jimmy's mother, "I told him that if he could explain how going through the same math two years in a row was good for Jimmy, I would listen. He couldn't. But he still didn't agree to see Jimmy got an appropriate book until I said I was ready to bring in a lawyer if necessary. It was not an idle threat."

The mother of Mike, a second-grader, was alarmed when he appeared at the kitchen door at 10:30 on a school morning. "Are you sick?" she asked. "I'm okay, but I wasn't having any fun at recess, so I came home," Mike told her. His mother, who was new to the United States and still learning English, decided to go to the school to find out how a seven-year-old could just walk off and come home. A friend suggested that she wait, assuring her it probably wouldn't happen again. Mike's mother said, "The next time he'll get hurt, or some other child will." She asked for a meeting with the teacher and the principal and made her point. The next day there were two more teachers on the playground.

You can stand up for your rights as a parent once you know what they are. You can complain successfully, too, if it's necessary to help your child and others.

A CONCERNED EDUCATOR'S "FIVE RIGHTS OF PARENTS"

Parent advocates and many concerned educators believe that parents have made it too easy for the schools to shut them out and ignore their rights. Dr. J. Cy Rowell of Texas Christian University says, "Parents need to remind themselves that they are consumers of education and that the schools are not doing them a special favor by giving them information." Writing in the professional education journal *Phi Delta Kappan*, he lists five rights he believes parents should have in dealing with the school. What follows is a summary.

1.   Parents need information about the training, previous employment, and accomplishments of teachers and principals. This is the other side of the school's request for family information. The school should make it a routine practice to give parents biographical information about school staff.

2.   Parents are entitled to know what is being taught, how the curriculum is organized, how students are grouped for instruction, and what teaching methods are used. Elementary parents need to know how reading is taught. Parents of high school students should be told the content of courses.

3.   Parents should be told, without having to ask for this information, about school policies regarding discipline, attendance, and arranging to visit the school.

4.   Parents should be able to commend teachers and principals and should also have the right to protest incompetent teachers without fear of recrimination.

5.   Parents should also have the right to influence policy not only by electing school board members and speaking at meetings, but also by serving on committees which shape curriculum, determine discipline policies, and set school priorities.

You and other parents can use the list of rights suggested by Dr. Rowell as a goal to aim for in gaining more control over your schools.

LEARN THE SCHOOL SETUP

In this chapter we'll take an overall look at your school system and find out who is responsible for what in operating your schools. You already know a good deal about the people most directly concerned with your child's learning—the teacher, the principal, and the counselor. At times you may need to go beyond these people in getting help for your child. You'll be a more effective advocate if you've learned the setup beforehand. We'll also look briefly at the role of state education agencies, teachers' unions, and the federal government in your child's school. Understanding the system is essential if you and other parents want to work for school improvement.

KEY PEOPLE IN THE SYSTEM

The governing body in your school district is the school board (which may be called the board of education, the school trustees, or the school committee). The school board is responsible for levying taxes to support the schools, hiring the superintendent of schools, overseeing the school budget, and setting policy for the school district. School board members are citizens elected for a term of several years. (In about 10 percent of the nation's school districts members are appointed.) They usually serve without pay. Because the citizens who serve on the school board—and not the professional educators—by law have the final authority in school matters, we say that we have "lay" control of schools. Because you and other citizens elect your school board, we also say that the board represents the people in exercising control over their schools. If your school board is like most, though, it probably falls far short of this ideal of representing citizens and exercising authority over the schools. Later in this chapter, once you're familiar with the setup as it *should* be, we'll take a closer look at how it really is, and why.

The board hires a superintendent of schools, sometimes called the "general superintendent," a professional educator, to run the school system. The superintendent's job is to see that the school board's policies are carried out in educating children. For example, if the board decides children in grades 4, 5, and 6 should learn a foreign language, the superintendent is responsible for planning the program, hiring the teachers, and fitting language study into the schedule.

The superintendent and the staff of professional educators who work under his direction to carry out school board policies are known as the school administration. A city school system may have an administrative staff of several thousand people in the "central office." In a small school system, the superintendent may perform nearly all functions himself (or herself). In most school districts, the superintendent has at least one staff member to assist him in each of these areas:

Financial matters—assistant (or associate) superintendent for business.

Student testing and guidance—assistant superintendent for research or director of guidance.

Planning curriculum (what is taught in class)—assistant superintendent (also called coordinator) for curriculum.

Managing individual schools—building principals (and perhaps assistant principals).

Looking in on the Superintendent of Schools

In addition to overseeing the work of the specialists on his staff, the general superintendent sees that district programs operate properly and assigns and supervises principals in each district school building.

Superintendents are apt to be content with the status quo if things appear to be going smoothly. Above all, they want to avoid dissension in the teaching ranks, knowing that a teachers' strike may result in nonrenewal of the superintendent's contract. Many superintendents won't press for improvements in the classroom— no matter how beneficial these might be to children—if they feel teachers will object. To cite an all-too-common example, if teachers don't want to grade written papers, a superintendent probably won't insist that writing get priority in district classrooms.

Yet some superintendents do lead the way in bringing needed change to their schools. Looking for a way to improve reading achievement, Charles Micciche, school superintendent in Groveton, New Hampshire, studied reports on the effectiveness of direct (intensive) phonics and arranged to have it introduced to a small group of teachers in voluntary workshops. Their enthusiasm sold the program to other teachers in the district. Micciche reports that during the first two years of the new reading program, test scores improved substantially. Within five years the school district was able to begin phasing out remedial reading classes.

How the Administrative Staff Affects Your Child's Classroom

Except for principals, the specialists on the superintendent's staff work largely behind the scenes. You and your child may never see most of them. Yet they profoundly influence your child's education, and they are among the highest paid workers in your school district.

Each assistant superintendent (coordinator or director) is responsible for district-wide programs in his or her special area. Next to the general superintendent (who may perform this function himself in a small district), the staff member in charge of curriculum is the most important person in the district, since what children will be taught depends largely on his (or her) knowledge, judgment, and educational philosophy. The curriculum specialist develops plans of study (a curriculum guide) and chooses teaching materials for reading, math, social studies, and so on. The guidance director oversees standardized testing, supervises guidance counselors, and may also be in charge of special programs, such as those for gifted children.

If you have questions about curriculum, testing, or special ed and can't get satisfactory answers from the teacher, counselor, or principal in your child's school building, you can call or make an appointment with the central district office to talk with the director or assistant superintendent in charge of the area you're concerned about. Some school districts issue parent handbooks listing these staff people by name and function. If your district doesn't do this, a secretary in the central office should be able to give you a copy of the organizational chart (with names) or a staff list. Update your chart or list at the beginning of each school year so you'll have the information when you need it.

Your Principal Is Chosen by Your Superintendent

The board may also select principals, and in a few school districts, including Chicago's, parents have a say in the choice. A parents' committee interviews candidates and gives an approved list to the superintendent for a final decision. As you know, the principal's job is to see that the building is safe and well maintained and to supervise teaching.

As we saw in chapter 9, many principals find it more expedient to ignore teaching problems than to solve them. Often they don't know how to rescue a teacher who is floundering. A veteran midwestern teacher remarks, "Usually the principal hasn't been in the classroom for years, and he may not have very good teaching skills himself." This is typical of comments I heard from teachers in elementary and high schools around the country. Many principals are content with keeping the building quiet and orderly and staying on the good side of the teachers.

Of course there are exceptions—principals who take a stand and refuse to put up with bad teaching. Joe Clark of Eastside High, Paterson, New Jersey, is an inner-city principal hailed for bringing order to a school which had severe problems with drugs and violence. Clark does paperwork before school hours. Once the day begins, he is highly visible, in and out of classrooms, patrolling the hallways, greeting students by name. Commenting on weak principals, Clark says, "They're afraid of their teachers. They're afraid of their students. . . . They make alibis [but] never really try to make things better. . . ."

WHOM DOES YOUR SCHOOL BOARD
REALLY REPRESENT?

Now that you are familiar with the school setup in your district, you're ready to take a closer look at how the school board operates.

You'll recall from the beginning of the chapter that the school board's job is to make policy, which the school superintendent, hired by the board, is supposed to carry out. As you'll also recall, by law school boards are ordinary citizens elected by the public. The intention here is to give you and other citizens a say in how your schools are run.

But this description of how the board is *supposed* to operate does not give us an accurate picture of what really happens, or where the real power is—and why. You need to know this in order to influence the school board, or run for the school board—or simply understand how your schools operate.

First, the school board often doesn't make school policy. As much as 96 percent of the time, according to one study, the school board lets the superintendent make policy. Instead of making proposals themselves, discussing them, and voting on them, school board members vote to approve the superintendent's suggestions, often with little discussion.

Second, the members of the school board seldom represent the public. Instead, they usually represent the professional educators, the school superintendent and his staff, often defending school practices the public objects to and in effect siding with the superintendent against the public when there is a question about how well the schools are doing their job. The most comprehensive survey of school boards to date states: "Rather than being representatives *of* the community, boards are more likely to be spokesmen *for* the superintendent *to the community*."

This relationship between the board and the superintendent is an outgrowth of the way most board members see their role. As surveys of school boards consistently show, members usually consider themselves elite trustees of education. They defer to the professional educator's judgment in decision making, and in many cases act as a buffer between the superintendent and the community. Yet studies also show that the public wants board members to act as the people's representatives in making decisions about education. This is not the hopeless stalemate it seems. As we'll see in the next chapter, there are effective ways for you and other people in the community to gain access to the board, and it is possible to identify and elect the types of board candidates who really will represent you and the rest of the community, instead of the school superintendent.

THE STATE AND FEDERAL ROLE IN YOUR SCHOOLS

The responsibility for educating children rests with individual states. Every state (except Hawaii, which has a single school district) has delegated much of this responsibility to its local school districts. But the state governments regulate such matters as school funding, standards for teacher certification, school attendance, general curriculum requirements, high school graduation requirements, and competency exams. In approximately half the states, local districts must choose books from a state-approved list. Districts in the remaining states choose their own books.

State legislatures make laws affecting education. State boards of education set policy and choose a chief state school official, who may have a title such as "commissioner of education" or "state superintendent of public instruction." A state department of education sees that schools throughout the state meet minimum guidelines. As we've mentioned in earlier chapters, your state's department of education can be an important information source if you have questions about such matters as parents' rights, education for gifted children, or special education.

A substantial portion of money spent on schools comes from local property taxes, as you're probably aware. The trend in recent years has been for more state spending on education, which usually brings with it more state control.

Though education is not mentioned in the Constitution as a function of federal government, Congress has passed a number of laws granting federal money to schools. Beginning with the National Defence Education Act in 1958 and the Elementary and Secondary Education Act (ESEA), formerly Title I, now Chapter 1, in 1965, there has been a steadily increasing flow of federal money into local schools. You are already familiar with the Rehabilitation Act of 1973 and the Education for All Handicapped Act passed in 1975 (see chapters 6 and 10). The federal government has also given schools money for educational television, drug abuse programs, audio visual equipment, and a host of other purposes. Often these programs have had little to do with real learning. In 1979 a costly federal Department of Education was set up. No public school today is without federal money and the federal regulation which goes with it.

In 1982 the Education Consolidation Improvement Act combined twenty-nine already-existing federal funding programs for schools into block grants under Chapter 2, which is designed to give states and local districts more control over federal money in their schools. But this has not decreased outlays of federal money for elementary, secondary, and vocational education, which increased from $4.2 billion in 1976 to $7.16 billion in 1981. The estimated outlay for 1985 is $7.66 billion, according to the Office of Management and Budget.

How does federal money affect your child's education? Unfortunately, federal funds have often promoted school programs that distract both children and teachers from the central task of schooling—learning reading, writing, and math. On the whole, federal programs aimed at improving these skills have not been successful.

In *Toward a Literate Society: The Report on Reading of the National Committee of Education,* a committee of educators examining the failure of Title I (ESEA) to solve the illiteracy problem and deliver better education to the underprivileged reported in 1975: "It is not cynical to suggest that the chief beneficiaries of the Elementary and Secondary Education Act have been members of the school system—both professional and paraprofessional—for whom new jobs were created. Seven years and as many billion dollars later, the children of the poor have not been 'compensated' as clearly as the employees of the school systems through this investment." Schools received more than $41 billion under Title I between 1965 and 1984. National scores on the Scholastic Aptitude Test (SAT) fell 43 points between 1966 and 1981.

Federal money has been used to encourage psychological experiments in the schools, including the model teacher education program called Behavior Science Teacher Education Program (BSTEP), set up in 1969. This doesn't refer to helping children "behave" in the commonly accepted sense of that term. Rather, it trains teachers in behavioral science and psychological manipulation, introducing into classrooms such activities as role playing, sociodrama, encounter groups, "Magic Circles," and other strategies originally developed to treat mental patients. These activities not only steal time from legitimate learning, but also tend to tear down traditional values and frequently disturb children by pressuring them to reveal private feelings to classmates and teachers.

Funds for schools came predominantly from local districts until the mid-'70s, when the combination of federal and state tax money spent on schools outstripped local funds in the U.S. as a whole. Despite increasing control of education by state and federal governments, many decisions vital to quality education are still left up to individual school districts, provided they meet minimum state requirements. For example, your superintendent and school board can still decide what teachers and principals to hire, how reading will be taught, and whether to stress the basics.

HOW TEACHERS' UNIONS FIGURE IN THE SCHOOL SETUP

The two major teachers' unions are the American Federation of Teachers and the National Education Association. The AFT, which has much of its strength in cities, numbers 580,000 members in 2100 local affiliates. NEA affiliates are often found in towns and suburbs and usually have names similar to the national group, the Lakeview Education Association, for example. Members of local education associations must also belong to the state education association and the NEA. The NEA is the largest union, with 1,600,000 members in 9200 of the nation's 15,300 school districts.

While the AFT became interested in teachers primarily to bolster the membership of organized labor, the NEA is dedicated to promoting a philosophy of education, as well as to getting better pay and working conditions for its members. Since critics believe this philosophy is largely responsible for many of our educational problems, it's important to have a clear idea of the NEA's role.

Since the early 1900s, the leaders of the NEA have been educators known as "progressives," as Samuel L. Blumenfeld points out in his recent book on the history of the union. Progressives believe the school's major function is to "socialize" children, teaching them to be useful members of a group. Like John Dewey, generally recognized as the father of progressive education, these educators believe that teaching academic skills is secondary.

Dewey, who believed in socialism, wanted education to promote it. In *The School and Society,* considered a classic by many educators, he wrote: "There is no obvious social motive for the acquirement of mere learning, there is no clear social gain in success thereat." When modern educators criticize the "back to basics" movement or warn against putting too much emphasis on academic subjects, they testify to the enduring influence of Dewey's contempt for "mere learning."

Modern progressives leading the NEA oppose many of the current proposals to improve the teaching of academic subjects and to make schools accountable to the public. In 1973 the union went to court to block release of statewide achievement test scores in New Jersey. The NEA has consistently lobbied for federal funds which help to make possible the psychological experimentation taking place in today's classrooms. The NEA objects to Department of Education regulations giving parents the right to inspect teaching materials, stating that this will lead to "classroom meddling" by parents and others who do not agree with NEA's philosophy. The union does not explain why it believes that parents who pay for the materials used in educating their children should not see those materials.

In addition to its other interests, the NEA, like the AFT, bargains hard for more pay, more influence in running schools, and improvements in working conditions for teachers. School boards often give in too easily to union demands. In bargaining, as in other matters, boards often do not question the superintendent's advice. This means your interests as a parent-taxpayer may be left out of the bargaining when the board and the superintendent agree to a contract with the teachers' union local of the AFT or NEA.

William Rioux of the NCCE suggests "trilateral" bargaining—allowing parents and other citizens to have an equal voice with school boards and unions in the negotiations. This system is a reality in Rochester, New York, where a parent-citizen representative has bona fide bargaining power.

In some districts parent-citizens can review or observe contract negotiations. A Florida law allows the public to attend collective-bargaining sessions and citizens have some part in the proceedings. Four or five other states provide for citizen review or observing of negotiations. California's Rodda Act provides that before negotiations begin, the school board must state at a public meeting what it plans to offer the union. Citizens have an opportunity to review other proposals during the bargaining process. But these states are exceptions. In many states with "sunshine" laws (laws requiring official acts to take place in public) public contract bargaining is exempted.

You can find out from your local school officials or from the office of the county superintendent of schools whether citizens in your district and state can review or observe teachers' contract bargaining. If parent-citizens could review proposals or observe bargaining sessions, they would learn how effective the board is in getting more real education (as opposed to overstaffing or protection of teachers' jobs in questionable school programs) for their tax dollars.

THE TERRITORY: DISTRICTS, SCHOOLS, AND CLASSES

It is impossible to understand the school setup—districts, schools, classes—without speaking of numbers and size. In 1945, there were 160,000 separate school districts throughout the United States, according to the National Center for Education Statistics. Today, after nationwide consolidation, there are 15,300 districts, serving roughly twice as many students as in 1945. More than half of today's students attend school in districts of 10,000 students or more. The number of school districts varies widely from state to state, ranging from Hawaii's single, state-controlled school district to 1000 districts each in Illinois, California, Nebraska, and Texas.

Most states have between 200 and 400 separate school districts, instead of the thousands of smaller districts that existed before World War II. School consolidation, the movement to combine schools under larger administrative units that began in the '40s and gained momentum in the '50s, is largely completed now. The term "unified" is sometimes used to refer to smaller school units combined to form larger ones. "Unified" can also mean that a school district includes both elementary and high schools, as is the case in more than two thirds of the nation's school districts.

Turning small schools and districts into large ones was supposed to make school operation more efficient, giving us better education for less money. Yet in terms of 1983 dollars we spent only $866 to educate the average public school student in 1950, while in 1983 we spent $2948, according to latest NCES figures. And in 1984, with costs still climbing, achievement scores dropped in New York City and in California, which have two of the largest groups of students in the nation. New York reading scores declined by 2.6 percent from 1983. In California, twelfth-grade reading scores "declined by the largest margin in seven years," according to a report in the May 16, 1984 issue of *Education Week*. The average achievement of high school students nationwide is lower now than it was in the mid-'60s. We can't know what the costs or the achievement record might have been without consolidation, of course.

But it's plain that education is both far more costly in real dollars and far less effective than it was four or five decades ago.

Bigness Means Less Control for Parent-Citizens

Parents and citizens find it more difficult to exercise control over their children's education as schools and districts get bigger. A study by Dr. Cliff Eagleton of school districts having more than 10,000 students points up three "large district" problems of special interest to parents who want to be involved:

1.   School boards are less likely to be representative of the community, because running huge districts takes special expertise in finance, policy making, and so on. Ordinary citizens may feel reluctant to run for board seats. Board members feel far removed from what goes on in the classroom.

2.   Superintendents and principals in a large bureaucracy are more apt to react to inquiries by being defensive and secretive. The survey compared the leadership styles of principals and administrators in small districts with those in large districts. Possible styles ranged from open, organized, and task oriented (best) to a closed style that included playing favorites (worst). In small districts (approximately 1500 to 5000 students) half of the principals and administrators showed the more desirable characteristics, while the other half showed less desirable characteristics. In an extremely large system, nearly all of those surveyed showed a preponderance of the worst leadership traits. "This doesn't mean that there are no talented administrators in big school systems," Eagleton says. But he adds, "The system defeats them, so even the best ones eventually say, 'Why should I fight it?' "

3.   Unions find it easier to wield power in huge, consolidated districts. They usually oppose attempts to break up or "decentralize" large school districts.

Dr. Eagleton recommends breaking up large districts. In a magazine article, he writes: "No one person or policy board is smart enough to manage massive-sized school districts. Smaller school districts should have two consequences. First, boards of education made up of ordinary people will be able to direct their purposes. The return of grass-roots involvement will reinstill strong decision-making capacity at the local level of society. Second, smaller school districts will allow the leadership to respond more quickly to situations that arise . . . and resolve problems before they have time to fester and become unnecessarily complex."

Some large city systems, including those in Los Angeles, New York, and Detroit, have been decentralized in an effort to give citizens some control over their schools. Yet even if local neighborhood groups throughout the city have a voice, decentralization is not the same as having separate districts, each with its own power to tax and the control that goes with it.

Bigness at the school level is criticized by several educators who have written recent commentaries on school problems, including Ernest Boyer and John I. Goodlad. Dr. Eagleton notes that in large high schools only a small percentage of students can be part of student government or play any role in decision making. A big high school may offer only 2 percent of its students an opportunity to take part in athletics, while a small one, despite limited facilities, may get as many as 20 percent of its students involved on teams. A common argument in favor of large high schools is that they can offer a richer assortment of courses. But offering too many choices often leads students to bypass the rigorous courses in favor of the trivial.

Bigness also affects students in more subtle ways. The nurse in a high school of several thousand students says, "We get a lot of kids coming in here just because they're lonely. Some are freshmen, but there are older ones, too. I think they feel lost in the crowd. They know that if they come in here, someone has to talk to them."

The two groups that have benefitted from the trend toward bigness in education are school administrators and teachers' unions. Administrators draw higher pay for running big districts and big schools. In addition, building a bureaucracy encourages specialization, increasing the need for high-salaried administrators. Teachers' unions favor big systems and big schools because it is easier to bargain with and to gain control of a few large units than many smaller ones.

Being aware of the arguments against big schools, you and other parent/citizens may be able to inform board members that moves to combine school units for "economy" may actually result in higher costs and a less satisfactory school environment for students.

Do Smaller Classes Help Children Learn?

When it comes to class size, administrators and unions do not look kindly on bigness. How big should a class be? Is a class of thirty too large? If we could reduce class size to ten students per teacher, would children learn better? Most educators would answer yes to the last two questions. To many noneducators, as well, having fewer students per teacher seems like a logical way to boost learning. Yet this is not supported by research. In fact, the well-known comparative study of private and public schools by sociologists James Coleman, Thomas Hoffer, and Sally Kilgore shows that students learn more in Catholic schools, which have larger classes than do their public school counterparts. Of course, this doesn't mean that larger classes per se help students to learn. Rather it suggests that factors other than class size play the major role in determining student achievement.

National figures show that in the early '60s, before the current achievement decline began, there were twenty-six pupils per teacher. By 1975, when achievement was careening downward, there were only twenty pupils per teacher. As the decline in student achievement continued on into the '80s, so did the decline in the number of pupils per teacher. Latest available NCES figures (1982–83) show only eighteen to nineteen pupils per teacher in our schools.

Why is smaller class size not a guarantee of better learning? A parent whose child "wasn't learning much" in an advanced Spanish class of only eight students (this in a private school) had it figured right when she said, "That teacher ran the class as if there were forty students." Learning won't increase with fewer students per teacher unless the teacher adjusts his or her approach to take advantage of the smaller-sized classes, giving more homework, more individual attention, more time for recitation, and so on.

Assuming teachers make these adjustments, there are two areas where a lighter teaching load may be justified: in beginning reading classes and in high school English composition classes. In Florida it is state law that high school English classes have fewer students so teachers can give proper attention to writing assignments. If your schools reduce class size, promising parent/citizens that better learning will result, ask for test scores or other hard evidence that students are learning better. Without such monitoring, smaller classes may result only in less work for the teacher and higher cost for the taxpayer, which so far have been the only discernible results of decreasing the number of students per teacher in our public schools.

NEW APPROACHES TO SCHOOL MANAGEMENT AND PARENT INPUT

One antidote to many of the ills of centrally controlled schools is a system of management known as "shared governance." Salt Lake City, Utah, has used shared governance to run its schools since the mid-'70s. Every school has two councils that make decisions about operating the building and planning the academic program. Though major decisions about the curriculum are made by the principal and teachers, who make up the "improvement council" for each school, parents do have a voice. Eight parent representatives and the school principal sit on the "school-community council." As we've noted before, educators in general have resisted giving parents any meaningful role in curriculum decisions, but the Salt Lake City plan is an encouraging step in the right direction.

Dr. M. Donald Thomas, who instituted shared governance as superintendent of schools in Salt Lake City, believes it is responsible for the rise in student scores on national tests and the drop in absenteeism in the district over the past decade. Only a few other cities, including Jackson, Mississippi, and Tulsa, Oklahoma, have a similar system of school management.

In recent years approximately three fifths of the states have acknowledged the need for greater parent participation in public schools by passing laws requiring that parents and other citizens (in addition to school board members) be involved in the schools in some way. But these laws usually fail to give parents policy-making power or the influence they are likely to have in systems using shared governance. In most cases, the parent-citizen groups have names like "Citizen Advisory Committee," which indicate a nonpolicy function. Among other states requiring advisory groups are Alaska and Pennsylvania.

School-based or on-site management, as the name implies, decentralizes control of schooling so that those closest to individual groups of students do the planning for them. Under this system, principals usually have more control over who is hired to teach in their schools. Although school-based management can be set up with the principal in his traditional role as sole school decision maker, some believe the system is more effective if a council of parents and teachers share in making decisions for each school.

This system of management began attracting attention in the late '70s and is now mandated in California, Florida, and South Carolina. Other states are considering similar legislation, and Boston is in the process of putting school-based management into operation in some of its schools. In South Carolina, each school must set up a "school advisory council" consisting of the principal, parents, teachers, students (in the case of a high school), "other members of the community," and "other persons" selected by the principal. Two thirds of the council must be elected. The law states that "each council shall assist in the preparation of the annual school reports . . . and shall provide such assistance as the principal may request as well as carrying out any other duties prescribed by the local school board." This means that the influence of the council in each school, and therefore of parents, aside from their role in preparing the report, will be largely determined by the board and the principal.

In California, two out of three elementary schools have school improvement councils made up of parents, teachers, and staff members elected to the councils by their peers. The function of the council in each school is to identify problems that prevent children from achieving and to come up with solutions.

There are numerous other variations of school-based management, depending on who does the planning and what decisions are left up to individual schools. A switch to school-based management may simply mean giving the principal control over hiring teachers for his building, rather than having them chosen by the central district office.

Now that you know a bit more about the school setup than you knew before, how can you put this knowledge to work for your child and your schools? First, use this chapter as a resource for information and evidence about what changes in schools are most likely to result in real improvements in education. As we've seen, some changes, shared governance, for example, can result in giving parents more of a voice and in raising student achievement. Other changes, such as smaller classes, often don't deliver the improvements they promise. Ask for evidence. Second, remind yourself how the setup is *supposed* to operate in your school district, with the board representing the community and making school policy, which the superintendent then carries out. Although things do not work this way, the shared assumption that they do can make it possible for citizens like you to influence what happens in your schools. In the next chapters, we'll take a close look at how you and other parents can bring about needed school improvements.

12

HOW TO USE PARENT POWER
TO IMPROVE YOUR SCHOOLS

Many parents—you may be one of them—are convinced they're not qualified to judge. The premise of this book is that your common sense, your own years in school, and your experience as your child's first teacher are important qualifications. You as a parent can tell the difference between good teachers and ineffective teachers, between good school programs and bad ones. In fact, parents are often better judges of what will work and what won't than professional educators are.

Consider the open classroom craze which began in the late '60s and early '70s. Educational experts decided that classrooms didn't need walls, that students from kindergarten right on through junior high school should be free to move around at will, and that children should be allowed to choose what, when, and how they would learn. Instead of instructing students directly, teachers were to play a passive role as "facilitators" of learning. Educators introduced open, unstructured learning without careful testing to find out whether it really helped children achieve.

Very few parents thought the open classroom idea would work. They were dismayed—but not surprised—to find that open classrooms and the new teaching methods too often resulted in confusion and the waste of valuable learning time. Skeptical parents were told by educators that the new methods would help children become more creative. Educators largely ignored the possible relationship between the general decline in academic achievement and the experiments with open learning. They also ignored research, including an extensive four-year study, which showed that structured, disciplined teaching helps all types of children to make greater gains in reading, math, and other academic skills than they can make in an open classroom setting. The same study showed that open learning does not help children to become more confident and creative.

The open classrooms experiment would have been short-lived in most schools if parents had had more of a say. You do have a right to speak up, to comment directly on what goes on in the classroom. You're paying for it now. Your child will pay later if the school isn't doing a good job.

Children whose parents are active in school and develop good rapport with the school people show higher levels of self-esteem and reading achievement, according to several studies. Parents who are interested and involved in the school often transfer their own confidence and sense of control to their children. Teachers and principals will get the message, too. Having a parent who's concerned, helpful, and visible is bound to bolster a child's image with school people.

At this point you may be convinced being involved in your child's school is worthwhile—and equally convinced that you can't spare the hours it takes to sew costumes for the class play or run the spring fund-raiser. There are other ways to let the school know you're there. This chapter covers the recent concern about upgrading schools, which has encouraged parents' groups across the country to take a more aggressive stance working for changes in their schools. You'll find you don't have to attend meetings to make your presence known at school or to donate your talent as a volunteer.

THE NEW LOOK IN PARENTS' GROUPS
Parent Teacher Associations exist in every state and in the District of Columbia. The PTA and similar organizations for parents have spent much time and energy raising money for new slide projectors and serving refreshments at holiday parties. Pleasant as these activities are, they don't affect what happens in the classroom. One parent advocate speaks of these parents' groups as "company unions." They can be counted on to support any proposal of the school administration with no questions asked.

More than ten years ago, the national PTA eliminated a bylaw stating that PTA groups would not "interfere" in school administration, so local PTA's now have more freedom to work for school improvements. A number of local PTA's have taken a more aggressive stance in dealing with school problems in recent years. Some have provided parent advocates. If your school has a PTA, joining can give you an entrée into the system, and help you learn about local issues, board policies, and state and federal school legislation.

Despite these changes, the PTA has not overcome its image of being too eager to cooperate with educators at the expense of holding them accountable to parents. Critics point out that having school people as part of the group stifles parent efforts to discuss and remedy shortcomings in local schools. Now many separate, local parents' groups shun cupcakes and busy work in their determination to make a real contribution to upgrading their schools. Some exemplary groups:

Philadelphia Parents' Union. This 4000-member group sprang up in the mid-'70s during the rash of teachers' strikes. A group of parents responding to a television editorial which said parents didn't care about the strikes sparked interest in forming the Union. Says Director Christine Davis: "Parents had no voice, and they were not aware of their rights in dealing with public schools. We try to educate them." The Union holds parent workshops and acts as an advocate for individual parents in solving school problems.

The Parent Educational Research Committee (PERC) of Verona, Wisconsin, provides a core of ten or twelve volunteers who serve as a resource and back-up group for parents who need help in dealing with a wide variety of school issues. Study and work by PERC leaders led to reapportionment of the school district, giving a voice to residents who had not been represented.

United Parents Associations of New York City serves as an "umbrella" for 350 parents' groups, about one third of the parents' groups in New York City public schools. UPA policy is set by delegates from member groups voting in a monthly assembly. The UPA trains parent leaders and represents parents at school board meetings.

United Parents for Neshaminy in Langhorne, Pennsylvania, was organized to deal with parents' problems during a teachers' strike. Afterward, though the group dwindled, Parents for Neshaminy helped solve a textbook shortage and persuaded schools not to drop foreign language courses.

In the past eight or ten years local school-improvement groups have succeeded in tackling such difficult problems as school discipline and removal of incompetent school personnel. Here are samples from NCCE files:

Parents in a western school district found the superintendent unwilling to deal with their requests for needed changes. Though he had powerful allies on the school board, these parents banded together and managed to get the superintendent replaced.

Though the law in their state permits corporal punishment, parents in one district abolished it in their schools.

In an elementary school where children and parents were confused by arbitrarily invoked rules for behavior and discipline, a parents' group persuaded the principal to explain the disciplinary policy and supply guidelines for students, teachers, and parents.

Perhaps you're fortunate enough to have a parents' group working to improve schools in your area. By joining it, you may boost your child's performance in school and help to make the school a better one. If there is no such group, you can join with other parents to start one. These tips come from William Rioux and the staff of the NCCE:

1. Contact parents through the school, through community organizations, or by writing a letter to the local newspaper.

2. To gauge the reaction of school officials to such a group, inform them of plans to start one, perhaps inviting a top administrator to attend a meeting as a guest, not as a member.

3. Elect officers for short terms at first, to keep leadership flexible.

4. Begin by tackling a problem you have a good chance of solving. For example, convincing the school that children need more time to use the school library may seem like a small beginning, but you can build on it. Avoid issues that might require more strength and knowledge than your new group has.

Starting with a large enthusiastic group and having it shrink is a problem common to many parents' groups. Says Daniel Safran of the Center for the Study of Parent Involvement in Oakland, California: "Parents who are active must accept that many parents won't be active, but there is a need to keep *all* parents well informed. Have a newsletter that lets parents know what's going on in school, written from the parents' point of view."

What if you already belong to a school support group, but it isn't accomplishing much in the way of constructive change in your school? You and other parents could start a new one. A number of parents' groups began this way. In a small New England school district which already had a parent-teacher organization (PTO), several parents decided they needed a "parents-only" group to examine the budget and other possible problem areas. Other parents joined them. Suspecting that administrative costs for their schools were too high, the new group launched a full-scale budget study to find out how their district compared with similar districts in administrative costs.

You may not have to start a new group to accomplish your goal. "Try to use a cadre within the group to ignite enthusiasm," says Anne Henderson of the NCCE. If even a few other members feel as you do, perhaps you can work from within to urge members to take a firmer stand on school problems. This strategy often works, and even if it doesn't, it may prove worthwhile, because the members who feel change is necessary can form the core of a new group.

The NCCE serves as a source of information and as a clearinghouse for more than 350 independent school groups with a wide variety of goals. To find out about the parents' group nearest you, contact the NCCE (see Glossary for address).

BEING A VOLUNTEER CAN MAKE YOU AN INSIDER

"Can you tell me what's different about this picture?" the woman asks. As third-graders watch intently, she holds up a reproduction of a painting that shows people in a nineteenth-century park setting.

"I know!" A tiny girl waves her hand. "It's got dots all over it. Everywhere you look it has dots. We never had a picture like that before."

"That's right." The woman motions the children in the back rows to come up so they can see better. "Georges Seurat, who painted this picture, dotted the paint onto the canvas, instead of putting it on in brush strokes . . ."

The woman is a school volunteer, part of the Picture Lady program, which brings reproductions of famous paintings into elementary-school classrooms. Other school volunteers may offer students one-to-one tutoring or help teachers conduct field trips. Parents with unusual travel experience can add special interest to classes in geography, language, and history. In some schools volunteer parents help school nurses and other staff people screen children for hearing or vision problems.

Even if you have no time during the school day, you may still become part of an existing volunteer program. The school may need adults who can arrange for tours of their office or factory to help students learn about careers. At least one volunteer program—INVEST in District 65 in Evanston, Illinois—enlists parents and other citizens to talk with students over the phone about special interests or school projects.

As a volunteer you can add a plus to school programs, and at the same time enhance your image as a helpful, interested parent. Working inside the school, you may have a chance to observe the following:

How it feels to answer questions from twenty or thirty second-graders whose hands shoot up at exactly the same instant.

How teachers and other school people cooperate with one another.

How the general atmosphere of the school—quiet or noisy, friendly or strained—affects the way children behave and learn.

How classrooms differ: One is all business, the next disorganized. In one, children learn eagerly; in the next they plod or gaze out the window.

The prime purpose of school volunteer programs like INVEST in Evanston is to match what the community and its citizens have to offer with the needs of its schools. INVEST, organized in 1980, asks potential volunteers to fill out a questionnaire noting talents, training, occupation, or travel experience that they could share with students in local elementary classrooms. Teachers are kept informed about the types of help or programs volunteers are prepared to give and ask INVEST to match them with someone who can present the program or give the assistance they need in class. In a recent year INVEST provided volunteers to help with staging and costumes for a play, speak to students about city planning, help children with projects, work in the school library, tell stories, and act as guides for school field trips. The program's volunteers include not only parents, but also students from nearby Northwestern University and employees of local businesses.

Your superintendent's office can tell you whether there is a volunteer program in your district. If it doesn't use volunteers, maybe the district would be willing to consider starting such a program. An existing parents' group might act as a catalyst and provide the initial pool of volunteers. Keep these tips in mind:

Some school districts without a full-fledged volunteer program simply send home questionnaires in September asking parents to contribute time and talents, and then let teachers know that these people are available.

State law, the union representing teachers in your district, or district policy may limit the use of volunteers in the schools. Check with the district or county superintendent's office or the state board of education.

Once you have preliminary plans for starting a volunteer program—a statement of purpose, volunteers available, a list of services you could perform for students and teachers—the next step is getting school board approval. As the governing body of the school district, the board makes policy and approves new programs.

Some volunteer programs are highly organized, long-standing efforts to bring citizen help into the schools. Rhode Island, for example, has a statewide program, Volunteers in Rhode Island Schools (VIRIS), which stresses individual tutoring of students. Other volunteer service may be temporary and informal. One midwestern school district about to set up a computer program asked for input from people in the community who had special expertise in the use of computers. School people were able to get the advice they needed in two or three evening planning meetings with the volunteer group.

There are more than 1100 school volunteer groups throughout the country with 4.3 million members, according to the National School Volunteer Program, Inc., which offers training for directors of these groups. For more information about school volunteering, contact the NSVP (see Glossary for address).

HOW THE DIRECT APPROACH PAYS OFF

Joining with other parents can be essential if there's a problem to solve at school, or if you want to have a part in school activities and be counted publicly as a supporter. But if your schedule makes it impossible to attend meetings, you do have other options. As an individual, you can use the direct approach.

The idea of the direct approach is simple. You take a good look at how the school is helping your child to learn, and you let school people know when you think they're doing a good job and when you think there's room for improvement. The direct approach works best if you follow a few ground rules: be positive, be specific, and put your comments in writing.

Praising good teachers and good school programs is a good way to get more of the same. Psychologists call it positive reinforcement, and it does work. One father tells his experience: "Sue enrolled in a new class for students who wrote well and wanted to improve their writing skills still further. The students in the class also tutored students who had problems with writing. Sue liked tutoring, and she told me she had learned more about writing in a few weeks in this special class than in her previous two years of English. She said other students in the class felt the same way. Then we heard rumors the class might be discontinued. I let the teacher and the principal know how enthusiastic Sue, other students, and I were about this class, and it was not discontinued. I can't claim I saved it singlehandedly, but I think my comments helped."

I have heard parents say they feel their compliment to a child's teacher might be misinterpreted. "What if he thinks I'm only trying to help Eric get a better grade?" Frankly, I wouldn't worry too much about this if your comment is sincere and specific, and if your communication with the teacher is good.

If you are concerned, wait until all the reports are in before you send the teacher a note. Bad teachers deserve bad publicity, but good teachers deserve recognition. Here's a sample appreciative note:

Dear Mr. Jones:

My son Tom was in your seventh-grade social studies class this past year. He enjoyed the class and I think he learned a lot. We were impressed by the way the projects fit in with the rest of the work students did, and we also liked the idea of giving students many quizzes instead of just a few long tests.

Thanks for your hard work.

Sincerely,
Ted and Alice Smith

Specific comments not only sound more sincere, they also let the people at school know you pay close attention to what's going on in class. Is your third-grader, who used to hate math and have trouble with it, learning well and loving it this year? Is your sixth-grader's geography book interesting, clear, well organized? In a note to the teacher, tell her how pleased you are that her approach to math has helped your child. Let the sixth-grade teacher know exactly why you think the geography book is such a good one. As you can see, these messages are different from saying to the teacher on parents' night, "You're doing a great job!"

A note gets people's attention, and it's literally something for good teachers to hang on to. When you send the teacher a complimentary message, send a copy to the principal and perhaps to the superintendent and president of the school board, too. Don't make this mistake: A superintendent was pleased to receive a note from a parent praising the work a third-grade teacher had done with her child. When the superintendent mentioned the note to the teacher, he discovered she knew nothing about it. The parent had sent the note only to the superintendent!

Sending copies is important, not only to tell administrators that a teacher is doing a good job, but also to let them know what parents want. A principal who gets a letter telling him you're pleased with the way Ms. R. teaches reading may decide to take a second look at how well reading is taught in other classrooms in his school.

A final note on the direct approach: When you think school people are doing a good job, when you feel a good school program needs support, spread the word by writing a letter to the editor of your local paper. Let everyone know that teachers at your school have worked hard to strengthen the science program. If you think your school needs a new library instead of the new gymnasium that's been proposed, a letter to the editor may help to sway opinion your way.

Teachers do appreciate helpful suggestions from parents. My son's fourth-grade teacher had been teaching only a year or two when he was in her class. During a conference I mentioned her effective method for helping students learn the multiplication tables. She gave a certificate to each child as he passed a series of short tests on multiplication facts. "I got the idea of giving awards from a parent last year," she told me. "Frankly, I wasn't having much luck getting them to learn multiplication until I tried this." Like many other teachers, she had been taught by education professors that it was poor practice to have children memorize or to give them awards for learning. It took a tip from a parent to remind her that some things can be learned only by committing them to memory and that children often do learn better if there's a reward.

Often you can start on a positive note even when you feel something is definitely wrong with the school program. Your note to the principal might read: "Last year, in fifth grade, my son was very enthusiastic about the science program, and I felt it was a good one, too. This year he's disappointed because the sixth-graders get so little work in science. Would it be possible to spend more time on science in sixth grade so that students would be better prepared for junior high work in science? . . ."

A message like this gets the point across without ruffling feathers unnecessarily. You may want to meet with the principal to find out what she thinks would be needed to improve the sixth-grade science program, and whether parents could help by talking with the district's curriculum supervisor or other school officials.

One parent told me about her own even more direct approach to involvement with her children's schooling. During the year she keeps a record of her children's progress, of their teachers' strengths and weaknesses, and of the general atmosphere of the school. At the end of each year she makes an appointment with the principal and talks over her findings.

I asked her how the principals reacted. She said, "They're usually surprised, but they always listen." She adds, "Schools send report cards to parents, and I think parents should pay enough attention to what goes on in school to do some reporting of their own."

If you decide to follow her example, be sure to make an appointment. Point out what pleases you about the school, as well as what you think needs improvement. And, once again, be specific. "You and the teachers here all do a wonderful job for our children," may be an accurate comment about your school, but this comment is more meaningful: "Jane has done a lot more reading in her free time this year, thanks to the minilibrary Mrs. Y. set up in her classroom. This seems like an idea that would work well in any class."

CITIZENS TAKE DIRECT ACTION

Direct parent action has often filled a void left by educators.

Parents in Birmingham, Michigan, alarmed at the number of children who seemed to have reading problems, founded the National Forum for Educational Awareness. The Forum will sponsor courses by reading specialists who can help teachers learn the most effective methods of reading instruction. Teachers, who say that colleges of education did not train them to teach reading, welcomed the chance to learn. By special arrangement with a major university, they will receive college credit for Forum courses.

Gail Kessler tells of a Boston high school in which administrators refused even to acknowledge racial violence, though there had been incidents of bloodshed and parents feared for children's safety. A parent task force went into the school and documented racial tensions. They publicized the problem, held court hearings, and finally managed to get new administrators who dealt with the situation.

The role played by publicity in this case is worth noting. If only a small group of parents are aware of and concerned about a school problem—whether it's violence or lack of good reading instruction—it is easy for school officials to do nothing. But if you publicize the problem, you will gain allies in the community at large. Remember that all citizens pay taxes and all have a stake in getting full value for education dollars. Business people need well-educated employees. When schools do a good job of teaching the basics, fewer people will need welfare.

Businesses as well as parents have pitched in to improve schools. Large and small corporations have made important contributions, donating money and employee time and know-how in volunteer programs. Few have been better targeted or more successful than a project sponsored by the publisher of the *Northeast Mississippi Daily Journal* in Tupelo, Mississippi. He pledged to donate $1 million to county schools over a ten-year period, provided they use the money to improve the teaching of reading. The funds bought new textbooks and a testing program to monitor results and made it possible to hire teachers' aides for first-grade classes. Since Mississippi teachers were not unionized, the uncertified aides were able to do some of the actual teaching which helped boost children's reading achievement.

The results were impressive. In 1976 students in county public schools scored in the 23rd percentile (below 77 percent of students nationwide) on the California Achievement Test (CAT) in reading. By 1982 their reading scores on the CAT had climbed to the 62nd percentile (below only 38 percent of students nationwide). In 1982 the state legislature appropriated money to put the program in every school in Mississippi.

In the final chapter you will learn how you and other parents and citizens, working through your elected representatives, can press for fundamental changes in your school system.

13

MAKE YOUR VOTE COUNT FOR BETTER EDUCATION

> "If Johnny can't read, call your governor,
> school board member, legislator and council-
> man. If Johnny can't read after one more year,
> get a new governor, school board member,
> legislator, or councilman. You'll be surprised
> how well that system works."
>
> —LAMAR ALEXANDER,
> Governor of Tennessee

Elected officials are more responsive to public opinion than are school administrators, who often refuse to accept—or even listen to—the views of "nonexpert" parents and other citizens. Parental input to school board members (or other elected officials) can spur dramatic improvements in school programs. For example, a few years ago, following its usual practice, a suburban elementary school tested sixth-graders to decide which children could enroll in seventh-grade foreign language class. Administrators said two thirds of the children scored too low to succeed. The parents of one of these students, Jim, asked that he be allowed to enroll anyway on a trial basis. The principal refused. When the parents asked him to explain just how the tests predicted success in studying a foreign language, they discovered that the tests were not specifically designed to do this. They also found that the "cutoff" score was fixed arbitrarily to exclude the majority of students. The school superintendent also refused to listen to their plea. They were told it was board policy to follow this procedure in choosing students for foreign language classes.

Jim's parents decided to appear before the school board to explain what they had learned about the tests. They also pointed out the unfairness of presuming students would fail at foreign language study without first giving them a chance to try. They noted that in all other school courses and activities, including advanced math classes, cheerleading, and the school band, students were not excluded until they had been given a fair chance to try out.

Jim's parents made only two brief appearances before the board, but members were sufficiently impressed with their arguments to study the issue on their own. Several months later they changed the policy for admission to junior high foreign language classes, giving parents a say in the decision. Now many more seventh-graders get a two-year head start in learning a second language.

Will your school board listen when you present your case? That depends not only on how you approach the board but also on the makeup of the board itself. Let's take a closer look at how Jim's parents succeeded in persuading their school board to reconsider the foreign language class policy:

1.   They began by talking to the principal and the superintendent, following the lines of authority. In some cases it may not be wise to tell administrators you plan to go to the board, since they can put your case in an unfavorable light by speaking to board members first.

2.   The issue involved policy. Is the policy valid? Should students be judged incapable of studying a foreign language without being given a chance to try it? Should parents have a say in whether children are allowed to enroll in such a class? Policy is officially the board's responsibility.

3.   Jim's parents had done some investigating and came to the board prepared to report the facts. They had found that the tests being used were not intended to predict who could and who could not succeed in learning a language. They pointed out the discrep-

ancy between the procedure used in selecting students for foreign language classes and that used in selecting students for other classes and activities in the school. They were able to show that the policy was unfair to the majority of students.

Follow these guidelines and you have a good chance of convincing at least one member of the board that the problem you point out needs attention. You can approach the board as an individual or with a group of parents. Because school board meetings are not very well attended by the public most of the time, even a relatively few parents concerned about the same issue can seem like an imposing group. As one parent said, commenting on his successful appeal to the school board, "We took along ten or twelve people—enough to outnumber the school board members and administrators."

Surprisingly, a study reported by the Institute for Responsive Education (IRE) found that *individual* presentations to the board or individual private contacts with school board members (or with the superintendent) often get better response than group presentations and contacts. This means that simply talking to an individual board member may be more effective than marching into a board meeting with a delegation of parents. The reason for this may be that a private talk with a board member does give you the obvious advantage of not having to compete for attention with a busy agenda. This doesn't explain why individual parents appearing at a public board meeting are apt to do better than a group in swaying board opinion. But it does show that what you have to say may be even more important than how many people you can bring to a meeting— good news for busy parents, since organizing a group takes time.

When you decide to bring a problem to the school board, you can choose from among four approaches: An individual or a group contacting a board member; an individual or a group appearing at a board meeting. Your choice, of course, will depend on the problem, the people involved, and what your aim is. For example, if you want to gain widespread attention for an issue, appearing at a public meeting is essential. The IRE study notes that in general, it's best to present *information* in formal public settings and use private contacts with board members (or the superintendent) to make *requests* or *proposals*.

No matter which approach you choose, consider these comments from a longtime board member who has also served on the Federal Relations Network of the National Association of School Boards: "Most school boards want to stay in tune with public goals, but they're leery of narrow special-interest groups. From the board's standpoint, the trick is to get past the special interests and see the overall needs . . . If you plan to go to the board with a problem, don't begin by airing it in a letter to the editor of the local paper, or by just showing up at a public meeting. School boards don't like surprises. The best approach is to write a brief, factual letter stating your concerns and asking to be put on the agenda."

As you'll recall, Jim's parents were told by the superintendent that the foreign language class selection procedure was a matter of board policy. Hearing this, many parents would have given up, believing the superintendent was making excuses to deny their request. Very likely he was. But don't be too quick to assume an administrator is stalling deliberately. The IRE study suggests some administrators are genuinely uncertain of whether they have authority to deal with a policy matter or grant a request. The problem arises because the school board often gives the superintendent such broad powers that the line between its authority and his is blurred.

Often, as in the case of Jim's parents, when administrators say something is a matter for the board, they are both telling the truth and trying to discourage parents from going any further. An administrator may urge parents to "take it up with the board," assuming, of course, they will not. Remember, communicating with your school board may be easier than you expect.

WHERE TO GET HELP WHEN YOU NEED IT

If you and other parents want to present a problem to the school board (after determining that it is a policy issue and after following the lines of authority from teacher to principal to superintendent), the first step is organizing. Chapter 12 contains suggestions about forming an independent parents' group or convincing your present parents' group that action is needed. If you have the interest and support of a large group behind you, so much the better, but it doesn't take a large group to gather information and talk to school administrators or board members. A handful of determined parents is better than a hundred with lukewarm commitment.

Once you have a working group, your greatest need will be

facts and information. This is particularly true if you and other parents feel improvements are needed in your school's academic program. Board members are used to going along with the directives of the superintendent's staff people when it comes to curriculum. In the eyes of the board, these professionals are experts who have all the answers. To be convincing when you ask for changes in academic programs, you'll need solid evidence there is a better way of doing things.

For example, perhaps parents in your school have found that many children are in remedial reading classes and reading scores in general are low. Children are taught primarily by being asked to memorize "sight" words. Much "reading" time is spent on busy-work dittos and workbooks, which will not help them learn to read. How can you convince the school board that direct (intensive) phonics would be better for children? You can get the information you need—usually at little cost—by making a phone call or writing a brief letter. For reading information, write or call the Reading Reform Foundation (RRF) (see Glossary for address). The RRF can send you statistics showing the gains in reading scores made by a number of schools in many parts of the country which have switched to direct phonics. They can also put you in touch with school superintendents, principals, and teachers who have seen how this reading method improves children's learning. Testimony from other school people is the most effective evidence you can offer board members, administrators, and teachers in your schools that they should consider a change. RRF can send a list of intensive phonics programs suitable for use by parents or teachers.

For any questions you have about your school's (elementary or high school) academic program, an excellent source of information is the Council for Basic Education (see Glossary). For reading information, ask for publication OP17, "Phonics in Beginning Reading: A Guide for Teachers and Parents." The CBE is a nonprofit group dedicated to promoting greater emphasis on and better teaching of academic subjects. Their Occasional Papers are aimed at parents and other noneducators who want to promote basic learning in local schools. Other CBE publications deal with such subjects as minimum competency testing, written composition, mathematics teaching, elementary-school science, and more. Send for a publications list.

When you and other parents ask for changes in the school's

academic program, you can expect resistance from the superintendent and his curriculum staff. They have invested a good deal of professional ego, not to mention a good part of the school budget, in the programs you are trying to change. Charles Micciche, the New Hampshire school superintendent mentioned in chapter 11, offers this advice for suggesting a change to school officials (he is advising teachers, but parents can heed the same advice): "Everyone resists change, and school administrators tend to be a most conservative lot. Go slowly, propose trials, keep the threat of permanency out of your plan; this will more readily gain acceptance. Timing and patience are critical."

If you and other parents want to push for a change in the reading program, you could present copies of the *updated* edition of Dr. Jeanne Chall's *Learning to Read: The Great Debate* (McGraw-Hill 1983) to a school board member, the superintendent or curriculum coordinator, and a teacher or two. Ask that the method Dr. Chall recommends be given a trial by having one or two teachers trained in direct (intensive) phonics for teaching primary children.

In suggesting any change, avoid downgrading current programs or the people responsible for them. Concentrate on calling attention to the probable advantages of trying out a new method of doing things.

When you and other parents present suggestions to the board, you'll be in a stronger position if you can anticipate objections and plan your strategy accordingly. No two school situations are exactly the same, of course, but here's how you may be able to handle two of the most common objections:

"The budget is tight. We can't consider changes because we just don't have the money." If you're trying to promote better teaching of the basics, your answer to this objection should please every member of the board. Consider the cost figures for one school that switched reading programs. The cost per pupil for reading materials in 1978 was $23.42. Then teachers were trained in direct (intensive) phonics, and by 1981 this school was spending only $8.50 per pupil for reading materials, according to Dr. George Roche, chairman of the National Council for Educational Research (NCER). More important, reading scores for this school were higher than for any other school in the district.

Looking at the cost of improving writing instruction, you can point out that grammar workbooks (which do not teach real writing skills) cost several dollars per pupil, while plain sheets of paper required for real writing cost only pennies.

Marva Collins, who founded Chicago's successful Westside Preparatory School, cites *too much* money as a cause of poor teaching in many schools. Appearing on nationwide television several years ago, she said, "[T]he more money we get, the more junk we put in. The more junk we put in, the less we teach. And the less we teach, the less children learn."

"There isn't time. The school day is too full already." The school day probably is full. You need to find out whether it's really filled with essentials. One approach might be to ask school administrators to show you typical class schedules for each grade. Then you can see how much time is devoted to basics, and how much to less essential learning.

If you're given a schedule with big blocks of time labeled "language arts," ask to have this broken down into time spent actually reading and writing, as opposed to time spent on workbooks. It's essential to see these breakdowns, since far too much time labeled "reading" or "writing" in elementary-school schedules is really spent on workbook busy work. The same approach applies to time labeled "social studies." Are children learning history and geography or a hash of current events, sociology, and "relevant" topics? Here it would help to see a curriculum guide and the textbook.

You may find what appears to be too much time spent in elementary school on learning not directly connected with reading, writing, and math. Unfortunately, some of this (gym every day, in addition to recess, or health or consumer ed may be required by state law. Talk to your state legislator about that. "Enrichment" is another problem you should be aware of when school people say there isn't enough time to improve teaching of essential subjects. Are children spending several hours a week in a "learning center" playing computer games, looking at slides, listening to tapes? If so, ask for evidence (test scores) showing that this "enrichment" really does boost learning in basic subjects.

The bottom line on learning time is results. You and other parents have a right to ask for evidence that learning time in your child's school is *productive* and to ask for changes if it is not.

What if the matter you want to discuss with the school board does not involve your school's academic program? Regardless of the problem, reliable information is your best ally. Whether your question involves parents' or students' rights, a possible change in governance of schools in your district, or how to go about analyzing the school budget, these groups can help you get the facts:

The National Committee for Citizens in Education (NCCE) (see Glossary for telephone hotline and address). The NCCE is dedicated to improving schools through informed participation of parents and citizens. The NCCE hotline can provide brief answers to questions on school practices and parents' rights. The NCCE also monitors education legislation and publishes a monthly newsletter and a variety of books and booklets on subjects ranging from testing to analyzing a school budget and starting a school improvement group. Send 25 cents for a publications list.

The Institute for Responsive Education (IRE) (see Glossary for address). The IRE is a national, nonprofit group that conducts research and provides technical assistance on school-community relations. IRE was founded to give citizens access to educational information and research. Its publications include "A Handbook for Parents and Citizens on School Effectiveness" and "Parents as Educators: Home-School-Community Partnerships for Learning." Write for a free publications list.

WHAT TO DO IF YOUR SCHOOL BOARD IS UNRESPONSIVE

If you don't attend a school board meeting now and then and speak up about school issues, you are voluntarily putting up with taxation without representation. If your school board is unresponsive to parents, you are being forced to endure taxation without representation.

In the course of talking to parents, I heard some infuriating reports of unresponsive, and irresponsible, school boards. A Wisconsin school board suggested that a parents' group circulate a petition showing support for a reapportionment of the school district that parents had requested. After the group had worked for weeks collecting hundreds of names on a properly signed petition, which a small group of parents presented at a meeting, the board decided that a petition was not sufficient. They would not consider the issue unless all signers of the petition were present at the *next* meeting.

The NCCE reports cases in which school boards have denied citizens a chance to speak at meetings, held meetings at inconvenient times, or excluded citizens altogether by holding un-justified "executive sessions." Of course there are school boards, like the one in the case described at the opening of this chapter, which do listen when parent/citizens want to discuss a possible change in the established ways of doing things. Unfortunately, however, as a survey of more than eighty school districts has shown, boards of education usually do not govern their school dis-tricts. They simply legitimize the policies of the school superinten-dent. Even when parents and other citizens do speak up at board meetings in these districts, they have no real voice in school affairs because the people they elect have delegated their authority to the superintendent.

Is it possible to have a school board that truly represents par-ents and the rest of the public, rather than the school administra-tion? According to the studies cited by the IRE, the key to getting a representative school board is electing members who are "vulner-able" to public opinion. As the IRE study notes, the move to get the school board out of politics, which dates back to the early part of the century, has resulted in boards made up of apolitical leading citizens who see themselves as elite trustees of education and who rely heavily on professional educators to tell them what's best for the community's schools.

Such boards are not usually vulnerable to public opinion and often have little interest in hearing parents' views for several rea-sons:

Members have no larger political ambitions, and no personal need to gain the public's approval.

Though they often do want to be reelected to the board, many because they sincerely want to serve the community, and a few to enhance their leading citizen image or business prospects, mem-bers are justified in saying that board membership is a community service, that they donate their time, and it is often a thankless job.

In some communities, the scarcity of school board candidates underscores the truth of these claims. If few people want to serve, the public has little choice. In addition, the considerable investment in time required to serve on the board contributes to a board's being unrepresentative of the community as a whole. For example, men who must hold two jobs to support their families, and women who work and run a household often don't have the hours to spare.

If these characteristics describe the board members in your school district, and if that board is not as responsive as it should be, you may want to consider electing candidates of a different type. In a foreword to *School Boards and the Communities They Represent,* IRE president Don Davies writes: "The Report . . . concludes that the democratic potential of school boards can best be realized if they become *more not less political,* and if citizens act so as to elect politically ambitious members, and if their members have their base in a special interest constituency rather than in a vision of an objective public interest. The research evidence . . . confirms Joseph Schlesinger's comment that 'no more irresponsible government is imaginable than one of high-minded men [or women] unconcerned for their political futures.' "

The studies also suggest that the following measures would result in more responsive school boards.

Limit candidates to one term of office. New members almost invariably act more like representatives of the public than do long-time members, and single terms are likely to attract candidates who want to use the office as a political stepping stone and will therefore be vulnerable to public opinion.

Schedule school board elections to coincide with general municipal elections.

Have another government official, a village president, for example, serve as a school board member or chair.

Instead of electing members at large, have each neighborhood or subdistrict within the larger district elect its own candidate.

Almost any one of these proposals would result in a larger field of school board candidates. Naturally your community would be unlikely to make all of these changes, but even one or two of them—in particular choosing politically ambitious people who will listen to what you and other parents have to say—would result in a more responsive school board.

If you plan to work for these changes to make your school board more responsive, expect some opposition. School people will point to dire consequences of "injecting politics" into the schools. Keep in mind that school administrators are well aware that one consequence of these changes will be a school board that listens to parents and taxpayers—and exerts more control over the schools. The net effect will be to make school people more accountable to the public. Naturally, administrators would prefer the status quo. James Koerner, a former executive director of the CBE, writes: "The superintendent of schools in most communities has accumulated an unconscionable degree of control over basic educational policy. This adverse situation has come about for several reasons. It has come about, first, by default; by the local board's silence and its failure to carry out its responsibilities in the most important areas of the educational system, such as curriculum, academic standards, and personnel. If it yields its authority in these quintessential matters to the superintendent, it destroys its main *raison d'être.*"

Others in the community who sincerely believe in "nonpartisan" elections may also object to these changes. You can point to the IRE studies which show that under such a system citizens have had far too little say in their schools. Remind them that taxation without representation runs counter to our national tradition.

Below are some publications you will find helpful in dealing with school board elections and related education issues in your community (see Glossary for addresses).

National Committee for Citizens in Education:
Finding Out How People Feel About Local Schools (1982). $2.60, plus $1 postage.
How to Run a School Board Campaign and Win (1982). $5.95, plus $1.
Parents Organizing to Improve Schools (1976; revised 1984). $3.50, plus $1.
School Budgets. It's Your Money. It's Your Business (1979). $4.95, plus $1.

Council for Basic Education:
How Effective Are Your Schools? A Checklist for Citizens. $.50.
What Is Basic in Education? A Model Curriculum $.50.

Institute for Responsive Education
School Boards and the Communities They Represent (1984). $7.
A Citizen's Notebook for Effective Schools (1984). $13.

CONTACT YOUR ELECTED REPRESENTATIVES

Money is power, as the saying goes. The trend today is for more and more money for local schools to come from state rather than local taxes—which is likely to result in greater state control of education. This means you and other parents have good reason to get in touch with your state legislator and let him know your views on school issues. For example, about half of our states adopt school textbooks statewide, requiring every school in the state to select books from the state-approved list. If this is true in your state, do you think the law should be changed to allow districts freedom in choosing their own books? The states control teacher certification. Has your state upgraded certification requirements as much as it should?

Your state legislator most likely has an office in his home district, perhaps only a few miles from where you live. You don't have to go to the state capital. If you're not sure who your legislator is, or how to get in touch, you can find out by calling the nearest chapter of the League of Women Voters. If you and other parents are concerned about a school issue that is a matter of state law, go as a group to see your legislator. Write or telephone him (or her) at the home office, explaining the problem as you see it and what you think should be done. Will your ideas have any impact? Says Mary Lou Cowlishaw, Republican leader of the Elementary and Secondary Education committee in the Illinois House of Representatives: "I can't emphasize enough that ordinary citizens should make their views on education known to legislators. Parents can't accomplish anything sitting at home complaining to one another. To get the changes they want, they must put organized, orderly pressure on state legislators of *both* parties. Yes, legislators do pay attention to calls and letters from citizens."

This also applies to members of Congress. A legislative assistant to a U.S. Senator says, "Legislators often get their information from the [educational] establishment because they have no other source. They can't know all the issues and how you [parents and citizens] want them to vote unless you tell them. Their staff people are paid to listen to you. When you talk to a lawmaker or someone on his staff about any issue, keep in mind that they need basic information." Speaking of proposed education legislation the Senator had recently sponsored, she adds, "That bill came about because a group of parents who were very concerned about the problem paid him a visit in his office back home to discuss it. Until then, he hadn't been aware that there was a problem. What these parents said convinced him action was needed."

Legislators get both information and pressure from paid lobbyists hired by the NEA, the AFT, and other groups. The state affiliate of the NEA is widely recognized as the most powerful lobby in nearly every state capital. Much of the information they give legislators is aimed primarily at protecting members' jobs and increasing union power. For example, the NEA has long promoted the idea that smaller classes mean better learning, though as we've seen, research has shown smaller classes often guarantee nothing except more teaching jobs and higher cost to taxpayers.

Education establishment pressure groups like the NEA use their funds and large membership both to cultivate legislators and to intimidate those who refuse to go along with union policies. In *Today's Education* (April–May 1982) the NEA president wrote: "We also know those who are not our friends. . . . When, next November, we enter the voting booth, we will remember how they acted." Such a statement is well calculated to whip legislators into line. With as many as 5000 members in each Congressional district, the NEA is a formidable political adversary. If lawmakers are to buck such pressures from the union, they need to be assured of support from you and other parents.

A legislator who gets a substantial number of letters from people in his or her district on the same issue (individual letters or postcards count more than "canned" messages), takes the opinions of these voters very seriously, indeed. In the eyes of your legislator, the few people who feel strongly enough to write represent thousands of voters who hold the same views—and this often determines how he or she votes on upcoming legislation.

YOU CAN PROPOSE SOLUTIONS

If anything good can be said for the current crisis in education, it is that we have been shocked into seeing that it is not a crisis at all, but a long-standing problem we have at last faced and one which has many causes. As parents, as voters, and as taxpayers, you and I have a right both to propose solutions through our elected representatives and to approve or disapprove of those proposed by them.

The following proposals, I believe, would give all of us more of a say in the schools we pay for and would make school people more accountable to the community they serve.

Pay for School Board Members

We can elect school board members who are "vulnerable," as the findings of IRE studies suggest. We could go one step further in attracting more school board candidates who would be willing to represent the public. Though a full-time salary would not be possible or even advisable in most cases, I believe that all school board members should be paid. According to a 1983 National Association of School Boards survey, seventeen school boards in metropolitan areas pay members salaries ranging from a few hundred to a few thousand dollars a year.

A paid board would have three advantages. First, it would help make school board membership a sought-after job, rather than a thankless one. Second, board membership would be more representative of our communities if it were opened up to people who could not afford to serve without pay. Finally, and perhaps most importantly, if we are determined to have better schools, our school boards will have to play an active role in such vital matters as curriculum planning and examining test results. They must also learn to look closely at educators' claims that reducing class size and spending for the latest fads and gimmicks will result in better learning for children. We should not expect school board members to do this demanding job without pay.

Bypass Colleges of Education

We should work toward revising state regulations so that candidates with college degrees, but without training in colleges of education, can be hired to teach in public schools. They now teach successfully in private and parochial schools. School districts hiring teachers without education courses would be taking no more of a chance than they do now in hiring candidates from colleges of education, since some are incompetent and others are only marginally able. By eliminating the education requirement, school districts will have a far larger pool of academically able applicants from which to choose.

Some critics have suggested trying to upgrade colleges of

education, but these institutions are insulated enough from public pressure to be able to resist such attempts at reform. If graduates of these colleges had to compete with holders of bachelor's degrees in other fields, those who run our colleges of education would be compelled to raise entrance and graduation requirements. In addition, this might force colleges of education to at last make use of educational research in developing "methods" courses that would be truly helpful in training prospective teachers of reading, writing, and math. At present, though there is abundant research to show what works and what does not work in the classroom, colleges of education commonly ignore this research in training teachers.

New Jersey has instituted a Provisional Teacher Plan that allows the hiring of candidates with bachelor's degrees, and without "education" courses, who pass a state competency test. California has also revised its certification laws to allow college graduates without education training to teach in public schools. In 1984 eight states introduced bills to allow noneducation majors to teach in public schools, according to the National Conference of State Legislatures. New York City has hired 3500 public school teachers who have college degrees but not the usual education courses. A 1984 Louis Harris survey shows that only 10 percent of teachers who have taken these courses feel that they are useful preparation for teaching children in the classroom. The increasing recognition that colleges of education do not train teachers effectively has given rise to a number of volunteer, privately supported groups, such as the Reading Reform Foundation and the National Forum for Educational Awareness, which can offer help to in-service teachers.

Check Achievement Test Scores
School boards should learn to use achievement scores to check school output in a variety of ways. They should ask not only for comparisons of current scores in their districts with national norms or with similar school districts, but they should also examine the output of schools in their district over time. This method of measuring school effectiveness was suggested by Frank Armbruster in a Hudson Institute report in the late '70s. If it had been widely used and the results heeded, many schools might have abandoned ineffective teaching practices that led to continuing slump in academic achievement from the highs of the mid-'60s. To check school

put over time, the board might compare the reading or math scores of this year's fourth- and sixth-graders with those of students in the same grade five, ten, or more years ago. Significant changes would prompt questions about relative merits of teaching methods and materials "then" and now. To do this, of course, it would be necessary to use the same version of the same achievement test for a reasonably long period, taking any re-norming into account (see chapter 4).

Such efforts to check school output are not popular with educators, who protest that tests are not perfect and that schools teach much that cannot be tested in this way. No sensible person would argue these points. Yet educators have not shown us better tests, nor have they given us cause to trust that they will teach our children well if only we support the schools and leave educators alone to do their work. Imperfect as they may be, achievement tests can tell us whether students are learning to do long division, or to read and comprehend. They can also tell us whether School X does better at teaching these things than School Y and whether School X does a better job of teaching basic subjects now than it did ten years ago or five years ago. The alternative appears to be unquestioning payment of ever increasing costs for schooling that may be—and often is—doing less and less to help our children realize their potential. No sensible person should expect us to accept this alternative.

As we've seen, cheating has occurred both in giving achievement tests and in reporting of scores to the public. Henry S. Dyer, a former vice-president of the Educational Testing Service, raises the question of cheating in discussng the use of tests to hold school people accountable in *Parents Can Understand Testing*. Certainly there is a conflict of interest when school people are asked to preside over the testing used to check their own performance. Perhaps it is time to consider having these tests administered by people outside the school system who have no vested interest in the results.

Investigate the Causes of the Reading Problem
Establish in every state a commission to study the cause and extent of the reading problem. Poor reading skill is central to nearly every one of our other educational problems. Children who have

not been taught to read cannot learn anything else. As we have seen, poor reading is not a problem unique to minority or disadvantaged children. Even the "best" schools find it necessary to hire remedial reading teachers and to label children "learning disabled" (most commonly in reading).

If we instead focus on preventing reading problems, we could save millions of dollars, and we could save millions of children from the frustration of being taught by an ineffective method.

Poor reading skill causes numerous problems, both in and out of school. Dr. Hilde Mosse, psychiatrist for the New York City school board for more than twenty years, writes: "All types of reading disorders play a major role in the violent behavior of school children. The close relationship between violent and non-violent juvenile delinquency and reading disorders has been well-documented. . . . The causative chain starts with the fact that the child is not taught reading properly and that his reading disorder is not corrected early enough. . . ."

These state commissions could survey the teaching of reading in their state's schools to determine whether children are being given the benefit of learning to read by the method which research has proved to be most effective. To answer this question they could compare reading scores and other data from schools which use the intensive (direct) phonics method with schools using the "look-say" (indirect phonics) approach. The commissions would discover which schools had higher reading achievement scores and which schools had more children in LD and remedial reading classes. The commissions could then publicize their findings. Parents and school boards in local districts should be allowed to decide which method would be used to teach children in their schools.

The commissions should be broadly representative of parents and other citizens, including members of school boards, from all types of communities, and business people. To avoid any possible conflict of interest, educators (teachers, professors of education, administrators, counselors, and so on) should comprise no more than a small proportion of any commission, nor should they become leaders of the commission, since its work would involve passing judgment on methods and teaching materials developed or recommended by educators.

Support Incentives for Good Teaching

Traditionally, pay increases for teachers have been based on length of service and credit for taking extra courses (which often do not increase their knowledge or improve their teaching skill). Failure to tie pay increases to actual performance in the classroom can demoralize good teachers and discourage others from trying to become more effective. Many observers believe that this failure to reward superior effort also discourages able young people from choosing teaching as a career.

Incentive plans recently proposed include "merit pay," "career ladders," and "mentor teacher programs." All are intended to reward the better teachers and to encourage all teachers to upgrade their performance. In addition, the hope is that improving the status and pay of effective teachers will encourage them to stay in the classroom, instead of leaving it to become administrators, as some now do.

At this writing, fourteen states have enacted laws setting up incentive plans or pilot programs to develop such plans. An additional two dozen states are considering plans to reward good teaching. You can find out from your state legislators whether your state is among them. These incentive plans badly need support from parents and other citizens. Though many individual teachers favor such programs, the NEA has opposed paying teachers on the basis of performance. The AFT favors incentive proposals which combine course credits, length of service, and performance as a basis for raising teachers' salaries.

Develop a Parents' Lobby

Independent parents' groups should develop statewide networks to share ideas and to promote their mutual interests in improving schools. Teachers have unions; principals and administrators have professional associations. Parents need a political voice, because what happens in the state legislature increasingly determines not only how much money will be spent on education but what children will study, what books they will use, what tests they must pass, how well qualified their teachers will be, and much more. A central aim of such a parents' network would be to lobby for legislation to promote school practices that would benefit students. The educational establishment has long been lobbying for laws to benefit teachers and school administrators, without regard for the real interests of parents and children.

Protect Private Schools and Home Schooling

Protect your right and the rights of other parents to educate their children at home or send them to a private school, *regardless of whether you intend to exercise these rights yourself.* A monopoly of education, like other monopolies, works to the disadvantage of consumers. As long as alternatives to public education exist, there will be incentive for the people who run public schools to do a better job. Comparisons like the 1981 Coleman report, showing that private schools educate children better for less, spotlight the flaws in the public system. Union leaders feel the heat of competition.

Expect legislative pressure backed by the NEA to make it difficult for parents to teach children at home. The union claims they are concerned about the quality of education children will get at home. Critics of the union claim it is far more concerned about teaching jobs and union power that will be lost if enough parents choose to teach their children at home.

Unions also oppose any proposals for a voucher plan to give parents a choice between public and private schools. They speak of the danger of killing the public school system and of the "chaos" that would result. Allowing citizens free choice in selecting cars and dental care has not resulted in chaos. Why should it be any different in education? If public schools, massively funded and often over-staffed, can be "killed" by private schools operating on a shoestring and by individual parents teaching children at home, the system is not workable. In a free society, parents should not be coerced into sending their children to tax-supported schools where educators do as they please.

Your child can't afford to wait for educators to reform the system from within. Improvements will come only if parents insist on them—school by school and district by district—for the sake of their own children. Ask questions at school and ask for changes if necessary. Choose school board members who are willing to make educators accountable to the public. Take advantage of the information and resources in this book, and ask other parents to join you. You can begin now to help your child get the best possible education.

NOTES

CHAPTER 1

Page

8 John I. Goodlad, *A Place Called School* (New York: McGraw-Hill Book Co., 1984), p. 39.

9 Robert F. Biehler and Jack Showran, *Psychology Applied to Teaching* (New York: Houghton Mifflin, 1978), pp. 312–313.

9 Barbara Lerner, "American Education: How Are We Doing?" *Public Opinion,* Fall 1982, p. 64.

CHAPTER 2

15 Gordon and Patricia Sabine, *Books That Made the Difference* (Hamden, Conn.: Library Professional Publications, 1983), p. 79.

24 Robert L. Thorndike, "Causation of Binet IQ Decrements," *Journal of Educational Measurement,* 14:3, Fall 1977, pp. 197–202.

CHAPTER 4

42 Andrew Strenio, *The Testing Trap* (New York: Rawson Wade, 1981), p. 81.

43 George Weber, "Uses and Abuses of Standardized Testing in the Schools," Council for Basic Education (CBE) Occasional Paper 22, 1974, p. 8.

44 Mitchell Lazarus, "Coming to Terms with Testing," in *The Myth of Measurability,* Paul L. Houts, ed. (New York: Hart Associates, 1977), pp. 188–189.

45 Edward B. Fiske, "Some Colleges Question Usefulness of S.A.T.'s" (quoting William C. Hiss, Bates College, Lewiston, Me.), *New York Times,* Oct. 9, 1984.

46 Henry S. Dyer, *Parents Can Understand Testing,* (Columbia, Md.: National Committee for Citizens in Education, 1980), p. 8.

Page

50   Edwin F. Taylor, "Science Tests," in *Myth of Measurability,* Houts, ed., pp. 291–308.

50   *Ibid.,* p. 304. Item from Stanford Achievement Test, Intermediate Level I, Form A (New York: Harcourt Brace Jovanovich, 1972).

52   Dyer, *Parents Can Understand Testing,* p. 30.

54   David Harman, "Reading Tests," in *Myth of Measurability,* Houts, ed., p. 312.

54   Banesh Hoffmann, *The Tyranny of Testing* (New York: Crowell Collier, 1962), p. 106.

55   Judah Schwartz, "The Illogic of IQ Tests," in *Myth of Measurability,* Houts, ed., p. 91.

61   Hoffman, *Tyranny of Testing,* p. 97.

56   William B. Fetters, George H. Brown, and Jeffrey A. Owings, *High School and Beyond: A National Longitudinal Study for the 1980's* (National Center for Educational Statistics, 1984), p. 19.

57   D. E. Megivoren, "Why Can't Sonja Fail Algebra?" *Network* (National Committee for Citizens in Education), February 1979, p. 5.

59   Strenio, *Testing Trap,* p. 78.

60   J. Parker Damon, "Questions You Should Ask About Your Testing Program," in *Myth of Measurability,* Houts, ed., pp. 348–363.

CHAPTER 6

84   Robert Benjamin, *Making Schools Work* (New York: Continuum, 1981), pp. 15–16.

84   Louise Bates Ames, Clyde Gillespie, and John Streff, *Stop School Failure* (New York: Harper & Row, 1972), pp. 188–189.

88   *Ibid.,* p. 63.

88   William B. Fetters, George H. Brown, and Jeffrey A. Owings, *High School and Beyond: A National Longitudinal Study for the 1980's* (National Center for Educational Statistics, 1984), p. 21.

90   Jeanne Chall, *Learning to Read: The Great Debate,* updated ed. (New York: McGraw-Hill, 1983), p. 22.

93   *Ibid.,* p. 28.

95   Linda G. Fielding, Paul T. Wilson, and Richard C. Anderson, "A New Focus on Free Reading: The Role of Trade Books in Reading Instruction," in *Contexts of Literacy,* T. E. Raphael & R. Reynolds, eds. (New York: Longmans, in press).

96   "Factors in Reading Comprehension," Speech Report, *Reading Informer* (Reading Reform Foundation, September–October 1983), p. 18.

96   Norman E. and Margaret Silberberg, "Myths in Remedial Education," *Journal of Learning Disabilities,* February 1969, pp. 209–217.

Page

99 "Evaluating Workbooks," Reading Education Report No. 52, University of Illinois, August 1984, pp. 3–4.

100 "Third National Mathematics Assessment," National Assessment of Educational Progress, April 1983, p. 31.

100 "One Man's Solution to U.S. Education Problem" (article on John Saxon), *Human Events,* July 16, 1983, p. 1.

102 Barbara Kuczen, *Childhood Stress* (New York: Delacorte Press, 1982), p. 181.

102 Gerald S. Coles, "Learning-Disabilities Test Battery: Empirical and Social Issues," *Harvard Educational Review* 48:3, August 1978.

CHAPTER 8

125 Theodore Sizer, *Horace's Compromise: The Dilemma of the American High School* (Boston: Houghton Mifflin, 1984), p. 37.

128 John Goodlad, *A Study of Schooling,* (New York: McGraw-Hill, 1984), pp. 152–152, 156.

131 Frank Armbruster, *Our Children's Crippled Future: How American Education Has Failed* (New York: Quadrangle/New York Times Book Co., 1977), pp. 110–111.

132 Dennis W. Chalmers, letter to author, June 22, 1981.

136 This item is based in part on an article by Chip Shields, "Surprise: Good Grades Not a Must for College," *Homewood-Flossmoor Star,* Dec. 6, 1984.

CHAPTER 9

141 James Stigler, Harold Stevenson, and Schin-Ying Lee, "Cultural Context of Academic Achievement in Japan, Taiwan, and the United States." Phone interview with Dr. James Stigler, March 18, 1985.

143 *Ibid.*

150 W. Brookover and L. Lezotte, *School Characteristics Associated with Changes in Student Achievement,* (East Lansing, Mich.: The Institute for Research in Teaching, Michigan State University, 1979).

157 Samuel L. Blumenfeld, *How to Tutor* (New Rochelle, N.Y.: Arlington House, 1973).

CHAPTER 10

171 David Schimmel and Louis Fischer, *The Rights of Parents in the Education of Their Children* (Columbia, Md.: National Committee for Citizens in Education, 1977).

Page

174 Letter from Harold M. Voth, M.D., to Irvin W. Myers, Superintendent and school board members of Auburn-Washburn Rural District 437, Kansas, Feb. 14, 1981.

176 U.S. Department of Education, "Part 98—Student Rights in Research, Experimental Programs, and Testing," *Federal Register,* vol. 49, no. 174, Sept. 6, 1984, p. 35321.

CHAPTER 11

184 Jim Gallagher, "From 'Jungle' to 'Model': One School's Transformation," *Chicago Tribune,* Sept. 25, 1983.

185 Ross Zerchykov, *School Boards and the Communities They Represent,* Institute for Responsive Education (IRE), June 1984, p. 38, 19.

185 L. H. Zeigler, M. K. Jennings, and G. W. Peak, *Governing American Schools* (North Scituate, Mass.: Duxbury Press, 1974), p. 250.

185 Zerchykov, *School Boards,* p. 4.

187 John B. Carroll and Jeanne S. Chall, eds., *Toward a Literate Society: The Report on Reading of the National Academy of Education* (New York: McGraw-Hill, 1975).

188 Samuel Blumenfeld, *N.E.A. Trojan Horse in American Education* (Boise, Idaho: Paradigm, 1984).

188 John Dewey, *The School and Society,* rev. ed. (Chicago: University of Chicago Press, 1915), p. 15.

189 *New York Times,* Aug. 4, 1974, Sec. E, p. 9.

189 *NEA NOW* Newsletter, April 1984, p. 1.

192 Cliff Eagleton, "Return Schools to Local Control," *USA Today,* September 1984, p. 44.

193 James Coleman, Thomas Hoffer, and Sally Kilgore, *High School Achievement: Public, Private, and Catholic Schools Compared* (New York: Basic Books, 1982).

CHAPTER 12

198 Introduction by Jerome Bruner to Neville Bennett's *Teaching Styles and Pupil Progress* (Cambridge, Mass.: Harvard University Press, 1976), pp. ix–x.

200 William Rioux and the Staff of the National Committee for Citizens in Education, *You Can Improve Your Child's School* (New York: Simon and Schuster, 1980), pp. 235–237.

207 Gail Kessler, "Parents and Schools Form a New, Powerful Partnership," *Family Learning,* March/April 1984, pp. 29–31.

CHAPTER 13

Page

211 Ross Zerchykov, *School Boards and the Communities They Represent: An Inventory of the Research* (Boston: Institute for Responsive Education, June 1984) p. 57.

211 *Ibid.*, p. 69.

214 Charles Micciche, Speech Report in *Reading Informer,* September–October 1984, p. 25.

218 Zerchykov, *School Boards,* p. v.

219 James Koerner, *Who Controls American Education?* (Boston: Beacon Press, 1968), p. 141.

225 Hilde Mosse, M.D., *The Complete Handbook of Children's Reading Disorders,* 2 vols. (New York: Human Sciences Press, 1982), vol. 1, p. 284.

GLOSSARY

ACT Assessment (ACT). Standardized tests intended to show how well students will succeed in doing college work.

Achievement tests. Standardized tests to measure and compare what students have learned in academic subjects, e.g., math, reading, social studies.

Alternative schools. Those that differ from the majority of schools in a district, allowing parents to choose whether children will attend "academic" schools, "open" schools, schools catering to students with special talent in science or in the performing arts, and so on.

American Federation of Teachers (AFT). One of the two major teachers' unions, having most of its locals in large cities.

Association for Children with Learning Disabilities (ACLD). Provides support and information for parents of children said to be learning disabled. 4156 Library Rd., Pittsburgh, PA 15234; (412) 931–7100.

Center for the Study of Parent Involvement. Studies and promotes parent involvement in public schools. 5000 Manila Ave., Oakland, CA 94609; (415) 658–9040.

Council for Basic Education (CBE). Promotes emphasis on the academic disciplines, offering speakers and consulting services (for a fee); also prepares citizens' guides to help parents and citizens evaluate local school programs. 725 Fifteenth St. NW, Washington, D.C. 20005; (202) 347–4171.

Direct phonics (code emphasis, intensive phonics, phonics first, synthetic phonics). Reading instruction which begins by teaching children systematically all the letters and letter combinations necessary for sounding out words; it is the teaching method research has shown to be most effective for teaching all children to read.

Family Educational Rights and Privacy Act (FERPA). The law defining parents' rights to examine children's permanent school records and to control who sees these records.

FERPA office. U.S. Department of Education, Room 3017, 400 Maryland Ave. S.W., Washington, D.C. 20202; (202) 472–6032.

Financial Aid Form (FAF). Questionnaire which must be filled out by families applying for loans and grants to help with college expenses.

Hatch Act (1984 regulations), also known as Pupil Rights Amendment. States that school people must have written parental consent before students can take part in psychological examination, testing, or treatment (which may include activities carried on in the classroom), if the primary purpose is to reveal private information about students or their families in federally funded research projects. Also requires that parents be allowed to examine *all* instructional materials used in such a program.

Hatch Act office. U.S. Department of Education, Room 3021, 400 Maryland Ave. S.W., Washington, D.C. 20202; (202) 472–5123.

Heterogeneous class or grouping. Teaching students of varying academic abilities in the same class or group.

Home and School Institute. Offers supplementary materials for home learning. Trinity College, Washington, D.C. 20017; (202) 466–3633.

Homogeneous class or grouping. Teaching students thought to have approximately the same academic ability in the same group or classroom.

Individualized educational program (IEP). A plan for teaching a child enrolled in special education.

IQ (intelligence quotient) tests (general aptitude tests). Intended to measure ability to do academic work.

Indirect phonics (meaning emphasis, eclectic method, psycholinguistic method, look-say, analytic phonics). Reading instruction which requires children to memorize whole words, with incidental teaching of letter sounds spread out over several years.

Institute for Responsive Education (IRE). A nonprofit research group that studies and promotes community participation in public schools. 605 Commonwealth Ave., Boston, MA 02215; (617) 353–3309.

National Assessment of Educational Progress (NAEP). Periodic testing of representative groups of U.S. students in various subject areas, e.g., math, writing, reading. Sponsored by the Education Commission of the States.

National Association for Gifted Children (NAGC). 5100 N. Edgewood Drive, St. Paul, MN 55112; (612) 784–3475. Promotes legislation, sponsors conference, and provides an information clearinghouse for education of the gifted and talented.

National Center for Educational Statistics (NCES). Gathers and reports statistics on schooling throughout the nation.

National Committee for Citizens in Education (NCCE). Promotes parent-citizen involvement in public schools, offering publications, information, and consultation for parents, citizens, and educators. 410 Wilde Lake Village Green, Columbia, MD 21044; (301) 997–9300. Hot line: 1–800–NETWORK.

National Education Association (NEA). One of the two major teachers' unions, having many of its locals in towns and suburban areas.

National Institute of Education (NIE). Promotes and supports educational research.

National School Volunteer Program (NSVP). Provides information about volunteer programs in public schools and trains coordinators for these programs. 300 N. Washington St., Alexandria, VA 22312; (703) 836–4880.

Parent Teacher Association (PTA). A school organization affiliated with the National Council of Parents and Teachers.

Parent Teacher Organization (PTO). An independent local school organization.

Reading Reform Foundation (RRF). A nonprofit volunteer group dedicated "to restoring intensive [direct] phonics to the teaching of reading throughout the nation"; provides information on phonics programs to parents, citizens, and schools. 7054 E. Indian School Rd., Scottsdale, AZ 85251; (602) 946–3567.

Scholastic Aptitude Test (SAT). Standardized tests intended to show how well students will succeed in doing college work.

Standardized tests. Tests intended to measure general aptitude, knowledge, or some other quality of large numbers of people. The tests are "standardized" by first giving them to a sample group representative of all those who will take them.

Tracking. Grouping of students, according to academic ability, into "low," "average," and "accelerated" classes or into "academic," "general," and "vocational" programs.

United Parents Associations of New York City, Inc. (UPA). An umbrella organization for parents' groups in 350 New York City public schools. 95 Madison Ave., New York, NY 10016; (212) 619–0095.

SUGGESTED READINGS

LISTS OF CHILDREN'S BOOKS

American Library Association, *Notable Children's Books 1940–1970* (1977) and *Notable Children's Books 1971–1975* (1981).

Z. Sutherland, editor, *The Best in Children's Books—1966–1972* (1973) and *The Best in Children's Books—1973–1978* (1980). University of Chicago Press.

J. Trelease, *The Read Aloud Handbook*. (1982). Penguin.

M. L. White, editor, *Adventuring with Books*. (1981). Urbana, IL: National Council of Teachers of English.

H. E. Williams, *Independent Reading, K-3* (1980). Bro-Dart.

CHILDREN'S READING

Diehl, Katherine and G. K. Hodenfield. *Johnny Still Can't Read— But You Can Teach Him at Home*. Reading Reform Foundation (RRF). $2.50, plus postage.

IMPROVING YOUR SCHOOLS

Finding Out How People Feel About Local Schools. National Committee for Citizens in Education (NCCE), 1982. $2.60, plus $1.00 shipping and handling.

How Effective Are Your Schools? A Checklist for Citizens. Council for Basic Education (CBE). $0.50.

How to Run a School Board Campaign and Win. NCCE, 1982. $5.95, plus $1.00.

Parents Organizing to Improve Schools. NCCE, 1976 (revised 1984). $3.50, plus $1.00.

School Budgets. It's Your Money. It's Your Business. NCCE. 1979. $4.95, plus $1.00.

What Is Basic in Education? A Model Curriculum. CBE. $.50.

Zerchykov, Ross, *School Boards and the Communities They Represent*. IRE. 1984. $7.00

Zerchykov, Ross et al., *A Citizen's Notebook for Effective Schools*. Institute for Responsive Education (IRE), 1984. $13.00 (deluxe edition: $20.00).

Selected Bibliography

Abbott, Robert. "Circles, cycles, and circumventions . . . yet there is an answer." Speech reprinted in *Reading Informer.* Reading Reform Foundation (RRF) (October 1980).

Adler, Mortimer. *Paideia Problems and Possibilities.* New York: Macmillan, 1983.

————. *The Paideia Proposal.* New York: Macmillan, 1982.

American Education. Spring 1984.

Ames, Louise Bates, Clyde Gillespie, John Streff. *Stop School Failure.* New York: Harper & Row, 1972.

Anastasi, Anne. *Psychological Testing.* New York: Macmillan, 1977.

Armbruster, Frank. *Our Children's Crippled Future: How American Education Has Failed.* New York: Quadrangle/New York Times Book Co., 1977.

Association for Supervision and Curriculum Development (ASCD). *Synthesis of ASCD Resolutions Through 1984.* Alexandria, Va.: ASCD, n.d..

Austin, G. and H. Garber. *The Rise and Fall of National Scores.* New York: Academic Press, 1982.

Bateman, Barbara. "Teaching Reading to Learning Disabled and Other Hard-to-Teach Children." In *Theory and Practice of Early Reading,* Vol. 1., Resnick, Lauren B., and Phyllis A. Weaver, eds. Hillsdale, N.J.: Lawrence Erlbaum Associates, 1979.

Benjamin, Robert. *Making Schools Work.* New York: Continuum, 1981.

Bennett, Neville. *Teaching Styles and Pupil Progress.* Introduction by Jerome Bruner. Cambridge, Mass.: Harvard University Press, 1976.

Biehler, Robert F. and Jack Showran. *Psychology Applied to Teaching.* New York: Houghton Mifflin, 1978.

Blumenfeld, Samuel L. *How to Tutor.* New Rochelle, N.Y.: Arlington House, 1973.

Blumenfeld, Samuel L. *N.E.A.: Trojan Horse in American Education.* Boise, Idaho: Paradigm, 1984.

Boyer, Ernest L. *High School.* New York: Harper & Row, 1983.

Bronfenbrenner, Urie. Speech reprinted in *The Innovator.* University of Michigan School of Education (September 1984).

Brookover, W. and L. Lezotte. *School Characteristics Associated with Changes in Student Achievement.* The Institute for Research in Teaching. East Lansing, Mich.: Michigan State University, 1979.

Carroll, John B. and Jeanne S. Chall, eds. *Toward a Literate Society: The Report on Reading of the National Academy of Education.* New York: McGraw-Hill, 1975.

Chall, Jeanne S. *Learning to Read: The Great Debate.* Updated edition. New York: McGraw-Hill, 1983.

Chandler, Jean et al. "Parents As Teachers: Observations of Low Income Parents and Children in Homework-Like Tasks." Research Report. Harvard University Graduate School of Education (1983).

Coleman, James, Thomas Hoffer, and Sally Kilgore. *High School Achievement: Public, Private, and Catholic Schools Compared.* New York: Basic Books, 1982.

Coles, Gerald S. "Learning-Disabilities Test Battery: Empirical and Social Issues." *Harvard Educational Review* 48:3 (1978).

College Entrance Examination Board. *On Further Examination: Report of the Advisory Panel on the Scholastic Aptitude Test Score Decline.* New York: CEEB, 1977.

Cooper, Lynne Eickholt, and Mary C. Jackson, *School Advisory Councils.* School Advisory Council Assistance Project, College of Education, University of South Carolina (1983).

Copperman, Paul. *The Literacy Hoax: The Decline of Reading, Writing, and Learning in the Public Schools and What We Can Do About It.* New York: William Morrow, 1978.

Cronback, Lee. "Five Decades of Controversy Over Mental Testing." *American Psychologist* (January 1975).

De Vito, Alfred and Gerald H. Krockover. *Creative Sciencing: A Practical Approach.* Boston: Little, Brown, 1976.

Dewey, John. *The School and Society.* Chicago: University of Chicago Press, 1915. rev. ed.

Diehl, Katherine and G. K. Hodenfield. *Johnny Still Can't Read—But You Can Teach Him at Home.* Reading Reform Foundation, n.d. [$2.50 plus postage; see Glossary for address.]

Dunn, Rita S. and Kenneth J. Dunn. "Learning Styles/Teaching Styles:

Should They . . . Can They . . . Be Matched?" *Educational Leadership* (January 1979).

Dyer, Henry S. *Parents Can Understand Testing.* Columbia, Md.: National Committee for Citizens in Education, 1980.

Eagleton, Cliff. "Return Schools to Local Control." *USA Today,* (September 1984).

Feder, Bernard. *The Complete Guide to Taking Tests.* Englewood Cliffs, N.J.: Prentice-Hall, 1979.

Feistritzer, Emily. *The Condition of Teaching.* New York: Carnegie Foundation for the Advancement of Teaching, 1983.

Fetters, William B., George H. Brown, and Jeffrey A. Owings. *High School and Beyond: A National Longitudinal Study for the 1980's.* Washington, D.C.: National Center for Educational Statistics, 1984.

Fielding, Linda G., Paul T. Wilson, and Richard C. Anderson. "A New Focus on Free Reading: The Role of Trade Books in Reading Instruction." In *Contexts of Literacy,* T. E. Raphael and R. Reynolds, eds. New York: Longmans (in press).

Gallagher, Jim. "From 'Jungle' to 'Model': One School's Transformation." *Chicago Tribune,* Sept. 25, 1983.

Goldberg, Debbie. "Attracting the Best with Incentive Plans." *New York Times Education Winter Survey,* Jan. 6, 1985.

Goodlad, John I. *A Place Called School.* New York: McGraw-Hill, 1984.

Henderson, Anne. "The Evidence Grows: Parent Participation— Student Achievement." National Committee for Citizens in Education, 1981.

Hoffmann, Banesh. *The Tyranny of Testing.* New York: Crowell Collier, 1962.

Holt, John. *Teach Your Own.* New York: Delacorte Press, 1981.

Houts, Paul L., ed. *The Myth of Measurability.* New York: Hart Associates, 1977.

Kessler, Gail. "Parents and Schools Form a New, Powerful Partnership." *Family Learning* (March/April 1984).

Klein, Stanley. *Psychological Testing of Children.* Boston: Exceptional Parent Press, 1977.

Koerner, James. *Who Controls American Education?* Boston: Beacon Press, 1968.

Kuczen, Barbara. *Childhood Stress.* New York: Delacorte Press, 1982.

Lerner, Barbara. "American Education: How Are We Doing?" *Public Opinion* (Fall 1982).

Lightfoot, Sara Lawrence. *The Good High School.* New York: Basic Books, 1983.

London. Herbert I. *Why Are They Lying to Our Children?* Briarcliff Manor, N.Y.: Stein and Day, 1984.

Losen, Stuart M. and Bert Diament. *Parent Conferences in the Schools.* Newton, Mass.: Allyn and Bacon, 1978.

Mackay, David and Joseph Simo, *Teach Your Child to Read and Write, and More.* New York: Penguin Books, 1976.

Maddi, Salvatore E. and Suzanne Kobasa. *The Hardy Executive.* Homewood, Ill.: Dow Jones, Irwin, 1984.

McNeil, Linda. "The Impact of Student Employment on Classroom Knowledge," *Basic Education.* Council for Basic Education (June 1984).

Megivoren, D. E. "Why Can't Sonja Fail Algebra?" *Network.* National Committee for Citizens in Education (February 1979).

Micciche, Charles. "The Legacy of Language—A Foundation for the Future." Speech reprinted in *Reading Informer.* Reading Reform Foundation (September/October 1984).

Mosse, Hilde., M.D. *The Complete Handbook of Children's Reading Disorders.* 2 vols. New York: Human Sciences Press, 1982.

National Assessment of Educational Progress. "Third National Mathematics Assessment." Denver, Colo.: NAEP, April 1983.

National Assessment of Educational Progress. "Writing Achievement: 1969–1979. Results of the Third National Writing Assessment." Denver, Colo.: NAEP, 1983.

National Committee for Citizens in Education. "Eight Citizen Leaders Are Making A Difference for Local Schools." *Network.* NCCE (May 1984).

National Committee for Citizens in Education. "Parent Rights Card." Columbia, Md.: NCCE, 1982.

National Commission on Excellence in Education. *A Nation at Risk.* Washington, D.C.: 1983.

National Education Association. *NEA NOW.* Washington, D.C.: NEA (April 1984).

"NEA Tells Parents to Ask Questions About Schools." *Homewood-Flossmoor Star,* Jan. 20, 1985.

"One Man's Solution to U.S. Education Problem." *Human Events* (July 16, 1983).

Osborn, Jean. "Evaluating Workbooks." Reading Education Report No. 52. University of Illinois, Champaign-Urbana. (August 1984).

Reed, Sally. "Education Courses: Are They Useful?" *New York Times Education Winter Survey,* Jan. 6, 1985.

Remsberg, Bonnie and Antoinette Saunders. *The Stressproof Child.* New York: Holt, Rinehart & Winston, 1985.

Richardson, Charles M. "Learning Disability Procedures: A Human Rights Perspective." *Journal of Learning Disabilities* (January 1981).

Rioux, William and the Staff of the NCCE. *You Can Improve Your Child's School.* New York: Simon and Schuster, 1980.

Roche, George C. "See Dick. See Jane. They Can't Read." *St. Louis Post-Dispatch,* May 22, 1984.

Ross, Alan O. *Learning Disability: The Unrealized Potential.* New York: McGraw-Hill, 1977.

Rowell, J. Cy. "The Five Rights of Parents." *Phi Delta Kappan* (February 1981).

Ryan, Charlotte. *The Testing Maze—An Evaluation of Standardized Testing in America.* Chicago: National PTA, 1979.

Sabine, Gordon and Patricia. *Books That Made the Difference.* Hamden, Conn.: Library Professional Publications, 1983.

Samuels, S. Jay. "Factors in Reading Comprehension." Speech reprinted in *Reading Informer.* Reading Reform Foundation (RRF) (September/October 1983).

Sanoff, Alvin P. and Lucia Solorzano. "It's at Home Where Our Language Is in Distress." *U.S. News & World Report* (Feb. 18, 1985).

Schimmel, David and Louis Fischer. *The Rights of Parents in the Education of Their Children.* Columbia, Md.: National Committee for Citizens in Education, 1977.

Shields, Chip. "Surprise: Good Grades Not a Must for College." *Homewood-Flossmoor Star,* Dec. 6, 1984.

Silberberg, Norman E. and Margaret. "Myths in Remedial Education." *Journal of Learning Disabilities* (February 1969).

Sirotnik, Kenneth. "What You See Is What You Get." Arlington, Va.: ERIC Document Reproduction Series, #29, 1981.

Sizer, Theodore. *Horace's Com-*

promise: *The Dilemma of the American High School.* Boston: Houghton Mifflin, 1984.

Stebbins, Linda B. et al. *Education as Experimentation: A Planned Variation Model.* Cambridge, Mass.: Abt Associates, 1977.

Lee, Schin-Ying, Harold Stevenson, and James Stigler. "Cultural Context of Academic Achievement in Japan, Taiwan, and the United States." Center for Human Growth and Development, University of Michigan, Ann Arbor, Mich. (1984).

Strenio, Andrew. *The Testing Trap.* New York: Rawson Wade, 1981.

Thorndike, Robert L., "Causation of Binet Decrements," *Journal of Educational Measurement* 14:3 (Fall 1977).

"Teacher Excellence: Teachers Take Charge." *American Education* (Spring 1984). [Interview with Dal Lawrence, president, Toledo Federation of Teachers.]

U.S. Department of Education. "Part 98—Student Rights in Research, Experimental Programs, and Testing." *Federal Register* 49:174 (Sept. 6, 1984).

U.S. Department of Education. *The Nation Responds.* Washington, D.C.: 1984.

Weber, George. "Uses and Abuses of Standardized Testing in the Schools." Council for Basic Education Occasional Paper 22, 1974.

Weinberg, Richard L. and Lynn Goetsch. *Parent Prerogatives.* Chicago: Nelson-Hall, 1979.

Westin, Jeane. *The Coming Parent Revolution.* Chicago: Rand McNally, 1981.

Willoughby, Stephen S. "Teaching Mathematics: What Is Basic?" Council for Basic Education Occasional Paper 31, 1981.

Zeigler, L. H., M. K. Jennings, and G. W. Peak. *Governing American Schools.* North Scituate, Mass.: Duxbury Press, 1974.

Zerchykov, Ross. *School Boards and the Communities They Represent: An Inventory of the Research.* Boston: Institute for Responsive Education, June 1984.

Zimbardo, Philip. *Shyness.* Reading, Mass.: Addison-Wesley, 1977.

INDEX

AACD. *See* American Association for Counseling and Development

Ability grouping, 35, 93, 126
  achievement test scores used for, 50, 53, 55
  advantages and disadvantages of, 127–129
  in high school, 126–129
  for reading, 93–96

Abuse of children, 151

Achievement, and report cards, 85–86

Achievement tests
  coaching for, 45–46, 89
  for college placement, 59
  grade-equivalent scores, 94
  grouping by scores on, 50, 53, 55
  high school, 57–58, 59
  interpretation of scores on, 61–62
  kindergarten through eighth grade, 54–55
  legal rights of parents in relation to, 165–166
  norm-referenced, 44
  progress and, 89
  questions on, 49–50 (*see also* Multiple-choice questions)
  for reading, 94
  school districts and, 89
  school funding in relation to, 190
  school output and scores on, 223–224

similarity to intelligence tests, 55
switching, 89

ACSD. *See* Association for Supervision and Curriculum Development

ACT. *See* ACT Assessment

ACT Assessment (ACT), 51, 58–59, 63, 134

ACTION, 118

Adkisson, Janice, 126

Administrators. *See* School Administrators

Advanced placement (AP) tests, 59, 62

AFT. *See* American Federation of Teachers

Alcott, Bronson, 23

Alcott, Louisa May, 23

All About Letters (U.S. Postal Service), 23

Almanacs, 71

American Association for Counseling and Development, 123

American College Testing Program (Iowa City, Iowa), 49, 135

American Federation of Teachers (AFT), 188–189, 221, 226

Ames, Louise Bates, 84, 88

Anxiety, test-related, 81

AP tests. *See* Advanced placement tests

Aptitude tests, 133
  general (*see* Intelligence tests)

Armbruster, Frank, 10, 131, 223